BRITISH COLUMBIA
DISASTERS

BRITISH COLUMBIA
DISASTERS

DEREK PETHICK

MR. PAPERBACK®
LANGLEY, B.C.

MR. PAPERBACK®
P.O. Box 3399,
Langley, B.C. V3A 4R7

BRITISH COLUMBIA DISASTERS
First published by Stagecoach Publishing Co. Ltd. in 1978
Mr. Paperback edition—July 1982

Cover and format design—Garnet Basque
Cover artist—Kim Lafave

Canadian Cataloguing in Publication Data

Pethick, Derek, 1920—
British Columbia disasters

Bibliography: p
ISBN 0-919531-05-9

1. Disasters—British Columbia.
2. British Columbia - History.   I. Title.
FC3820.D5P48   971.1   C78-002175-4
F1087.P48

Contents

Introduction 7

1862: The Smallpox Epidemic 11

1864: The Bute Inlet Massacre 24

1868: The Barkerville Fire 46

1875: The Loss of the S.S. Pacific 56

1886: The Great Vancouver Fire 69

1887: The Nanaimo Mine Disaster 79

1894: The Fraser Valley Flood 91

1896: The Collapse of the Point Ellice Bridge 136

1898: The New Westminster Fire 145

1910: The Great Victoria Fire 155

1913 & 1914: The Fraser River Slides 161

1918: The Loss of the Princess Sophia 173

1918-1919: The Influenza Epidemic 180

1929-1939: The Great Depression 191

1948: The Fraser Valley Flood 203

Introduction

FIRE, flood, famine, epidemic, shipwreck, avalanche, mine cave-in. . .the forms of disaster are many. No community long escapes tragedy, as a glance at the record shows. Certainly British Columbia has known its share of disasters, both natural and man-made, over the years.

Perhaps the worst on record is also the first to be recorded. This is the infamous smallpox epidemic of 1862, when thousands—some have estimated as many as a third—of Pacific Coast Indians succumbed to smallpox. Ironically, a smallpox vaccine had been known for years and hundreds of white residents had availed themselves of its protection. But the Indians were left to fend for themselves. After an arrival from San Francisco was diagnosed as having "variola," as the scourge was known, the tribes encamped near Victoria were all but doomed. Within days, scores were dead and dying, the rest fleeing northward to their homes and carrying the disease with them, and a mighty civilization was on an irreversible decline.

"How the mighty have fallen." observed a Victoria newspaper. "Four short years ago, numbering their braves by the thousands, they were the scourge and terror of the coast. Today, broken-spirited and effeminate, with scarce a corporal's guard of warriors remaining alive, they are proceeding northward bearing with them the seeds of a loathsome disease that will take root and bring a plentiful crop of ruin and destruction to the friends who have remained at home. . ."

The deaths of as many as 25,000 men, women and children was tragedy enough; the callous indifference of white pioneers remains one of the blackest chapters in provincial lore.

At least one disaster saw the Indians enjoy a moment of revenge when, during the construction of a wagon road from Bute Inlet to the Cariboo gold fields, Chilcotin warriors massacred some of Alfred Waddington's work parties. Retribution was swift, "justice" severe.

There were other disasters which owed their occurrence to man's negligence. The Barkerville fire of 1868 was not an accident, but inevitable, due to the fatalistic attitude of many, open hearths, poor construction standards and small to non-existent firefighting facilities. Almost every community suffered fire, Mr. Pethick describing not only that of Barkerville but those of Vancouver, New Westminster and Victoria.

Human oversight contributed to other calamities. In November of 1875 the ancient sidewheel steamer *Pacific* slipped from her dock in Victoria. Hours after, off Cape Flattery, she collided with the sailing vessel *Orpheus.* The *Pacific* sank like a stone; all but two of her company perished in this shipwreck, one of the worst in Pacific Northwest history. Subsequent investigation showed that the collision had been avoidable; that the master of the *Orpheus* had sailed away, leaving the *Pacific's* company to their fate; that the passenger liner's officers and crew had been incompetent; that the *Pacific* had been rotten, her hull so thin that little more than a layer of paint had separated her unsuspecting passengers from the sea.

Whether or not human error played a significant role in the sinking of the Canadian Pacific liner *Princess Sophia* 1918 remains a matter of conjecture; only the loss of all 343 persons aboard is indisputable record.

Twenty-two years before, the collapse of the Point Ellice bridge in Victoria had claimed 55 lives. The plunging of a streetcar crowded with holiday-goers into the harbor shocked the nation. Examination of the bridge showed that the collapse of its center span had to occur sooner or later, so rotten were its pilings—rot which had been hastened by the indiscriminate test-borings of city engineers.

And so it went. In 1913 almost the entire Fraser River sockeye run was wiped out when railway construction crews blasting a right-of-way through the canyon all but dammed Hell's Gate and prevented the salmon reaching their upstream spawning grounds. This is one of the first—and worst—ecological disasters in provincial memory. But it served to draw attention to the fact that nature's storehouse was not inexhaustible, that man's irresponsible harvesting of resources could not continue indefinately.

Not all disasters, however, could be blamed on human negligenge or greed. Nature has exacted her due time and again with devastating effect. In the spring of 1894 the Fraser overflowed its banks and flooded hundreds of thousands of acres. Prime farm-lands, homes, roads, bridges and livestock were submerged or washed away, and several settlers lost their lives. More than half a century after, despite an extensive dyking system, history repeated itself. This time the damage toll was even greater as much of the Fraser Valley was turned into a lake. Damages totalled in the millions of dollars and required years of repairs.

In 1918 millions of lives were lost during the world-wide influenza epidemic. Residents of British Columbia were not spared and the resulting panic turned the province's largest cities into ghost towns as people avoided social contacts by sheltering in their homes.

Twenty years after a panic of a very different nature swept the land—depression. This economic disaster claimed people's savings rather than their lives, although tens of thousands experienced years-long hardship and privation before the Second World War brought full employment and hardships of an altogether different kind.

Throughout *British Columbia Disasters* Mr. Pethick has examined the causes and effects of the tragedies covered. *How* did they happen? *Why*? Could they happen again? Not content with a superficial look he has dug deeply to achieve a book that is enjoyable, entertaining and informative. The history of British Columbia disasters is in effect the history of British Columbia; the events and forces which made—and broke—many pioneers when they were faced with calamity. Most rose to the occasion with courage and determination; others lost their nerves and their lives. This paradox of human nature is made all the more intriguing by the knowledge that some of the worst disasters were avoidable and quite foreseeable. But greed, cowardice and ignorance are also human characteristics. Such are the elements of great drama.

Mr. Pethick has captured all of these elements in 15 chapters and over a period of almost 90 years. ●

1862
The Smallpox Epidemic

At the present rate of mortality, not many months can elapse ere the northern Indians of this coast will exist only in story.

The *British Colonist*, June 12, 1862

VICTORIA in the spring of 1862 held less than 5,000 people, but Governor Douglas had recently expressed the hope that, before the year was out, it would officially become a city, with its own mayor and aldermen. In that case, no doubt, it would cease to be called "the Fort," and indeed, the expression already seemed out of date.

The community had long since expanded well beyond the palisaded trading post which Douglas had founded in 1843. At that time he had been second-in-command at Fort Vancouver on the lower Columbia River, headquarters for all operations of the Hudson's Bay Company west of the Rocky Mountains. Soon after 1840, a tide of immigrants had begun flowing across the plains from the eastern United States toward the fertile valleys of Oregon and California, and officials of the company had realized that before long those areas would come under exclusive American control. Accordingly, Douglas had been sent north by Chief Factor John McLoughlin to found a new trading post on Vancouver Island which, it was hoped, would remain indefinitely under the British flag.

This done, Douglas left the post under the direction of Charles Ross, later Roderick Finlayson, and returned to Fort Vancouver. In 1849 Vancouver Island became a crown colony, Richard Blanshard was sent out from England as its first governor, and Douglas came north from Fort Vancouver to take charge of

trade with the natives. Blanshard soon resigned and, in the fall of
1851, was succeeded by Douglas. For some years the resource-
ful Scot exercised virtually sole authority in the colony. In 1856,
on instructions from London, a seven-man legislature was
elected to assist him. As the years went by, a small but steady
trickle of immigrants made the long journey around Cape Horn
from the British Isles. By 1858 the settlement held about 300
souls, nearly all of whom were in some way dependent upon the
fur trade.

Then, almost overnight, the little community was transformed. Gold was discovered on the lower Fraser River, and
thousands of miners streamed north from California to make
their fortunes. As Fort Victoria was the only port in the northwest where tools, clothing and other supplies were available, it
was soon caught up in a wild economic boom. Within a few
months, hundreds of houses and stores were hastily knocked together, tradesmen arrived to open a wide variety of businesses,
and the population leaped in a single year from 300 to 5,000. In
the fall of 1858 a new colony, named British Columbia, was
created on the mainland. Douglas, having severed all connections with the HBC, was appointed its governor, and divided
his time and energies between the two colonies.

The boom subsided somewhat in 1859, but the discovery in
the fall of 1860 of far richer deposits of gold in the Cariboo
brought renewed prosperity. By 1862, it was hard to remember
the little world of early 1858, so greatly had the gold rush
changed it.

For example, one of the two bastions which had defended
Victoria from possible trouble with the natives had already been
dismantled, while the other bastion and the remains of the
palisade were generally regarded as nuisances. The town now
had a newspaper: the *Colonist*, founded by the eccentric Amor
De Cosmos, had flourished since December 11, 1858. Its editor,
who was also its chief reporter, provided a lively picture of
events in the community, as well as denouncing Governor
Douglas for not moving the colony more quickly in the direction
of democracy.

There was indeed much for De Cosmos to write about in the
spring of 1862. In far-away England, Prince Albert had suddenly
died, and Queen Victoria had entered her long solitary widow-
hood. South of the border (determined in the Pacific Northwest
by the Oregon Treaty of 1846) the Civil War was raging, and
there were even occasional outbreaks of violence between
Northern and Southern sympathizers in Victoria. A gasworks
which, it was hoped, would illuminate the town before the year
was out was under construction; camels brought from distant

China via San Francisco and destined for the Cariboo were on view in Victoria; and the vigilant De Cosmos had even observed a woman in trousers!

Most important of all, perhaps, Governor Douglas had recently resolved to construct a wagon road from the lower Fraser all the way to the Cariboo, a distance of at least 300 miles. Thomas Spence was about to sign a contract with Colonel Richard Moody, commander of the Royal Engineers on the mainland, for construction of certain sections, and advertisements asking for 1,000 laborers were appearing in the *Colonist*. Nor was this the only great project envisioned. Alfred Waddington, a Victoria businessman with contacts in several parts of the world, believed that a road should be built westward from the Cariboo to Bute Inlet, and, in March 1862, had signed an agreement with Douglas' government by which, in return for constructing the road, he would be allowed to collect tolls on it for five years.

Clearly, then, it was a hopeful time for Victoria, and its white residents looked forward to another bustling year. But what of those of darker skin, once sole possessors of the land, now "wandering between two worlds", the old ways and the new?

When Europeans first reached the north Pacific coast in the 18th century, their arrival had often been beneficial to the natives they encountered. In exchange for furs, they obtained goods previously unknown to them, which were useful in further developing their already complex culture. The remarkable art of the region, for example, reached its zenith in the middle of the 19th century.

Yet not all the results of the mingling of two very different cultures had been happy; liquor soon took its toll, and guns, bought from white men, were used in savage tribal wars. Moreover, the confrontation of the natives by a society with entirely different aims, standards and beliefs from their own, caused much confusion. The white newcomers were obviously powerful and clever; should those who had been in the Northwest for untold centuries cast aside the immemorial wisdom and traditions of their ancestors and adopt the customs of these strangers? Faced with this choice, many inevitably lost their bearings and gave way to apathy or debauchery. Conditions thus existed for the disintegration of Indian culture; if any new danger were to be added to those already pressing on it, the results could well be disastrous.

In 1862, large numbers of Indians were encamped in the vicinity of Victoria. Lured by the attractions of the white metropolis, for some years visiting parties of natives had made their way down the coast in their big canoes, and often camped on

the very spot where the Empress Hotel now welcomes a different sort of tourist. Such tribes as the Tlingit from the Alaskan
Panhandle, the Haidas from the Queen Charlotte Islands, as
well as the Kwakiutl, Tsimsian and Nootka were well represented. Some of these groups were frequently at war with others
when on their home territory, but it was understood that they
must bury their differences while in the vicinity of the fort. In
addition to these visitors, there was a permanent settlement of
Salish (then called Songhees or Songish) in the Victoria area.

Already, history had suggested that any outbreak of disease
among the natives might have serious results. Even before 1800,
white traders along the coast had seen the marks of smallpox.
There had been an epidemic of malaria in California and Oregon
in the early 1830s; later that same decade, smallpox had carried
off many natives on the more northerly part of the coast.
Fortunately the disease had not spread farther south than Port
Simpson, a little north of present-day Prince Rupert. In the
1850s there had been numerous deaths from smallpox among
the natives of the Yakima Valley, not far south of British
Columbia. No one could be sure that the dread disease would
never strike Victoria, but it was hoped that, if it did, the new
medical technique of vaccination would do much to reduce its
effect.

The mild Pacific spring had already brought crocuses and
daffodils to southern Vancouver Island when, on March 19, the
Colonist first drew the attention of its readers to the appearance
in the area of variola, as smallpox was then often called. Only a
single case had been discovered, that of a recent arrival from
San Francisco who had shown symptoms of the disease at about
the time his ship reached Victoria. However the *Colonist*
reported that there were quite a few cases in the big seaport to
the south, then Victoria's main link with the outside world, and
warned that the matter should by no means be ignored:

"As our city is now in almost weekly communication with the
Bay City, the danger of contagion from that quarter is neces-
sarily very great, and we therefore hope that we shall not be
regarded as alarmists when we advise our citizens—and more
especially those who design proceeding to the mines, where
proper medical treatment and good nursing are not to be
obtained at any price—to proceed at once to a physician and
undergo vaccination. The cost is but a trifle when compared with
the perfect immunity from the loathsome disease which those
who may take this precaution will enjoy.

"The varioloid patient alluded to above is roomed, we understand, in a thickly populated neighborhood, and in a house
where several other persons reside. He is well looked after and

cared for; but from sanitary motives we would recommend his immediate removal, if possible, to comfortable quarters in the suburbs of the town."

The following day the *Colonist* reported that the sick man had been removed to a house in the suburbs, that doctors had declared his case to be a mild one, and that he was expected to recover in a few days. On March 22, however, the newspaper reported a case in New Westminster, also that of a recent arrival from California; on the 26th De Cosmos urged prompt action by the government:

"We call the attention of the authorities to the fact that small pox has been introduced into this country from San Francisco... The most stringent regulations ought to be enforced, and enforced without a moment's delay. If a case occurs, the parties ought to be placed beyond the reach of communicating the infection to others. Imagine for a moment what a fearful calamity it would be, were the horde of Indians on the outskirts of the town to take the disease...We have no wish to be an alarmist, but we believe there is danger, if the smallpox be allowed to spread through the neglect of the authorities."

Some residents of Victoria evidently took the matter seriously, for soon the *Colonist* was noting that "a large number of citizens were vaccinated during the day by the several physicians."

The paper warned again of the dangers lurking in the native encampments around the town:

"The disease, we fear, will make sad havoc among the Indians unless stringent sanitary measures are adopted."

On March 28, not only did the *Colonist* report that the chain gang was cleaning out the gutters of the town as a sanitary precaution, but also gave the first hint that the situation was becoming serious:

"It is reported, but with how much truth we cannot say, that the loathsome disease has already broken out at the Songish village, and that several children have been attacked. The physicians are daily besieged by applicants for vaccination, who have become alarmed at the prospect of the spread of the disease. . . By order of the government, some 30 Indians were vaccinated on Wednesday by Dr. Helmcken."

As April dawned, De Cosmos noted that more and more of the white residents of Victoria were taking steps to protect themselves:

"Nearly everybody goes in for vaccination nowadays, and it is safe to say that at least one half of the resident Victorians have had the cuticle of their left arm slightly abraded and vaccine matter insinuated. More people with lame arms may be met on the thoroughfare any hour of the day than there were crippled

warriors after the battle of Bull's Run to be seen on the streets of
Washington."

Many Indians were also starting to avail themselves of the
white man's magic; in the next three weeks, Dr. Helmcken,
Victoria's pioneer doctor and son-in-law of Governor Douglas,
vaccinated more than 500 natives. Rumors of an epidemic in
Victoria were evidently spreading, for, near the end of April
". . .several Nettinett (Nitinat) Indians, who live near Cape
Flattery, called on the Governor, and said that they had been
deputized by their tribe to ascertain whether there was any truth
in a story told them by some white scamps that Gov. Douglas
was about to send the smallpox among them for the purpose of
killing off the tribe and getting their land. They were assured that
they had been hoaxed and left the next day for their home."

By this time, however, there could be no doubt that the
situation in the Victoria area was dangerous. There was an
encampment of Tsimsians near the fort, and soon the *Colonist*
had to report the most somber news so far:

"Some 20 deaths have already occurred in their village, and
so far as we have learned every case has been fatal.

"The chances are that the pestilence will spread among our
white population, a fit judgment for their intolerable wickedness
in allowing such a nest of filth and crime to accumulate within
sight of their houses and within hearing of our church bells. . . .
The Indians have free access to the town day and night. They
line our streets, fill the pit in our theatre, are found at nearly
every open door during the day and evening in the town, and
are even employed as servants in our dwellings, and in the
culinary departments of our restaurants and hotels.

"The entire Indian population should be removed from the
reservation to a place remote from communication with the
whites, whilst the infected houses with all their trumpery should
be burned to ashes, and the graves of the dead covered so
thoroughly as to make the escape of effluvia impossible."

It was now plain that the community faced a crisis, and
accounts of the situation began taking on increasing vividness
and urgency:

"Two deaths occurred on Saturday night, and several of the
patients appear at their last gasp. . . . As soon as a death occurs
in a hut and the body has been removed, the house is torn down
by its owner and the lumber removed to a new site, and re-
erected. The blankets and clothing used by the deceased are not
destroyed.

"Yesterday morning we noticed one of the sufferers
apparently in the last stage of the disease—his body covered
with corruption and sores and the death-rattle sounding in his

throat—while not five paces away sat a dozen or fifteen young bucks, his late associates or maybe his relatives, engaged in gambling, quite as unconcerned and indifferent as if the smallpox were a thousand miles away."

The first natives to take alarm were apparently the local Salish, for at the end of April they suddenly left for their traditional fishing grounds in the San Juan Islands. The Tsimsians, however, were not allowed time to make their own decision; they were given one day to leave the Victoria area, and the *Colonist* noted that "one of the gunboats will assist in the enforcement of these orders." A day or two later, the paper reported, their camp "was fired in the afternoon and every vestige destroyed." By this time the Tsimsians had embarked on the long journey up the coast—taking the dread infection with them.

Early in May there were 11 serious cases in the local encampment of Fort Rupert natives. By this time a special hospital had been built for whites and another for Indians, but the death toll continued to mount. By May 8 even the formidable Haidas were suffering from smallpox, and De Cosmos declared that every single Indian must be removed from the Victoria area at once. However, Governor Douglas was absent on the mainland, and for the moment no one else felt equal to enforcing so drastic an order.

More natives now moved of their own free will to islands in Haro Strait, but others refused to leave the vicinity of the fort, and on May 13 its white residents took drastic action. As the *Colonist* reported the next morning, "Yesterday the Northern Indian huts on the reserve were fired by order of the Police Commissioner and burned to the ground. Probably 100 huts were thus destroyed. . . . The Indians were notified to leave on Saturday last, and three days having elapsed and no notice being taken of the warning, fire was resorted to for the purpose of compelling them to evacuate. . . . We should not be in the least surprised if the disease were to visit and nearly destroy every tribe of Indians between here and Sitka."

It is a remarkable commentary on human nature in times of crisis that even though on Queen Victoria's birthday "the bodies of three Indians were. . .reported festering in the sun on the beach at the rear of the Government buildings," the traditional celebrations of the holiday went ahead as usual. It comes as rather a shock to read that "The numerous representatives of other countries and nationalities joined heart and soul in the festivities of the occasion. . . . The (Beacon) Hill was alive with young and old people, on horseback or afoot, and general enjoyment seemed the order of the day."

There were still some 70 Indians encamped at Ogden Point, on the extreme southern tip of the island. Thirty of them were found to be dying, and De Cosmos estimated that "If the mortuary statistics could be obtained, it would be ascertained that at least one third of all the northern Indians who were until lately encamped on the reserve or resided with townspeople as servants have already died under its influence. At the present rate of mortality, a northern Indian will be an object of curiosity in two years from now."

A new problem now faced the community. If every native was to be forced to leave the area, should this include Indian women living with white men? If so, should their white protectors suffer the same fate? De Cosmos believed he had an answer which was morally, if not medically sound:

"The question becomes a knotty one, and the knots to our view can only be untied by drawing them still tighter with the assistance of a clergyman. Humanize yourselves, civilize your paramours, and legitimize your children without delay!"

Soon afterwards, the *Colonist* reported how this problem had been solved:

"The sweeping order issued last week from the Police Department to compel all northern Indians and squaws to evacuate the city limits has been so far modified as to exclude from its provisions those squaws who are living as the mistresses of white men. Each mistress on application at the Police office is provided with a registered permit, which she can show in case of any attempt being made to enforce the original order by policemen. We understand that a bill to license the keeping of squaws will shortly be introduced into the Assembly."

A few days later, two policemen were sent to the Indian encampment at Ogden Point to report on conditions there. To their surprise they found no natives at all, only "a deathlike stillness reigning over the neighborhood, and a strong smell of decaying animal matter pervading the atmosphere."

As numerous possessions were scattered about, and the doors of the native huts were open, the officers concluded that their owners would shortly return. After a considerable time, however, they were informed by a passing native that nearly the entire encampment had died, and that the remainder, numbering perhaps a dozen, had left the area. An examination of the huts revealed that as the disease had taken its relentless daily toll, the natives had buried their dead under the very huts in which the survivors continued to live.

Yet, again, the white citizens seemed to be able to blot out these dreadful sights from their minds. The same issue of the *Colonist* which reported these horrifying developments in detail, also noted that a new church was about to be consecrated at Nanaimo, and urged its readers to seize the opportunity for a steamship excursion "to enjoy the beautiful scenery of the coast and the delightful weather at this season, in combination with rendering support for a good work. . . . The fare there and back will be $3."

Events in the Cariboo, where one of the greatest gold rushes in history was at its peak, received at least as much space in the press as the smallpox. A letter, often reprinted since, from a miner to a friend in Victoria, first appeared at this time in the *Colonist*:

"I am well and so are all the rest of the boys. I avail myself of the present opportunity to write you half a dozen lines to let you know that I am well and doing well—making from two to three thousand dollars a day! Times good—grub high—whiskey bad—money plenty."

In mid-June the authorities supervised the enforced removal of the last northern Indians from the Victoria area. About 300 Haidas set sail in 26 canoes for the Queen Charlottes. At the request of Chief Edensaw they were accompanied by a gunboat as far as Nanaimo, lest their traditional enemies ambush them in the Gulf of Georgia. There were now no Indians near the fort, and the *Colonist* made a sober assessment of the dimensions of the tragedy:

"How have the mighty fallen! Four short years ago, numbering their braves by thousands, they were the scourge and terror of the coast. Today, broken-spirited and effeminate, with scarce a corporal's guard of warriors remaining alive, they are proceeding northward, bearing with them the seeds of a loathsome disease that will take root and bring a plentiful crop of ruin and destruction to the friends who have remained at home.

"At the present rate of mortality, not many months can elapse ere the northern Indians of this coast will exist only in story."

This judgement was to prove accurate. Each group of natives returning to its village brought with it the plague, and soon the remotest inlets were filled with the dead and the dying. A ship's captain who came down the coast to Victoria reported many such sights along the way, and declared, "All Indians not vaccinated will die this summer." This roused De Cosmos to ask:

"What were our philanthropists about, that they were not up the coast ahead of the disease two months ago, engaged in vaccinating the poor wretches who have since fallen victims? Who among our missionaries will volunteer to save the aborigines from utter extermination?"

Such questions were academic; all that remained was to calculate the magnitude of the disaster. On July 7 the *Colonist* declared:

"The northerners as tribes are now nearly exterminated. They have disappeared from the face of this fair earth at the approach of the pale-face, as snow melts beneath the rays of the noonday sun. . . . In a few years the sight of an Indian in these parts will be considered as great a curiosity as if a mastodon were to suddenly rise from the grave which he had occupied for centuries, and claim his ancient prerogative as lord of the brute creation."

A few groups of natives had escaped the full force of the plague. A Roman Catholic priest had vaccinated most of the Cowichan tribe in time. The Anglican misssionary, William Duncan, had recently taken a group of his Indian converts from near Fort Simpson to a new location at Metlakatla, where he established a remarkable community and taught the natives many useful skills, while endeavoring to protect them from the moral dangers which the white man had also brought to the coast. Because he vaccinated his followers, the epidemic affected very few of them. Natives in other areas were not so fortunate; as late as August, the chief of the Sooke tribe, some 20 miles west of Victoria, died, as did many of his people. Some members of the white community also perished, including one of the policemen who had examined the ghostly encampment at Ogden Point. He had not been vaccinated.

Nevertheless, the white inhabitants of Victoria, who had seen much of this tragedy unfold before their eyes, seemed able to forget it once it was no longer before them. The Fourth of July was celebrated with enthusiasm (the First would have no significance in this area until well after 1867); a well-filled excursion steamer sailed from Victoria to Olympia for the holiday. On August 2 Governor Douglas signed the bill which officially made Victoria a city, and, on August 16, after a brief but lively election campaign, the portly butcher, Thomas Harris, became its first mayor. Good news continued to come from the Cariboo, as did exciting news from the American battlefields. In September the *Tynemouth* arrived from the British Isles with a cargo of prospective brides; the *Colonist* reported that "a large and anxious crowd of breeches-wearing bipeds assembled to see the women disembark, and generally expressed themselves as well pleased with their appearance." Meanwhile the gasworks was almost ready to illuminate the streets, and the question was widely debated: was it the appropriate moment to pave them?

As the year waned, more horse races were held in Beacon Hill Park, during the celebration of the birthday of the Prince of Wales; the new City Council set the speed limit at eight miles per hour and decreed that vehicles must keep to the left of the road. Real estate prices rose satisfactorily, street lights made their promised appearance, and De Cosmos asserted it was time to adopt the metric system, declaring that it "must ultimately obtain in all civilized countries." As winter set in, a few more cases of smallpox were reported from time to time in the vicinity of Victoria, but, by the end of the year, it was apparent that, at least in that area, the epidemic had passed.

Elsewhere, however, it was a different story. As each tribe of Indians had abandoned its dead and carried its dying back to their homes on the northern coast, they had carried the epidemic to even the remotest inlets. Often entire villages were wiped out, and trading vessels found familiar ports of call silent and deserted. One ship's captain who reached Victoria from the Stikine district in the summer of 1862, recounted his experiences for the *Colonist*:

"Captain Whitford, while on his passage from Stickeen to this place, counted over 100 bodies of Indians who had died from the smallpox between Kefeaux and Nanaimo. In some instances, attempts had been made by the survivors to burn the dead, by heaping brush over their remains and setting it on fire; but it had partially failed in most instances, and the fuel had burned out, leaving the blackened half-roasted bodies to rot, and pollute the air with their overpowering exhudations. On two islands, Captain Whitford saw four squaws. They had been attacked with the smallpox and were left on the islands to die with a small quantity of food and water at their sides; but had quite unexpectedly recovered and were subsisting on berries. They were subsequently taken off by Indians."

In the interior, too, the epidemic took its dreadful toll. A letter from a missionary to Governor Douglas gave some idea of the disaster:

"The native population around Lillooet have for the last two months been suffering under the visitation of smallpox. This disease has made fearful ravages amongst them, sweeping off whole families, and literally converting their camps into graveyards. It is ascertained that upwards of 150 have perished in this neighbourhood alone."

A government official in the gold-mining area reported even heavier casualties:

"The smallpox has been raging amongst the Indians throughout the district (with the exception of Williams Lake). At Beaver Lake nearly 50 have fallen victims, and one Indian now represents the tribe."

Lt. H. S. Palmer of the Royal Engineers, who explored the area between North Bentinck Arm and Fort Alexandria for the government in 1862, reported to Colonel Moody conditions in the regions he traversed:

"Smallpox has this year contributed a sad quota of death. During my stay there this disease, which had only just broken out when I arrived, spread so rapidly that in a week nearly all the healthy had scattered from the lodges and gone to encamp by families in the woods, only, it is to be feared, to carry away the seeds of infection and death in the blankets and other articles they took with them. Numbers were dying each day; sick men and women were taken out into the woods and left with a blanket and two or three salmon to die by themselves and rot unburied. Sick children were tied to trees, and naked, gray-haired medicine men, hideously painted, howled and gesticulated night and day in front of the lodges, in mad efforts to stay the progress of the disease."

It is estimated that when the 19th century opened, there were about 80,000 Indians in what is now British Columbia, most of them concentrated along the coast where the cedar and salmon provided most of the necessities of life. This population had declined slightly, although not enough to cause alarm. Between 1862 and 1864, however, about 20,000 natives perished. So great was the disruption of their culture that, even when the epidemic had largely spent its force, the population continued to decline. By 1885 it fell to about 28,000; almost 50 years after it reached a low of about 22,000, when it began a slow but steady rise which, in recent years, has accelerated.

More than numbers perished in the great disaster of 1862; a way of life, in which each knew his place in both his tribe and the universe, had also suffered shipwreck. Perhaps if there had been no epidemic, an accommodation might gradually have taken place between the age-old native ways and the customs brought by the white man; but the double pressure of the epidemic and the coming of new lords to the land had proved too much to withstand, and even those whose bodies remained healthy were often left sick in spirit. Flowers spring up quickly in the wake of a forest fire, but it takes longer for hope to revive. It would take several generations before the Indian began seeing himself as more than a survivor of a vanishing race, and again feel pride in his past and confidence in his destiny. Even then, the road back would prove long and rocky.

1862 had seen the first, and doubtless the greatest, disaster ever to strike British Columbia; but its white residents, forgetting the anxious days of spring and the horrifying days of summer, were soon viewing the year in a different light. As 1863 arrived, Governor Douglas spoke hopefully to the tiny legislature of new settlements at Cowichan and Comox, and of the likelihood that they would soon have regular steamship service from Victoria. Another outpost of white enterprise was also about to be founded at Quatsino, on the west coast of Vancouver Island, where coal mining and lumbering would be developed. The Governor hoped that a geological survey of the colony could soon be undertaken. His address was encouraging and covered a wide variety of topics; the epidemic, however, was not among them.

Nor was it mentioned in the editorial with which the *Colonist* greeted the new year. Looking back over the previous 12 months, its editor viewed them in what he clearly felt was the right perspective:

"Another year has passed over our heads. The year of grace, one thousand and eight hundred and sixty-three, today commences its career. We hope we may have to chronicle at its end the continuation of the progress that has characterized the past twelve months. For progress there has been to a most cheering extent. No matter from what point we view our development, there is every ground for congratulation. Everything shows a rapid and healthy growth. Everything tends to inspire confidence in the progress of the colony."   ●

1864
The Bute Inlet Massacre

*"I have rejected all offers of assistance from men bent on vengeance.
I aim at securing justice only."*

Governor Seymour, despatch of May 20, 1864

THE smallpox epidemic of 1862 had been the greatest disaster ever to strike the native peoples of British Columbia; yet the white residents of the two British colonies on the Pacific coast apparently soon forgot it. It was sufficient that the Indians who arrived each year with their furs at Fort Victoria were no longer dying before the eyes of its citizens; sufficient that they had fled back to their native villages, bearing with them the dread infection. In the deep coastal fiords laughter would fall silent, the long-houses stand deserted; but to the new lords of the land this mattered little. Their eyes were all turned elsewhere —toward the creeks of Cariboo, where the great gold rush which began on the lower Fraser in 1858 was now at its glittering peak.

In a few short years it had transformed a large part of the Pacific Northwest. Once a vast wilderness, dotted here and there with small fur trading posts, the gold rush was rapidly incorporating it into the busy 19th century world. Victoria now had 5,000 inhabitants, a newspaper, street lights; there was regular steamship service from San Francisco. New Westminster and Nanaimo, though much smaller, were also thriving. What the future might hold was of course unsure; but so much had happened in half a dozen years that very few were prepared to be pessimistic.

As 1864 opened, there were still not one but two British crown colonies on the Pacific coast, with the energetic Scot,

James Douglas, governor of both and dividing his time between them. Not until 1866 would the colonies of Vancouver Island and British Columbia be united, and not until 1871 would the colony of British Columbia become a province of the Dominion of Canada. Yet already a major change was impending: Douglas, knighted for his many services, was about to retire into private life, and the British government had decided that each colony should have its own governor.

Many problems would face the two new representatives of the crown, but one which had apparently been solved by Douglas was that of providing easy communication between the gold fields and the coast. The earliest route to the upper Fraser had been the Harrison-Lillooet trail. This left the Fraser at its junction with the Harrison River, and travelled up the Harrison to Harrison lake, at the far end of which was the small community of Port Douglas. The trail then continued past (or if boats were used, through) Lillooet Lake, Anderson Lake and Seton Lake. From there it was but a short distance to the Fraser at Lillooet, not far south of the gold fields. This rough trail had been greatly improved in the summer of 1858 by a large corps of laborers who had been promised by Douglas that when it was finished they would be the first to use it—a considerable inducement in the circumstances. By October of that year it was in general use.

In some ways, however, it had proven unsatisfactory. If boats were employed (and several steamers were soon in service on the lakes) it involved several portages, with the added dangers and costs which these entailed; moreover, the rocky terrain was damaging to the hooves of horses, which suggested that it could never be used by stagecoaches.

These considerations had caused Douglas to envision and then doggedly push through the greatest of his achievements—the Cariboo Road. This began at Yale on the western bank of the Fraser, later crossed the river over the famous Alexandra suspension bridge, and then moved northward along the other bank to Lytton (named after Lord Lytton, British Colonial Secretary and author of *The Last Days of Pompeii*). At this point the Thompson flowed into the Fraser, and the road, leaving the main stream, followed for a time the banks of its tributary. Later it left the Thompson as well. Eventually the road rejoined the Fraser near Lac La Hache, and from there continued north to Quesnel. It was completed to this point in 1864, and the following year was extended eastward from Quesnel to Barkerville, the center of mining activity.

Described by the *Colonist* after Douglas' death as "a monument to the genius of the great mind that conceived and executed it," the Cariboo Road was wide enough for stagecoaches, and soon there was a steady, two-way flow of traffic. A gold escort was organized to protect those travelling down to the coast with their winnings; and before long the freight and passenger service developed by Francis Barnard was operating on a regular schedule, with relays of fresh horses ready at each of the famous road-houses along the route.

Most residents of the two Pacific colonies were highly pleased with this great economic artery, but there was one Victoria resident who felt otherwise. He was determined that a completely new path should be opened from the gold fields to the coast, and to this cause was willing to devote both his energies and his fortune.

Alfred Waddington was unusual in another respect: he had first come to the New World not as a young but a middle-aged man. Born in London in 1801, his family had important business connections in both England and France, and he himself studied at both French and German universities. Later he became manager of an ironworks in Brittany. When the California gold rush began in 1849, the adventurous Waddington resolved to see it first-hand. He made the long journey to San Francisco, and soon became a partner in a prosperous wholesale business in provisions. When a second gold rush erupted a few hundred miles to the north in 1858, he promptly moved to Victoria and opened a branch of his firm.

Instead of leaving the new outlet in charge of a subordinate, he decided to remain on Vancouver Island and, before long, was a prominent figure in its affairs. Not only did he supply the new wave of miners with tools and provisions, but he found time to write the first book ever published in the area. Printed on the same small press which produced the *Colonist*, it not only gave its readers a vivid first-hand picture of the fantastic summer of 1858, but became the subject of the paper's earliest book review. This appeared in its first issue of December 11, 1858. Copies of this book (only about a dozen still exist) now fetch $1000, but the modest Waddington only asked 50 cents.

The main thesis of the book, *The Fraser Mines Vindicated*, was one which Waddington would untiringly proclaim for the rest of his life: that the future of Britain's Pacific colonies was unlimited. Some of those who had had no luck on the lower Fraser were declaring that the gold rush was a fraud; but Waddington correctly predicted that the boom was merely beginning.

Soon he was taking an active part in the public life of Victoria, and in 1859 published a pamphlet entitled *The Necessity of Reform*. Waddington's name did no appear on the title page; the author was merely given as "one of the people." The pamphlet pointed out that most of the members of the Vancouver Island

House of Assembly were past or present employees of the Hudson's Bay Company, and that the franchise, restricted to those owning 20 acres of land, excluded many worthy city-dwellers, including merchants and professional men. By way of correcting this situation, in 1860 Waddington successfully stood for election to the Assembly. Yet something evidently palled— perhaps the necessity of constant attendance—and before long he resigned. It soon became apparent that this was merely in order to pursue his cherished causes more vigorously.

Chief among these, it quickly transpired, was a new road from the gold fields to the coast. By 1861 the upper, not the lower Fraser, was the center of activity, and Waddington believed that a completely new route should be opened from that area to the coast. This would go westward from the Cariboo and over the coastal mountains to the head of one of the deep inlets along the Pacific. There a new community would develop, through which trade would flow back and forth between the gold fields and the larger world.

Not many people on the mainland felt much enthusiasm for Waddington's project, as it would inevitably reduce the importance and prosperity of such centers as New Westminster. By contrast, many Victoria citizens felt that their city would benefit by the proposed new trade route, and were prepared to give Waddington both moral and financial support. Among them were such prominent figures as Dr. J. S. Helmcken and Dr. S. F. Tolmie.

Some preliminary surveys of the area between the Cariboo and the coast had already been made by others. In early September 1858 Governor Douglas had sent Joseph McKay (a trusted employee of the HBC who, five years earlier, had opened up the coal fields at Nanaimo and built its famous bastion) to examine the country west of Lillooet. Leaving Fort Langley with a party which included three Indian guides, he went up the Fraser and later the Harrison River. His report on the country between Lillooet and Howe Sound did not suggest that it would ever contain a broad highway of commerce; Douglas informed Lord Lytton, the Colonial Secretary, that "the country examined is mountainous, with some fertile valleys and very fine timber, but not attractive as a place of settlement."

In 1859 the Governor asked Major Downie, whom he termed "a respectable Scotchman," to examine the area around Jervis Inlet. Downie had had considerable experience in the California gold fields, and had accompanied McKay in 1858. Downie spent the winter of 1858/59 in the vicinity of Desolation Sound, and returned via the Fraser Valley in the spring; however, nothing he had seen made him envision the area as the site of a major trade route.

Despite these adverse reports, Waddington's mind was made up, and late in the summer of 1861 he wrote to Governor Douglas to propose that, in return for building a road from Bute Inlet to the Cariboo, he should receive the right to charge tolls on it for five years. The Governor was agreeable to the proposition, provided that Colonel Moody, Chief Commissioner of Lands and Works, approved of it, that the road was at least 10 feet wide, and that it was completed "within a reasonable time, say 12 months from date of charter."

This was enough for Waddington, and on September 19 he left with a small party for Bute Inlet and went up the Homathco River for 32 miles. On his return he again wrote to the governor, informing him that the river ran for at least 120 miles into the interior, and that there was a good pass through the coastal range. He had also anticipated the realization of his vision by christening one of its lofty peaks "Mount Success."

Shortly afterwards, Waddington sent another small party under Robert Homfray to make a preliminary survey of the entire route of the proposed road. Homfray set out in the fall of 1861 with four white companions, two Indian guides and a lively prose style "in a frail canoe, on to the head of Bute Inlet, up an unknown river and through an unknown country, among mountains covered with snow, and surrounded by fierce and savage tribes who had never seen a white man, besides the great risk of being buried under avalanches, attacked by hungry wolves, not to mention the ever-to-be-dreaded grizzly, with the off chance of perishing miserably in the snow from starvation and exposure."

After many adventures, which included being captured by one band of Indians and rescued by another, the party eventually reached a point high in the coastal mountains. There seemed little hope of crossing them into the interior, and they retraced their steps. Their canoe was destroyed in some rapids, but they built a raft which they successfully floated down the Homathco to the head of Bute Inlet. Homfray was not hopeful about building a road through the area, but refrained from making his views known publicly; as he explained many years later, "Mr. Waddington feared my descriptions of the many dangers encountered would prevent parties joining him in making the road through the Cariboo."

Despite this latest adverse report on the area, Waddington did not turn back. On March 28, 1862, he signed an agreement with the government of the mainland colony (as represented by Colonel Moody), which guaranteed him, upon the successful completion of the proposed road, three farthings for every pound of goods carried over it, four shillings and a penny (i.e. a dollar) for every horse and mule that used it, two shillings for every goat and pig, and one shilling for every human being. Next Waddington secured the services of Hermann Otto Tiedemann, a civil engineer. Tiedemann, born in Berlin, had arrived in Victoria in 1858, and quickly attracted attention by his design for Vancouver Island's first legislative buildings, the famous "bird-cages." Though these combined without reconciling several styles of architecture, even their critics agreed that the total effect was arresting.

Tiedemann set out from Victoria on May 16, 1862 in a canoe containing himself, four other white men, and three Indians. After touching at Salt Spring Island and Nanaimo, the party arrived at the mouth of Bute Inlet and set up camp. Because of constant rains, the Indians refused to go any farther and Tiedemann's party was forced to proceed without them.

This was merely the beginning of their difficulties. Not only were they plagued by "muscuitos," but the terrain was very rugged. After going some distance up the Homathco River, Tiedemann recorded in his journal on May 25, "The navigation of the river is getting very dangerous. Had to walk most of the time to the waist in water, which is like ice, and cut trees down, to have a free passage for the line by which we were dragging the canoe upstream. The current is very strong. It rained the whole day besides."

Eventually the river became so clogged by driftwood that the party beached their canoe, buried part of their provisions, and proceeded on foot. Struggling up the mountains, and looking hopefully for the fertile grassland, for a long time all they saw was "nothing but peak after peak, thousands of feet in height and clad in perpetual snow."

Far below them the Homathco remained "a dark chasm, in perpendicular walls of granite," as the party slowly worked its way eastward, often under conditions of great danger:

"To get over one of the perpendicular walls we were obliged to keep upwards on a slanting crevice in the wall about one foot in width, like snakes pushing our axes and guns before us; the least move of our packs on the shoulder would have sent us down 800 feet deep to the river.

Early in June the men ran out of provisions; Tiedemann noting:

"Shot a grouse this morning, divided it in five parts, each man boiling his in his drinking cup to have some soup, and our last bread was also divided. Rained the whole day."

Later a goat was shot and eaten, but, by this time most of the men were ill. Nevertheless they finally got through the

mountains, and Tiedemann was able to record, on June 11,
"Crossed beautiful valleys, splendid grass. Good country for a
waggon road."

Some friendly Indians guided the party the rest of the way to
Fort Alexandria, which they reached in late June. After resting
there for a week, Tiedemann's four men, led by Henry McNeill,
son of the famous captain of the S.S. *Beaver*, made their way
back to the coast by the route they had recently traversed. Tiedemann did not accompany them, so presumably he returned to
Victoria by more orthodox means.

Tiedemann had conceded that part of the route was feasible
for a wagon road, and this was apparently enough for Waddington. He organized a well-attended public meeting in August
1862, in Victoria, at which he exhibited a large map of the Bute
Inlet area, and declared that much of the route through it was
"more like our English parks than a wild stretch of land." He
announced his intention of issuing 500 shares at $100 each to
finance his project, and showed his own good faith by sub-
scribing for 50 shares himself.

Having raised a fair amount of money in this fashion, Waddington engaged workmen, and, on January 2, 1863, registered
the "Bute inlet wagon road company." Among its directors were
Dr. Tolmie, an official of the HBC, Hugh Nelson, a lumberman
who would one day be lieutenant-governor of the province of
British Columbia, and Robert Burnaby, a businessman active in
a variety of enterprises, after whom a suburb of Vancouver
would one day be named. In April 1863, a new expedition
under Waddington's personal command left Victoria in the
steamship *Enterprise*.

The expedition consisted of 91 men, including some French-
Canadian voyageurs, 19 mules and a large quantity of provisions. Among those accompanying Waddington were Lieutenant Peter Leech of the Royal Engineers, and Frederick
Whymper, a globe-trotting British artist. Also in the party were
two hopeful souls who planned to become the first residents of
the metropolis (to be named Waddington) which they believed
would soon rise, like Venus from the foam, on the banks of the
Homathco.

The expedition, after touching at Nanaimo, reached Bute
Inlet, where the venture had a somewhat ominous beginning
when the ship went aground. It was refloated a day or two later,
and the friendly local Indians proved useful in unloading stores.
Their uncertain position between two worlds was reflected in
their appearance, for although their faces were liberally daubed
with black and red paint, "some of these Indians also aped civilization a little, by donning what seemed to be second-hand

soldiers' uniform of no nationality in particular, with all its regalia, and some even were apparelled in black cloth suits of the shabby genteel description, while those not inclined to the mode of civilized dress, still wrapt their stately forms within the folds of either a red, white, blue or green blanket."

No time was lost in marking out a townsite and building store-houses, bunk-houses and a wharf. As axe-men cleared the path previously marked out by Tiedemann, a band of Chilcotin Indians from the interior made their appearance. Their leader, named Tellot, began by producing, of all things in this world, a copy of the *Illustrated London News*. It was not the most recent issue, being dated 1847, but in the margin had been written "Tellot, Chilcoaten chief, a good guide—faithful and trust-worthy etc. Signed, Captain Price."

Events were later to show that Price, who had done some exploration in the Bute Inlet area in 1861, had been tragically mistaken in his estimate of Tellot, but the Chilcotins were soon employed in packing supplies along the trail.

By the middle of June the road, including numerous bridges, had been completed as far as "Boulder Creek," 15 miles up the valley from the inlet. Here Waddington and his men crossed to the other bank of the river in canoes, and soon found them-selves facing the hardest part of their task. As a member of the expedition later recorded, "We were at the feet of the huge mountains, and almost within the hearing of the torrent of water squeezing through the big canyon." The faithful mules continued to bring up supplies from the coast, and soon the faith that moves mountains was supplemented by dynamite:

"A great deal of exploring had yet to be done in this most difficult part of the country, to ensure the safest and best possible route, and at first sight of the difficulties to be overcome one would rather be inclined to turn away from the idea of its possi-bility—the immense walls of rock and terrible yawning gulches, and the huge round bluffs encountered—but the line once defined by our indomitable chief, who was ever scrambling and climbing, and even crawling, for different sights, and peeping over awful precipices, the big work of blasting commenced in real earnest, when every faithful shot gave confidence in removing the gigantic mass."

As the summer advanced, the work went forward, and, once, an advance party caught a glimpse of the promised land:

"Looking far into the distance coastwise, could be traced the deep, dark array of magnificent forest growth, fringing the bank of the winding river down the valley, hemmed in by innumer-able peaks of many heights; and when turning towards the interior, was to be seen distinctly, through a wide gap in the mountainous range, a gradual depression of the mountains, terminating into wide stretches of apparently verdant prairie land, presenting a scene of some relief as it were to the rugged, broken and entangled mass of the surrounding country."

During this period, another small group of men who had been sent on ahead became lost, and barely made their way back to comparative safety:

"They were in a pitiful state; their hunger was hard to appease with safety, as the only food they had had for some days consisted of a wood rat caught by strategem, and an old leather purse, which they cooked. One of the men was so weak when found he could only with difficulty stand erect, and if it had not been for the timely assistance of an Indian hunter, who at intervals packed the weakest on his back, they must all have succumbed to the fate of starvation; but they soon afterwards rallied with proper care and nourishment and often afterwards amused the camp with experiences of three lost travellers."

By autumn considerable progress had been made on the road, and Waddington decided that most of his men should return to Victoria for the winter. A party of 17 was left behind to continue blasting a path through the mountains, while one man, Timothy Smith, was detailed to guard the stores and the expedition's make-shift ferry at the point where the road crossed the river.

On his return to Victoria, Waddington reported his progress to the government. Douglas had never been unduly enthusiastic about the project, but he agreed to extend the deadline for completing the road to the end of 1866. He also gave Waddington permission to sell building lots in the Bute Inlet area, provided that the sales were conducted in Victoria, and promised Waddington "every assistance consistent with the public interest." Meanwhile Waddington declared publicly that the road would definitely be open for traffic some time in 1864, and would make a profit of $100,000 a year. In a prospectus dated December 7, 1863, he urged the public to invest their funds in the project while there was still time to get in on the ground floor.

So winter set in, and residents of Victoria busied themselves with a variety of matters. De Cosmos, in his last few months as editor of the *Colonist*, continued to advocate a wide range of causes. Among the needs of the colony, he declared, were a ferry from North Saanich to a spot further up the island, a history of the early days of the area, a smaller coin than the "bit," and a water system supplied from nearby Elk Lake. A letter from the governor appeared in the paper, in which Douglas declared that his decision to retire was irrevocable; a minor gold rush developed at Leechtown, about 20 miles west of Victoria; and a stock exchange was opened in the city. In the spring of 1864, the man who had founded the city in 1843 did indeed retire and set out at once on a long sea voyage to Europe. Inevitably, citizens in the two Pacific colonies began speculating as to what changes would occur under his successors.

Late in the afternoon of March 25, 1864, Arthur Edward Kennedy stepped ashore at Victoria, and it was soon made apparent that a new era indeed had opened. Whereas Douglas had been aloof and autocratic, Kennedy had an easy friendly manner; whereas Lady Douglas had lived in virtual seclusion, the new governor had a sociable wife and two attractive daughters. Douglas had worked his way up from obscurity, and had seen little of the centers of civilization; Kennedy had been educated at Trinity College, Dublin, was a retired British army officer of Irish extraction, and had previously been governor of Gambia, Sierra Leone and Western Australia. He received an enthusiastic welcome, to which he made a modest reply; and so began what was hoped would be a promising new chapter in the history of Vancouver Island.

New Westminster saw a similar transition from the old days to the new. On April 20 the new governor of the mainland colony arrived on H.M.S. *Forward*. When compared to Douglas, Frederick Seymour was physically unimpressive. A bachelor, he had earned a reputation as a kindly and generous man in other parts of the Empire. He arrived in the little mainland capital—it held about 300 inhabitants—in an atmosphere of general goodwill and, after appropriate celebrations, the colony settled down to its task of carving a civilization out of the wilderness.

It seemed plain that a new chapter had opened for the two colonies, one in which their primitive beginnings would rapidly recede into memory, while more and more they became part of the busy 19th century world of moral and material progress. Admittedly, one of Fort Victoria's two bastions and part of its palisade were still standing, but there was a rising demand that they be dismantled, both as obstacles to traffic and as unnecessary reminders of the days when trouble might be expected from the natives. Such was the scene, and the outlook of Victoria's citizens, when, on the morning of May 11, the steamer *Emily Harris* arrived from Nanaimo with news which in a moment threw all these hopeful assumptions into disarray.

The news was from Bute Inlet, and it was stark indeed: of the 17 men who had been working on the road from the inlet to the Cariboo, at least 12 had been murdered by Indians. Only three were known to have escaped with their lives, and two of these were badly wounded. Horrified readers of the *Colonist* soon learned the gory details of the massacre from the three survivors who had been taken to a hospital in Victoria.

One of them, a native of Denmark named Peter Peterson, told how he and his companions were awakened at dawn on April 30:

"About daybreak I heard two shots fired. I started up and rushed out of the tent. I saw two Indians firing into the tent next to me. One of them on seeing me rushed up and aimed a blow with the butt-end of his musket. I succeeded in warding off the blow, and jumped away, when another Indian came up with a large axe and struck at me with both hands. I jumped to one side and the axe struck the ground. I then ran to the bank of the river and got behind a tree to hide myself, as I saw the Indian who first struck at me coming up with a musket to shoot. The Indian waited for two minutes for a chance to shoot, and was gradually getting closer to me. At last he fired and shot me in the left arm, the ball passing through my wrist. I then jumped into the stream, which was running fast; the blood poured profusely from my wound and discolored the water.

"The Indians, possibly thinking I was killed, did not attempt to follow me, and I was carried down by the stream about a quarter of a mile, being much bruised by rolling over stones and snags. . . . I was stopped by a large stone in the stream and crawled out, and walked a few hundred yards when I was overtaken by Mosley, and as I was unable to walk fast, Mosley went on down to the ferry, and I found him there about an hour afterwards."

Mosley, an Englishman recently arrived from California, told much the same story:

"About daybreak I was awakened by two Indians coming to the door of the tent. They did not enter but raised it up and whooped; at the same time each of them fired on either side of me. I was lying in the centre. They let the tent down. The ridge pole fell on top of me and the tent covered all three of us.

"While lying in this position I saw knives on each side of me come through the tent and pierce the bodies of my two companions. I could see through the side of the tent, and observing Indians going to the other tents, I jumped up and plunged into the river which was about two steps from me. After going down the river about a hundred yards, I got out and saw the Indians, men, women and children, shouting and hallooing where the cook's tent and provisions were. I then turned away and proceeded towards the ferry, meeting with Peterson about two miles below."

The two men were unable to find Tim Smith, the man in charge of the ferry used by the expedition, and the ferry had also disappeared. They barricaded themselves in a small hut, armed themselves with clubs, and prepared to defend their lives. They were not molested that night, and in the morning were joined by another survivor, Philip Buckley. He had passed through much the same experiences:

"I was lying asleep in a tent with another man when about daybreak I received a severe blow on my head, dealt by an Indian who had stealthily entered the tent and struck me with the butt end of a musket. Though partially stunned and confused, I jumped up and rushed to the door of the tent, where I met two Indians who stabbed at me several times with long knives. I received one wound in the right loin, another in the left, and a third severe cut in my left wrist.

"I dropped down between the two Indians, who left me, imagining, no doubt, that I was dead. I then crawled into some brush-wood and there fainted away from loss of blood. In about an hour I came to my senses and heard a noise going on in the camp, but could not see what was being done. I fancied the men were engaged in packing away the things from our camp.

"I managed to crawl a distance of about 150 yards to some water, where I drank eagerly, and remained there till about five o'clock. I felt stronger after quenching my thirst, and started off for Brewster's camp. I had gone about half a mile when I detected the same Indians encamped, and I turned back and remained all night near the spot I left. The next morning before daylight I started off and made the best of my way, though very weak, to the ferry, where I was rejoiced to find Peterson and Mosley."

The three men were later discovered by friendly Indians, who paddled them down the Homathco River to the site of the proposed town on Bute Inlet. From there they were taken to Nanaimo in another canoe, where the steamer *Emily Harris* conveyed them to Victoria.

It was plain that little hope could be held for the rest of the work party, and those who, a short time before, had been ridiculing Victoria's remaining defences began asking themselves if the Bute Inlet massacre marked the start of a general Indian uprising. Even those who doubted this agreed that the murderers must be brought to justice at once, as an unmistakable warning that such crimes would not go unpunished. Governor Kennedy sent news of the massacre to New Westminster (by ship, as there was as yet no telegraph between the two capitals), and Governor Seymour quickly showed that neither his short residence in the colony nor his liking for the pleasures of social life were a hindrance to prompt action.

On May 15 he despatched 28 volunteers under Chartres

Brew, Chief Inspector of Police, to Bute Inlet in the gunboat *Forward*, with orders to advance inland from there. Seymour also sent instructions to William Cox, Gold Commissioner in the Cariboo, to organize a posse and march westward toward Bute Inlet. The two forces were expected to effect a junction in the vicinity of Puntzi Lake, the point where the trails inland from Bentinck Arm and Bute Inlet converged, and it was hoped that in the process they would capture the wanted men.

Brew's party advanced some distance into the interior. They found the going hard, and later reported that Waddington's proposed wagon road was a "fearful trail. . .with 80 zig-zags on each side and a grade of one in two in many places." Before long they had reached the scene of the massacre, where "blood was found on all the tent sites, and the trails to the edge of the river, made by dragging the bodies down, were distinctly visible."

A short time later Brew's men reached the site where an advance party of Waddington's men under William Brewster had been struck down. The corpses still lay where they had fallen; Brewster's heart had been cut out of his body, no doubt so that by eating it his qualities could be transmitted to the murderers. After a brief inquest the remains were buried. That done, Brew decided that it was impossible to advance further into the interior, and returned with his men to Victoria and thence to New Westminster.

Meanwhile the expedition under Cox had started westward from Alexandria on June 8. It comprised about 50 men, including Donald McLean, a retired official of the Hudson's Bay Company, and two of his sons. Cox marched westward, and on June 12 arrived at Puntzi Lake. McLean went in search of Alexis, a Chilcotin chief believed to be friendly to the whites. He located his tribe and convinced them that only the actual murderers were in any danger; whereupon the tribe promised that their chief would soon make contact with Cox.

Some Indians in the area, however, were hostile, as the expedition encountered sporadic sniping in which one man was injured. Cox decided to remain in a small fort at Puntzi Lake, where he flew a white flag continuously as a sign that he entertained no general hostility to Indians.

When Brew returned to New Westminster, Governor Seymour promptly decided that a much stronger expedition must be sent into the interior, this time by way of Bentinck Arm. H.M.S. *Sutlej* left the mainland capital on June 13, with Brew, 38 volunteers, and Governor Seymour himself on board. When they reached the head of Bentinck Arm on June 24, more bad news awaited them. A pack train of 42 horses with eight men under Alexander McDonald, carrying supplies for Waddington's men from Bentinck Arm, had been ambushed, and three men, including McDonald, had been killed. The five survivors had managed to reach the coast, but the question was once again raised: Was a general massacre of whites in the northern interior about to begin?

Seymour's party cautiously made its way inland, and soon came upon evidence of McDonald's last desperate struggle.

"For several miles scattered evidence of white men's industry prepared the way for the scene of the conflict where the 42 horses with their pack saddles became the property of the Indians. There a Siwash tomb of logs, pompously adorned with stakes and flags, showed where a Chilcoaten chief had fallen under a bullet despatched in a dying effort by McDonald.

"About 15 yards from the tomb lay the unburied body of a white man. The wolves had made sad havoc with it, stripped naked as it was, but the features were recognizable and the identity established. The corpse of Higgins, violently distorted but well preserved, lay half a mile off, and a few hundred yards beyond that again, the remains of McDonald. Dead horses in the last stages of decay lay upon the trail."

Pausing briefly to bury the bodies, Seymour's party continued its journey until, on July 6, it reached Puntzi Lake, where Cox was yet entrenched in his log fort. Here the two forces were amalgamated under Seymour's command, although the governor felt he could detect differences between them:

"The men raised in the gold district, mostly Americans, passed the greater part of the night in dancing or playing cards to the accompaniment of war whoops and the beating of tin pots. The New Westminster expedition, almost exclusively English and comprising many discharged sappers, spent the evening in their usual quiet soldierlike manner."

The whites suffered one more fatality in this period. Donald McLean, accompanied by an Indian guide, left the fort to reconnoitre, and on July 17 fell to a bullet from an unseen hand. Governor Seymour remained inside the fort, but patrols were periodically dispatched into the surrounding countryside in search of information and possible aid from the natives.

Eventually contact was made with a Chilcotin chief, Alexis, who came to the fort with a message from the ringleaders of the massacre, Klattasine and Tellot. They professed themselves ready to surrender to white justice, and Cox agreed to meet them at an abandoned HBC fort on the Clusko River, some distance away.

On August 11, accompanied by Chief Alexis and some of his tribe, Klatassine, Tellot and six of their followers came to the

rendezvous and surrendered to Cox. They brought with them a
horse, a mule, and presents of money and gold dust, which
were apparently intended as recompense for the lives of the
murdered men. The reasons for their surrender are still in
dispute (in so vast an area they could surely have remained at
large indefinitely) but it seems possible that the men were
induced to give themselves up as a result of some sort of verbal
guarantee given to them by Cox, perhaps that their lives would
be spared. Cox's account, published in the *British Columbian* of
August 24, 1864, says nothing about the matter; he merely
states that Klatassine declared, "I have brought you seven
murderers and I am one myself," and informed the whites that
the original attackers had numbered 21. Two, he said, had since
committed suicide and one had been killed by the whites; 10
were still at large. The official *Gazette* issued by the British
Columbia government went out of its way to state that "the
surrender of the Indians is unconditional," while Governor
Seymour, in a despatch to the Colonial Office, told his superiors
that Klatassine's men "found themselves obliged to surrender or
starve." He added that "they have given themselves up with the
solitary condition imposed by Klatassine that he should be
allowed to ascend the scaffold with his arms free, adjust the rope
himself, and take his final leap of his own accord."

Opinions were divided even at the time as to why the Indians
surrendered. The *Colonist* for September 1, 1864 said that "the
murderers gave themselves up in consequence of a message
sent them through one of Alexis' Indians, and to save the lives of
their wives and children, their fishing and hunting stations being
taken possession of by the expedition." On the other hand the
British Columbian for September 7 hinted strongly that the
Indians had been tricked by false promises. Father Morice, who
later compiled a valuable history of the area, declared that the
Indians were told that "as they had acted under provocation and
in ignorance of the white man's laws, their lives would be spared;
and if they would promise henceforth to behave well, they might
even receive presents." By contrast, Major Downie, who had
earlier explored the Bute Inlet area for the government, wrote
many years later that "they were surrounded in the mountains
and cut off from escape; fear and hunger forced them to
surrender into the hands of the law."

At all events, once the two ringleaders and their six followers
were in custody, no more was heard of any guarantee or conditions, and Cox returned with his prisoners to Alexandria.
Brew's party meanwhile marched westward to Bella Coola in
hopes of finding the others involved in the massacre. In this they
were not immediately successful, but a friendly chief named

Anaheim was able to recover and return to them much of the material stolen from the McDonald packtrain. Anaheim also promised that if he found any of the murderers he would deliver them to the whites.

The various elements of the expedition (which had cost $80,000, a large sum for the young colony to pay) now returned to their homes and their daily lives. In September, eight Indians were tried for murder at Quesnel (then called Quesnelmouth) by Judge Begbie. The judge recorded in his notes during the trial that "there was no inducement whatever held out to the Indians to come in. It was entirely voluntary on their part." Two testified for the crown and were spared, one received life imprisonment (though he escaped not long afterwards and was never found), and five were sentenced to be hanged.

While they awaited execution, an Anglican missionary, the Rev. R. Lundin Brown, reached the area and took an interest in them. He spent the next few weeks converting them to Christianity and then baptized them, giving his own name to Klatassine. On the last morning he told Klatassine that "he was my son and I should ever remember him; and that we should meet again in a place where we should understand each other better and need no interpreter."

The Indians were then led out in front of a large crowd of their fellow tribesmen, and after some short prayers, were blindfolded and the drops then fell together. The five were buried with Anglican rites in a wood near Quesnel, and as the Rev. Brown wrote later, "A wooden cross with a rude inscription was set up to mark the spot where those poor fellows sleep."

The following summer, two others who had taken part in the massacre surrendered to the authorities. One, named Ahan, was executed on July 18, the other was pardoned. The rest of the attackers were never found. Thus the story of the Bute Inlet massacre and the "Chilcotin War" was officially ended.

What had caused the sudden violent attack on Waddington's men? Many theories have been advanced, both at the time and since. As early as May 28, 1864, the editor of the *British Columbian* declared that "we also learn, with more regret than surprise, that enough has transpired in the evidence taken by Mr. Brew, to justify the assertion that the massacre was far from being unprovoked." On the first of June the same paper asserted that Waddington "had ample warning of the hostility of the Indians, and yet he kept men there unarmed, and so stinted in their provisions that they were led to starve the Indians employed in packing for them." A week later the paper placed part of the blame on the now-retired Sir James Douglas: "The fact is, the recent murders, so far from being the result of the

withdrawal of Sir James, are but the natural fruits of his policy."
Douglas, said the *British Columbian* (whose editor, John
Robson, had been an inveterate foe of Seymour's predecessor)
had not been strict enough with Indian law-breakers, often
allowing their offences to go unpunished. On September 28 the
paper repeated its assertion that the attack "was not by any
means unprovoked."

It was suggested by several observers at the time that the
smallpox epidemic of 1862 might have contributed to the
massacre. In its issue of March 4, 1865, the *British Columbian*
printed a report made to Governor Seymour by J. D. Ogilvy,
police and customs officer at North Bentinck Arm. Ogilvy told
the governor that some of the Indians in his area "were laboring
under the impression that the whites were going to cause the
smallpox to come among them again in the spring, and on
inquiring where they had picked up such an idea, they replied
that some of the whites at Victoria had threatened them with it.
This is a most dangerous threat to make use of, and might cost
the life of every white man on the coast should it obtain credence
among the Indians."

Waddington himself seems to have believed that the epidemic
of 1862 had been a factor in the massacre. In a letter to the
Colonist of June 13, 1864, he said that about one-third of all the
Chilcotin tribe had been carried off by the disease: "I myself saw
the graves of perhaps 500 Indians." He referred to stories then
widely current that whites had taken blankets from the bodies of
Indians who had died of smallpox and sold them to other
Indians, and asked, "Is it to be supposed that such diabolical
deeds did not arouse the hatred of the Indians?"

Waddington in the same letter suggested other possible
causes for the massacre. He admitted that white men had sometimes molested native women, but denied that his own work
parties had done so. He also claimed that Lieutenant Palmer, or
one of his companions, while examining the route from Bentinck
Arm to Alexandria for the government in 1862, had knocked
down an important native and threatened to shoot him, which
had caused much ill-will toward white people.

A year later, while trying unsuccessfully to secure compensation from the government of the colony for his losses,
Waddington put forward another set of reasons for the
massacre. In a petition to the Secretary of State for the Colonies,
he drew up a new list of causes:

"1st, the introduction of the smallpox, which carried off some
5000 of the Chilicoaten Indians out of 7000; and the outrages
committed by white settlers at Bella Coola, and which the
government made no attempt to repress, whether by appointing

an Indian Agent, or Justice of the peace, or constable, or otherwise.

"2nd, the projected opening up and invasion of the Chilicoaten territory, without any indemnity being paid to these Indians, or even offered them by the government.

"3rd, the impunity attending different murders of white settlers, which had naturally emboldened them to greater crimes.

"4th, the removal of Governor Douglas, whom the Indians had so long known in connexion with the Hudson's Bay Co., and whom they had learnt to respect and to fear.

"5th, the removal at the same time of the detachment of Royal Engineers under Colonel Moody."

Other commentators in this period mentioned some or all of these factors. The *Colonist* of May 12, 1864, thought plunder was the main motive of the attack, but conceded that the natives had often been badly treated. Chartres Brew, Chief Inspector of Police on the mainland, was aware of Waddington's explanations of the massacre, but disagreed with them. In a report to Governor Seymour, he said that "not one of the causes stated except perhaps in some measure the introduction of the smallpox had anything to do with the Indian outbreak." He spoke instead of "the injudicious treatment of the Indians by Mr. Waddington's foreman and men." His main conclusion was that "the cause of the outbreak was that the Takla Indians were in want of food. When they worked for Brewster they were badly paid and not fed. They stole provisions, for doing which Brewster threatened to send the smallpox amongst them, the most exasperating threat that could be used to them. Their women were interfered with."

This last point was also referred to by Robert Homfray, who had explored the Bute Inlet region in 1861 for Waddington. Writing a generation later, he declared that "the terrible massacre had been brought about by the ill treatment of the Indian women by Mr. Waddington's party who were making the road." Frederick Whymper, the artist who visited Bute Inlet just before the massacre, supported those who believed that short rations lay behind the attack. He reported to the governor that he had personally seen how the natives "disputed with their wretched cayota dogs anything we threw out of the house in the shape of bones, bacon rind, tea leaves and other suchlike luxuries."

Three historians of this period cast what light they could on the matter. The Rev. George Grant, who had accompanied Sandford Fleming, engineer-in-chief of the CPR, as his secretary in an epic cross-country journey in 1872, declared that "after spending $60,000 on surveys and trail-making, his (Waddington's) men were murdered in 1864 by a tribe of Indians to whom provocation had been given." Grant personally visited the site of the massacre, and found that, eight years later, tools and supplies were still lying about, and also "at least one pair of women's boots, too surely indicating the source of the trouble." The American historian Bancroft, who interviewed many of British Columbia's pioneers in this period, agreed with this diagnosis. He said that "interference with their women on the part of the white men had so exasperated the Chilkotins that they resolved to rid themselves of the evil by the most direct means." Father Morice, who devoted many years to gathering material on the early history of the interior, took a somewhat different view. He said that the natives had first approached the man guarding the ferry and asked for food. Upon being contemptuously refused, they had killed him, and the subsequent murders were intended to prevent retaliation by Smith's companions.

The explanation had earlier been given considerable support by Governor Seymour. The governor was naturally the recipient of testimony from a wide variety of people, including some of those mentioned above, and in his despatches to the Colonial Office he had sifted the conflicting opinions as best he could. It is apparent that he had no high opinion of Waddington, and was not sorry to see his venture fail. Whether this was because the prosperity of his beloved New Westminster would have suffered from its success is, of course, impossible to determine, but the rivalry between the two capitals was doubtless a factor in his reactions and reports.

In a despatch of May 20, 1864 he went into the matter in some detail:

"I have before me the depositions taken by the police magistrates in that town. They show no cause for the deadly hatred of the Chilicoaten Indians. The witnesses declare that there was no provocation given, no tampering with their women or abuse of the men. The incentive to the slaughter remains unknown, and the deponents fall back in their conjectures on cupidity.

"But this seems an insufficient motive. The property of small value, the rough clothes and poor provisions of the road-makers would offer but a small temptation to the commission of so terrible an outrage.

"Some people say that Mr. Waddington may have given offence by carrying the road into the territory of the Chilicoaten Indians without asking permission. But this again breaks down, inasmuch as the perpetrators of the massacre are, it is believed, the very Chilicoaten Indians who assisted them in their labours.

"Others throw out the conjecture that the proceedings previous to Sir James Douglas's departure have induced the Indians to believe that the white men are left without a head. Possibly so. We know that the more civilized tribes in the Fraser have been allowed to believe that they are now without a protector or friend.

"The most plausible supposition was made to me verbally by Moseley. There may have been, he thinks, a quarrel between Smith, the ferryman, and some Indian. Smith was a man of violent character and irregular habits. The quarrel may have led to blows, the blows to death.

"A dread of punishment may have arisen. Hence probably the throwing of the body into the river and the cutting adrift of the scow. To conceal the one murder, the general massacre may have been undertaken. This last hypothesis would assume a greater fear of the power of the white man than I venture to suppose exists in the breast of the Indians. All remains mere guesswork respecting the motives which caused this melancholy incident...."

A year later, again writing to the Secretary of State for the Colonies, Seymour had no fresh light to shed on the massacre, though he did say of Waddington's men that "they bartered away their arms to the Chilicotens and at the same time kept them short of food."

"The road party slept while the armed and starving Indians watched; abundance of food lay within reach of the latter. Its protectors were helpless. A range of mountains almost inaccessible to Europeans would preclude pursuit, should a force desire to avenge the fate of those who lay at their mercy. It is no matter for astonishment that an attack was made on the road party and nearly all of them murdered in their sleep."

The governor summed up for his superiors his judgement of the entire affair:

"An undertaking started in opposition to the wishes of the government, grossly mismanaged and utterly impractical, as far as we know, even in more skilful hands, has ended in pecuniary embarrassment to one and in a violent death to 30 (*sic*). It would be more discreet, in my opinion, for Mr. Waddington to keep silence respecting the whole unfortunate affair."

The executions in October 1864, and July 1865, did not bring the story to a complete close. Waddington endeavored for some time to obtain compensation from the government for his losses, but without success. The official view was that if the road had been completed, he would have received his reward by collecting tolls on it; as it happened, his venture had ended in failure, and he was therefore bound to bear the cost of it. One can hardly doubt that most residents of New Westminster had never wanted to see a rival route supplant the great Cariboo Road, and that the governor was to a considerable extent reflecting their views. In any case the authorities in London supported him.

Waddington, though never ceasing to picture himself as a ruined man, was soon active in other fields. In 1865 he was appointed superintendent of schools for Vancouver Island, and served in this capacity for about 18 months. However, he was soon pursuing larger visions. The two Pacific colonies were amalgamated in 1866, and it was evident that the confederation of all British North America was fast approaching. A few weeks before the first Dominion Day, Waddington published a pamphlet entitled *Overland Communication by Land and Water Through British North America*. In this he explained how the new nation could be welded firmly together by a series of alternating land and water routes.

Soon he left for the United Kingdom, where he presented a paper on this subject to the Royal Geographical Society. Another pamphlet followed, this time entitled *Overland Route Through British North America, Or, the Shortest and Speediest Road to the East*. Waddington was now urging the construction of a transcontinental railway, such as the Americans were about to complete in 1869. The western terminus of the line would, of course, be—Bute Inlet!

To support his national dream, he journeyed to Ottawa and put his ideas before Prime Minister John A. Macdonald. The old Scot was not unduly encouraging, partly because Waddington had let it slip that some of his principal backers were American, and Macdonald thought it better no railway at all than one controlled from outside the country.

Yet Waddington, though all of 70, never despaired, and continued to seek for those who would both share his vision and back it with their money. Once again he enlarged his plan, pointing out that the railway could actually be extended even farther west than Bute Inlet by means of a series of bridges to Vancouver Island. He was in the nation's capital in search of support for his project when, in February of 1872, he was suddenly taken ill and died of smallpox.

His name is still commemorated on the map. The highest mountain in British Columbia (13,260 feet, and not far from Bute Inlet), once known as Mystery Mountain, was renamed Mount Waddington about 1930; not far away, on the Homathco River, is Waddington Canyon. By contrast, a short narrow street in Victoria has for nearly a century been known as Waddington Alley.

Waddington was buried across the Ottawa River, in Hull. He never married but, on his tombstone, some admirer has boldly inscribed

ALFRED WADDINGTON
The original promoter of the
CANADA PACIFIC RAILWAY
Born at Crescent House,
Brampton, London,
Oct. 2, 1801
Died at Ottawa, Feb. 26th, 1872

1868
The Barkerville Fire

The conviction is gradually forcing itself upon my mind that not only Fraser's river and its tributary streams, but also the whole country situated to the eastward of the Gulf of Georgia, as far north as Johnstone's straits, is one continued bed of gold of incalculable value and extent.

—James Douglas

BARKERVILLE in the summer of 1868 was perhaps the strangest community in North America. For more than five years it had been the center of one of the greatest gold rushes in history. From the four corners of the earth, men had been drawn to the creeks of Cariboo by the hope of leaving them as millionaires. Already, enough men had achieved this goal, or close to it, for the rest to feel sure that their turn was next. Millions of dollars worth of the precious metal had been brought down to New Westminster and Victoria, and the fame of Cariboo had gone round the world. True, by 1868 there had been a slight decline in output, but few felt worried by this; for all anyone knew, the biggest strikes had yet to be made.

All this had happened in very short order. A little gold had been brought to the HBC post at Kamloops by Indians in 1852, and a few years later a little more was brought to Fort Alexandria, farther north. But these were considered to have been merely incidental; the economy of the interior (until 1858 called New Caledonia) was based on fur, and the HBC had no wish to see this change. Consequently the company was careful not to publicize these matters; the old days and the old ways were quite satisfactory and it was hoped they would last indefinitely, if not forever.

But their end was in fact at hand. In 1856 and 1857 there were minor discoveries of gold around Fort Colville, in what is now northern Washington state. Yet these proved to be merely the prelude to the gold rush which developed on the lower Fraser River in 1858. Increasing numbers of miners began to patiently "pan" its bars, and the results of their labors, although not spectacular, were sufficient to make up a shipment of gold which was sent to San Francisco. Californians at this time vividly recalled their own great gold rush of 1849, and the possibility of another, a few hundred miles to the north, was sufficient to set off a stampede in that direction.

Fort Victoria was the first port of call, but the treasure-seekers, having secured tools and provisions there, soon crossed the Gulf of Georgia in makeshift boats and began to stake claims on the Fraser. Perhaps 20,000 men passed through Victoria in the single season of 1858; although many were unsuccessful, enough gold was extracted from the river's banks and bars to sustain the boom.

Gradually prospectors moved further inland up the Fraser Canyon. Travel became much more difficult, as boats could not be taken past the cataracts above Yale. Moreover, the natives were not always glad to see their ancestral realms invaded, and sometimes resisted the newcomers by force. Often those making their way slowly up the canyon saw the bodies of those who had preceded them being carried downstream by the current. Yet, as Governor Douglas wrote to his superiors in London on May 8, 1858, "The others, nothing daunted by the spectacle of ruin, and buoyed up by the hope of amassing wealth, keep pressing onwards towards the coveted goal of their most ardent wishes."

Some of the treasure hunters arrived in the area by quite a different route—that once used by the fur brigades. They crossed the American border south of Okanagan Lake, moved up the lakeshore to Kamloops and from there up the Thompson River to the Cariboo. This avoided the dangerous rapids of the Fraser, but, on the other hand, created the possibility that the whole economic life of the interior would soon fall into American hands and eventually come under American political domination. If this occurred the grand design of Governor Douglas, to retain and develop the vast area of New Caledonia (after 1858 known as British Columbia) as an important possession of the British crown, would be defeated.

To counteract this possibility, he had energetically begun building roads into the interior; first the Harrison-Lillooet trail, later the grand artery of the colony, the spectacular Cariboo Road.

Long before its completion, however, the gold rush had transformed the area which the road was designed to serve. In the spring of 1860 the governor reported that "The great majority of these hardy wanderers were making their way toward Quesnel river, where it is confidently expected rich hill diggings will be found."

By the summer of that year, the governor estimated that there were 600 white miners, as well as many Chinese, working in the Quesnel area, and that their earnings were from 10 to 25 dollars a day. This was a substantial sum for the period, but not more than had often been made on the lower Fraser, so much nearer the centers of civilization.

The first really big strike in the area, that which transformed it forever, was made in the fall of 1860. Four men, George Weaver, W. R. Keithley, John Rose and Ben MacDonald, were exploring the Cariboo, pausing now and then to sample the creeks with their gold pans. One creek, since named after Keithley, proved encouraging, as did another rivulet (Snowshoe Creek). Eventually they came to a little stream which flowed through a narrow rocky canyon. Noticing gold ore in plain view in the rocks, they took a sample pan from the stream. When they examined the result, they realized that, in a matter of minutes, they had made a hundred dollars!

Nothing like this had been known before in the area; yet as the men followed up their discovery, they soon realized that they had stumbled on one of the richest finds in history. By the end of the day they had several pounds of gold, and it was plain that the creek (now called Antler) contained much more. They decided to remain in the area until their supplies ran out and then return with their earnings to the nearest land office and stake a claim. After building a rough shelter, they settled down for the night, although one can be sure that it was some time before they fell asleep.

They awoke the next morning to a stunning surprise: a foot of snow had fallen overnight. This was quite a setback to their plans, but the snow melted and they were able to resume work. When their supplies were exhausted, they decided to return to the nearest settlement to stake their claim and buy more provisions. Before doing so, they resolved to say nothing to anyone about the magnitude of their discovery.

However, word of their fabulous find soon leaked out—why else would men be so anxious to return to a remote area and spend the winter there?—and the rush to Antler Creek was on. Even the deepening snow was no deterrent, as men dug holes in it and lived in these through the winter.

Not many regretted their decision or the hardships they endured, for when the snow finally melted in the spring of 1861, Antler Creek made their fortunes. A hundred dollars a day was a commonplace return, and many men did much better. A small sawmill was built in the area, and numerous cabins soon dotted the creek. By mid-summer 1861, Antler had 60 buildings, including several stores, some of which, anticipating new lucky strikes, stocked champagne.

The great Cariboo gold rush now began in earnest. As the length of Antler Creek was staked, prospectors moved on to other streams in the area. Williams Creek was discovered in February 1861, by Billy Dietz and Edward Stout. The former gave it his name, and the latter, by living until 1924, achieved the distinction of being the last survivor of those roaring days. Lowhee, Grouse and Jack of Clubs Creek also yielded large returns, while, on Lightning Creek, one miner took out 900 ounces in a single day!

By this time small settlements had developed in the area and activity became centered in Cameronton, Richfield and Barkerville. The last mentioned took its name from Billy Barker, a Cornish sailor who had jumped ship in Victoria and made his way to the Cariboo. He was the first to sink a shaft down to bedrock, and, although his first efforts were ridiculed, he drew up a bucketful of nuggets from 54 feet down. All doubts were immediately drowned in a general celebration which lasted three days.

Soon Barkerville was the undisputed center of the gold rush; nearby Richfield and Cameronton, although, theoretically, separate communities, were really only extensions of it, all three being on Williams Creek. Here, for a few brief years, flourished one of the strangest communities on record.

Fortunes were made—and often spent—overnight. Prices were inevitably very high as all supplies had to be brought up from the coast. Flour was $300 a barrel, a pair of boots cost $50; even a small quantity of candles or matches cost several dollars; but as some of the creeks yielded a thousand dollars a day per man, these prices were cheerfully paid. Once the Cariboo Road was completed, the general price level fell drastically, while wages remained stable at 10 dollars for a 10-hour day.

Numerous hotels and saloons appeared, as well as theatres, libraries, churches and banks. The HBC opened a store under the management of John Wark, periodicals from several parts of the world were available, and Barkerville even boasted a "Cariboo Literary Institute." Entertainers of various kinds came up from the coast and gave performances and the town boasted several pianos and billiard-tables, brought all the way to the mines on the backs of patient mules. On June 6, 1865, the *Cariboo Sentinel* published its first issue, charging a dollar a copy and appearing once a week. It soon proved a strong advocate for the uniting of all British North American colonies into a single Dominion of Canada.

Also in 1865, the Cariboo Road was extended from Quesnel
to Barkerville, and the telegraph reached the goldfields. Meanwhile the photographer Frederick Dally arrived in the area, and
quickly found his services in demand. He also provided for
posterity a permanent pictorial record of the gold rush.

The Cariboo was indeed the Wild West, but not in the
American sense; the larger, more orderly world still made its
presence felt. As the *Sentinel* declared in the spring of 1867,
"Our jail has been empty during the winter, although most of our
doors are without locks and our locks without strength." There
was indeed very little crime, and the stern Judge Begbie dealt
harshly with the little there was. As he declared on one occasion,
"We have a law which prohibits the use of bowie knives, pistols
and other offensive weapons, and in those countries over which
the British flag flies there is no necessity for carrying or using
offensive weapons, and let me tell those who are in court that in
the course of my duty I will punish most severely all those who,
coming into this British colony, make use of such deadly
weapons."

Church services were well attended, and many miners would
not work their claims on Sunday. The distinction was rigorously
maintained between ladies and mere women, and the stagecoach service from the coast organized by Francis Barnard
operated on a regular schedule. The government appointed
officials to record claims and arbitrate the inevitable disputes, as
well as a handful of constables to uphold law and order. The
latter were the unsung heroes of this period; while those around
them were often reaping fortunes for a season's work, they
served for a mere 25 pounds a month—a sum barely sufficient to
support themselves. Indeed, some of them—the adventurous
younger sons of well-to-do English families—were dependent on
remittances from home. On such foundations was a vast area of
North America supported; yet they did not crumble.

The output of the Cariboo reached its peak about 1863, and,
even five years later, remained remarkably high. Several claims
had already produced a million dollars, and a few perhaps twice
that. The exact figures will never be known, as the government
imposed a tax on all gold brought down to the coast, which inevitably meant that much of it was never declared. A vivid
description of the area at the height of the boom has been left us
by R. B. Johnson, one of the first Englishmen to visit British
Columbia as a tourist:

"For two or three miles down Williams's Creek all the available ground appeared to be taken up, and the place bore a
wonderful resemblance to an ant's nest. The unfortunate little
stream had been treated in the most ignominious manner. A

little above the town it flowed along silvery and clear as it had been wont to do; but soon inroads were made upon its volume in the shape of ditches cut from it, and continued along the sides of the hills, to feed the huge over-shot water-wheels that appeared in all directions. Then its course became diverted into five or six different channels, which were varied every now and then as the miners sought to work the surface formerly covered by them.

"At intervals dirty streams were poured forth by the sluices, in which the earth dug from beneath was being washed by the water; and here and there the stream was insulted by being shut up for a few hundred yards in a huge wooden trough called a flume.

"On the sides of the hills the primeval forests had been cleared for a short distance upwards, to provide timber for mining purposes and logs for the huts. The town comprised the ordinary series of rough wooden shanties, stores, restaurants, grog shops and gambling saloons, and on a little eminence the official residence tenanted by the Gold Commissioner and his assistants and one policeman, with the British flag permanently displayed in front of it, looked over the whole.

"In and out of this nest the human ants poured all day and night, for in wet-sinking the labour must be kept up without ceasing all through the twenty-four hours, Sundays included. It was a curious sight to look down the creek at night, and see each shaft with its little fire and its lanterns, and the dim, ghostly figures gliding about from darkness into light.

"The mingling of noises was as curious as that of objects. From the hills came the perpetual cracking and thudding of axes, intermingling with the crash of falling trees and the grating undertone of the saws, as they fashioned the logs into planks and boards. From the bottom of the valley rose the splashing and creaking of water-wheels, the grating of shovels, the din of the blacksmith's hammer sharpening pickaxes, and the shouts passed from the tops of the numerous shafts to the men below, as the emptied bucket was returned by the windlass."

On July 4th, 1868, the Cariboo celebrated Independence Day. As British Columbia was not yet a part of Canada, only a formal nod had been given in the direction of July 1st. The holiday implied no yearning for annexation to the United States; it merely demonstrated that many of the miners were American, and the time of year was appropriate. By late the next day, everyone was back at work.

As summer advanced toward autumn, the hot sun beat down on the toiling treasure-seekers. All thoughts were fixed on the veins of precious ore and the fortunes concealed in them; few seemed to realize the danger to which the little communities were exposed.

In Barkerville, as in the other settlements, all the buildings were of wooden construction, and crowded closely together. There was no fire brigade, and no plan for coping with an emergency. Apparently the miners believed that as luck had so often proved their friend, the fickle goddess would not desert them.

One resident of Barkerville, however, did not share the general indifference to the danger of a serious fire. This was the photographer Frederick Dally, who, on the night of September 15, sat watching a remarkable display of the Aurora Borealis:

"It commenced at 8 p.m. by the shooting up of upright parallel rays in the west, and shortly after by the same appearance in the east; also the same in the north. The night was cold and frosty, the brilliancy of the rays increased quickly and seemed so close that an observer in Barkerville, which town is over 4000 feet above the level of the sea, seemed to be within 2000 feet of them or less, and could see all the changes minutely.

"The rays when buffeted by the cold south wind that came down the canyon on William's Creek appeared to throw out a wavering and unsteady light in the same way that a mark will, when made by a piece of phosphorous; in the south appeared a long fleecy cloud, and bore a striking resemblance to the form of a snake, which changed but little until it felt the effects of the wind when it began to waver and emit a bright irradience (sic) which spread so rapidly that the whole heavens was (sic) one grand aurora which was ever changing in parts, sometimes very bright and then gradually dying out so faint that it would be doubtful whether it had not entirely disappeared, and again it would shoot forth brighter and more glorious than ever."

Yet not even the remarkable display in the heavens could entirely divert Dally's thoughts from the community around him:

"Whilst viewing this grand spectacle, my attention was drawn to the town, which lay beneath me, where dancing and revelry was going on, by the number of stove-pipes very close together coming through the wooden roofs of the buildings at every height and in every direction, that were sending forth myriads of sparks, and numbers of them were constantly alighting on the roofs, where they would remain many seconds before going out, and from the dryness of the season I came to the conclusion that unless we shortly had rain or snow to cover the roofs, for they remain covered with snow all winter, that the town was doomed."

Dally had previously warned his fellow citizens of the dangers which threatened them, but had met with little response:

"When I mentioned the probability of a fire to the business men of the place, they answered me and said it had become their settled opinion that the wood the town was built of was different to other wood and that it would not burn; otherwise the town would have been burnt long since; for, said they, see the number of small fires that have occurred, and not one of them sufficiently destructive to destroy a house, and so they remained passive in their fancied security and had nothing done to guard against so dire a calamity."

The morning of September 16 dawned clear but cold; a reminder that autumn was fast approaching was provided by the icicles hanging from the numerous sluiceboxes of the miners. Dally took a walk through the town, perhaps in hopes of finding new customers, encountered a young man who turned out to have been a steward on the ship which had brought the photographer to British Columbia, then returned to his studio "and seated myself in a chair, and again meditated on the probability of a fire, when I heard several running on the plank sidewalk, and heard one exclaim 'Good God, what is up?' I ran instantly to see the cause of the alarm, and to my astonishment beheld a column of smoke rising from the roof of the saloon adjoining the steward's house.

"I saw the fire had a firm hold of the building, and as there was no water to be had I felt certain that the town would be destroyed; so I collected as much of my stock of goods as possible together and hastened with them to the middle of the creek, and left them there whilst I made several journeys after other goods. The fire originated in a small room adjoining Barry and Adler's saloon; one of the dancing girls was ironing, and by some means or other the heat of the stove-pipe set the canvas ceiling on fire, which instantly communicated with the roof, and in less than two minutes the whole saloon was in flames, which quickly set the opposite business of the Bank of British North America in flames, so the fire travelled at the same time up and down both sides of the street, and as fast against the wind as it did before it; and although my building was nearly 50 yards away from where the fire originated, in less than 20 minutes it, together with the whole of the lower part of the town, was a sheet of fire, hissing, crackling, and roaring furiously.

"There was in a store not far from my place 50 kegs of blasting powder, and had that not been removed at the commencement of the fire, and put down a dry shaft, most likely not a soul would have been left alive of the number that was then present. Blankets and bedding were seen to be sent at least 200 feet high when a number of coal-oil tins exploded, and the top of one of the tins was sent five miles and dropped at the saw-mill on Grouse Creek.

"Every person was thinking of his own property and using desperate efforts to save it, and some not placing it sufficiently far out of reach of the element had all consumed; and others again had it taken so far that during the time they were away trying to save more property, Chinamen and others were stealing from them as fast as they could carry it away. . . .

"The town was divided by the Barker flume crossing it at a height of about 50 feet, and as it was carrying all the water that was near, it kept the fire at bay for a short time from the upper part of the town; but the hot wind soon drove those that were standing on it away; the fire then quickly caught the other half of the buildings, also the forest on the mountain ridge at the back, and as the sun set behind the mountain, the grandeur of the scene will not be quickly forgotten by those who noticed it. And then the cold frosty wind came sweeping down the canyon, blowing without sympathy on the houseless and distressed sufferers, causing the iron-hearted men to mechanically raise the small collars of their coats (if they had been so fortunate as to save one) as a protection against it.

"Household furniture of every description was piled up along the side of the creek, and the people were preparing to make themselves as comfortable for the night under the canopy of heaven as circumstances would allow, and in the early morning as I passed down the creek, I saw strong men rise from their hard beds on the cold stones, having slept wrapped up in a pair of blankets, cramped with cold and in great pain, until a little exercise brought renewed life into their systems."

Barkerville had been completely destroyed, with property losses estimated at $670,000. However, there had been no loss of life, and the task of rebuilding began the next day. The local saw-mill had not been damaged, and lumber was available at $125 per thousand. More than 100 buildings had been reduced to ashes, but, within a few days, 30 had been rebuilt, and 20 more were under construction. The main street was widened, more space was left between the buildings, and a meeting was held to organize a fire brigade. The *Cariboo Sentinel*, after a brief interval, resumed publication at nearby Richfield, and as early as September 29 declared "Any person who had looked upon the townsite of Barkerville 10 days ago, and seen nothing but a mass of smoking ruins, were he now to revisit the scene would be inclined to doubt his senses, when he beheld about 40 well-roofed buildings standing in perfect order, and many of them occupied by their former owners, who are now busily engaged vending their various goods."

By late October the paper asserted that "Barkerville may now be considered virtually as rebuilt, and all its inhabitants are comfortably situated for the winter." The *Sentinel* declared that those who had shown their faith in its future in such a practical manner had revealed "a degree of sound judgement that will be fully justified by the events of coming years."

In some respects this would prove true, but not to the degree envisioned by the *Sentinel*. Gold mining continued in the area for many years yet, with a few good strikes, but the truly fabulous yields of the middle years of the decade were not repeated. Nevertheless, with the aid of machinery, including high-pressure hoses capable of moving gravel in very large quantities, the area yielded a considerable amount of gold over several decades.

Subsequent increases in its price have proved to be an important stimulus, and in addition, the area has recently become a major tourist attraction. Some buildings still survive from the days of Billy Barker and Judge Begbie, artifacts of the gold rush have been collected and are on display, and one is able to visualize with some accuracy the era which converted an almost unknown region into one whose fame went round the world.

Wherever men dream that by a single lucky strike they might abandon forever a life of toil for one of ease, the name of Cariboo is whispered, while imaginations turn like silent compasses toward its little towns where, for a few brief years, life burned so brightly. So many people now visit them that we may perhaps say that Barkerville has risen from its ashes twice. ●

1875
The Loss Of The S.S. Pacific

"She was innately rotten, but the paint and putty thickly daubed on covered much of the rottenness, as paint and powder hide the wrinkles and crow's feet of a society belle."

ONE way of picturing the history of British Columbia is to see it as passing through a succession of phases, according to the dominant economic activity of the period. Thus we may distinguish the ages of fur, gold and timber, with some signs in our own day of an approaching "post-industrial era."

Fur had been the main interest of nearly all those coming to the Pacific Northwest before 1858. By this date, some of the amenities of life were available in Victoria, but every other cluster of white people in this vast area was organized for the sole purpose of serving the fur trade. Then, in 1858, this situation changed almost overnight, as gold was discovered on first the lower, and later the upper Fraser, and thousands of men, whose sole aim was to make their fortunes from a lucky strike, swarmed up the coast from California.

Some indeed succeeded, and for several years a golden tide flowed down from the creeks of Cariboo into the shops and saloons of Victoria. Yet by the time of the great Barkerville fire of 1868, the peak of the boom had been passed, and the output slowly but steadily declined.

This was soon felt throughout the colony, and the entry of British Columbia into Confederation in 1871 brought no immediate prosperity; the promised railway from eastern Canada to the Pacific coast would not arrive for another 15 years. True, coal mines had been in operation near Nanaimo for some time, and agriculture was developing in Saanich and the Fraser Valley, but these were not providing sufficient employment. What was needed was some new industry which would prove a worthy successor to fur and gold.

As it happened, such an industry was already in its early stages. As long ago as the late 18th century, Cook and Vancouver had been greatly impressed by the great forests which blanketed the coastal area, and had suggested that they might supply masts for sailing ships. However, it was 50 years before much was done to develop this important resource. In 1848 a sawmill was built at Millstream, near Victoria, and the following year some of its lumber was exported to San Francisco. In 1850 Vancouver Island's first independent settler, Captain Walter Colquhoun Grant, had built a sawmill at Sooke, some 20 miles west of Victoria. After he sold it to the Muir family, they developed a good export business to California.

The Alberni Canal had also attracted attention and, in the 1860s, a mill was established in the area. However, before the decade was over competition from mills on Puget Sound had forced it to close.

One who had taken an active part in this short-lived enterprise was Captain Edward Stamp, who decided to try his luck in a new location. He chose Burrard Inlet. Having secured financial backing in England, he built a mill on the southern shore of the inlet, where he soon developed a prosperous export trade. He also had hopes that a profitable business in canned salmon might be started on the lower Fraser, and was in England attempting to raise capital for this project when he died suddenly in 1872.

By this time others had become attracted to the possibilities of the lumber trade. Among them was Sewell Prescott Moody. Born in New England about 1837, he had crossed the continent with his parents in a covered wagon. While still in his early 20s, he came north from San Francisco to New Westminster, and engaged in various enterprises supplying the gold mines of the Cariboo.

He was not unduly successful, and cast about for some other outlet for his energies. At first he believed that coal might be profitably recovered from the shores of Burrard Inlet (one part of which is still called Coal Harbour), but the superior qualities of the Nanaimo deposits proved an insuperable object. It was at this point that he decided to enter the lumber business.

The first sawmill on the inlet had been built on its north shore by three New Westminster men in 1862. The mill was driven by water power, and teams of oxen dragged the huge logs down the hillsides to the saws. The venture went bankrupt, but was bought at auction by another New Westminster man, a grocer

named John Oscar Smith. Cargoes were shipped not only to
Victoria and Nanaimo, but to such distant points as Chile and
Australia. British Columbia's export business had finally begun in
earnest.

Yet Smith, too, went bankrupt, and the mill was purchased by
Moody, who soon had it in operation again. With two experienced partners, Moses Ireland and James Van Bramer, he
developed a profitable operation. Large cargoes of timber were
shipped to Mexico and Australia, and later to Peru and
Shanghai. In 1865 Moody loaded only four ships, but in the next
year five, and in 1867, seven. Before long the fame and quality
of British Columbia lumber went round the world. Soon ships
were arriving in the inlet almost every week.

By this time a small community, unofficially named Moodyville, had developed around the mill. It was in effect a company
town, and Moody attempted to control the lives of its inhabitants. The sale of liquor was forbidden (i.e. carried on by boot-
leggers), and culture in the form of a library and a school were
provided instead. The school's first teacher was Laura Haynes, a
young New England miss who was to live until 1938.

Moody rapidly became a prosperous man. He had organized
a company under the name of Moody, Dietz and Nelson, and
his mill was now run by steam. It was capable of cutting 100,000
feet of lumber in 24 hours, and often did so. After his marriage in
1869 he had a fine house in Victoria. His wife was disinclined to
live in Moodyville, as two half-breed illegitimate children of
Moody were well-known members of that model community.
He made occasional visits to California in connection with his
business, and on November 4, 1875 embarked on the S.S.
Pacific for San Francisco.

The *Pacific*, a sidewheeler of 900 tons, built in 1851, was one of
several old ships which had been purchased by the San Francisco firm of Goodall, Nelson and Perkins, and put into service
on the route between the two most important cities on the Pacific
coast. In her younger days she had carried passengers between
Panama and San Francisco, and during the Fraser River gold
rush had brought miners up from California. In the early 1860s
she had run aground and been severely damaged, but had been
patched up and put back into service. From 1872 to 1875 she
had remained at her moorings; but the start of a new gold rush in
the Cassiar district resulted in her being put on the Victoria-Puget
Sound-San Francisco run. Throughout her career the ship had
seldom been inspected by any government official, and then
only in the most casual way.

How many she carried on her last voyage will never be
known, as many tickets were sold at the last minute. The fare

was only five dollars, as the owners of the *Pacific* were engaged in a price war with a rival firm, the Pacific Mail and Steamship Company. Sometimes these companies allowed passengers to travel free, merely in order to take business from their rival. As children paid no fare, it is possible that there were many more on board than the later official estimate of about 275.

Her captain was Jefferson D. Howell, who had the unusual distinction of being a brother-in-law of Jefferson Davis, first and only president of the Confederate states in the recent Civil War. Howell had been an officer in the Confederate Navy until the defeat of the south, when he had come west to start life anew.

The arrival of the *Pacific* in Victoria late in October 1875 attracted little attention. The general public was more interested in various signs of reviving prosperity. The mining boom in the Cassiar district in the extreme north of the province was underway. Survey crews had recently examined Bute Inlet as a possible western terminus for the promised transcontinental railway; a new water system for Victoria had recently been built. An imposing new city hall was projected, and designs for it were on public display. Also in the news was Father A. J. Brabant, a Roman Catholic missionary who had been critically wounded by a native chief at Barkley Sound, and a vessel had been sent to bring him down to Victoria.

Some of those who boarded the San Francisco bound *Pacific*, such as Moody, were men who had business connections in California. On the other hand, J. H. Sullivan, Gold Commissioner in the Cassiar district, was en route to a well-earned holiday in Ireland. Captain Otis Parsons had sold his interest in some Fraser River steamers for $40,000 in gold, and was on his way to San Francisco with his family to spend part of it. Some Victoria men who could not spare time from their businesses were sending their families to California for a holiday. In addition to these, about 50 Chinese huddled together in the steerage. There were also several fine horses on board, part of a circus touring the Pacific Northwest. The cargo of the ship was mostly coal and potatoes and, according to one Victorian (D. W. Higgins, editor of the *Colonist*) who saw her just before she sailed, the ship was "loaded to the gunwhale with freight, and so filled with passengers that all the berth room was occupied, and the saloons and decks were utilized as sleeping spaces."

On the morning of Thursday, November 4, 1875 the *Pacific* left Victoria. She was an hour late in sailing, as her captain had decided to sleep in. A man who slept in at his hotel arrived at the dock a few minutes late, and had to content himself with vainly shouting for the ship to return.

It was noticed that the *Pacific* was listing slightly, and by way

of remedying this defect, the lifeboats on one side of the ship
were filled with water! Later, when that side of the vessel seemed
too low, those lifeboats were emptied and some on the other
side were filled. Under such circumstances and direction, the
Pacific made her way through the Strait of Juan de Fuca and
around Cape Flattery at its entrance.

By 8 o'clock that night, the *Pacific* was 40 miles south of the
Cape. As it was late in the year, most of her passengers had
retired for the night. The sky was clear and, though the wind was
brisk, the sea was comparatively smooth. Suddenly there was a
violent jar, which made the ship shudder. Some passengers
hastily dressed and went on deck. Here they were told that the
Pacific had collided with another vessel, but that there was no
immediate danger.

The lights of the other ship (later identified as the sailing vessel
Orpheus) could be seen receding in the distance, and some
passengers returned to bed. They quickly realized, however,
that something was seriously wrong, and once more rushed on
deck.

Here they found a scene of complete confusion. It was
obvious that the *Pacific* was sinking, and efforts were being made
to launch the boats. However, no boat drill had been held, and
neither passengers nor crew knew what to do; moreover, the
mechanism which released the boats was jammed from long
disuse. Some of the boats were still full of water, and others had
no oars in them. Adding to the confusion, the ship's lights had
gone out. Nevertheless, by cutting their lashings with axes, the
crew managed to launch a few boats.

Disorder reigned. A group of women were herded into one
boat, and several members of the crew promptly got in beside
them. When they were criticized for this, they replied that they
were there to look after the ladies. A male passenger who had
entered the boat with his wife was promptly ejected, despite her
tearful pleas.

The ship settled fast, breaking in two just before she disappeared. Three hundred people struggled in the cold water,
seeking pieces of wreckage to which they could cling. Most of
the women quickly disappeared, as the voluminous clothing of
the time absorbed large quantities of water. It seems likely that at
least 20 people survived the sinking and managed to keep afloat
by clinging to large pieces of wreckage. However, all but two of
these were eventually benumbed by the cold and washed away.

One of the two survivors was a young man from Port Stanley,
Ontario, named Henry Jelley. He had been engaged on the
CPR survey, and was on his way back to eastern Canada by way
of the American transcontinental railway, in operation since

1869. Seeing the wheelhouse floating in the water with a single man clinging to it, he made his way to it and soon the two were drifting slowly up the Pacific coast toward Cape Flattery. Jelley's companion proved to be a young man from Maine who had done very well in the Cariboo and was now on his way home.

The two men survived the night, but, at 4 o'clock the next afternoon, Jelley's companion became delirious. Finally he lay back and quietly died. The two men had tied themselves to their raft, and Jelley cut his companion loose.

A few hours earlier he had seen a piece of wreckage on which a woman and two men were floating, but the distance had been too great for communication. On two other occasions he saw human beings at a great distance.

By early Saturday morning the mountains of Vancouver Island loomed up, and Jelley had hopes that before long he would be washed ashore on its desolate coast. When he was only three miles from the island, a ship came in view which proved to be the American bark *Messenger*. Jelley was able to attract the attention of those on board, and at 10 o'clock on Saturday morning he was rescued and brought to Port Townsend, from where he made his way to Victoria.

There had been but one other survivor, a member of the crew. He was a native of the Hebrides named Neil Henley, who was picked up by the American revenue cutter *Oliver Wolcott*. Henley had originally been one of a group of eight, including the captain and one woman, who had clung to a large piece of wreckage; but, one by one the others had either slipped into the water or been washed away.

By this time news of the disaster had reached Victoria, and the *Colonist* expressed the general grief of the community:

"We have no heart today to dwell on the disaster that has hurried into eternity so many of our fellow citizens with whom only a few brief hours ago we mingled on the streets or met in the social circle as full of life and hope and energy as any who may read the Colonist today.

"The catastrophe is so far reaching that scarcely a household in Victoria but has lost one or more of its members. In some cases entire families have been swept away...."

As other ships reached Victoria in the next few days, crowds gathered at the docks each time in the hope that there would be more survivors. A reporter noted that, "as the fitful rays of the lanterns fell on the faces present it seemed as if all Victoria was gathered there to mourn." One ship, the *Gussie Telfair*, arrived on the evening of November 10, and in response to a question from shore a deckhand cried out, "We've got two men and a woman, dead, but no one else." Even so, there was a general rush to view the corpses, in case any of them was that of a loved one:

"One of the faces was that of a man who had passed his prime, with grey hair and beard, but with a powerful muscular frame, who must have fought hard with death and yielded to the dread conqueror only after a long struggle. Another was that of a middle-aged strong man evidently trained to hard work. The last was that of a young woman, perhaps 25 years of age; a pleasant winsome face it must have been in life, and crowned with a wealth of sunny hair. As the corpse lay there so still and white and quiet, it appeared to make a mute appeal for recognition, but person after person shook his head and turned away."

The woman was eventually identified, and an inquest on the tragedy was convened under Augustus Pemberton. By this time the two survivors of the disaster had reached Victoria, and were questioned closely about their experiences. Some members of the crew of the *Orpheus*, which in the meantime had run aground in Barkley Sound, also testified regarding the collision of their ship with the *Pacific*.

It soon became apparent that the lost steamer had not only been incompetently operated, but should never have been allowed to sail. Moreover, evidence suggested that the same was true of many ships on the Pacific coast, including the *Orpheus*.

Jelley testified that the ship was already listing when she left Victoria, probably because her cargo was poorly stowed. He confirmed that he "saw water put in the boats between Victoria and Race Rocks" and that "there were oars in the two large boats but the two forward boats had no oars in them." He estimated that the 5 boats carried by the ship would hold a total of 145 people. This prompted the foreman of the coroner's jury to point out that "At least 155 persons would have had to stay and drown if the boats had got away." Jelley also said that the mechanism for launching the boats was complicated and proved hard to operate.

The other survivor of the *Pacific*, Neil Henley, also testified at length. He agreed that he had "seen water put in those boats to trim ship" and gave a vivid account of the last quarter hour of the *Pacific*:

"The wind was freshening from the southard when I went to bed. It was pretty dark. Saw a few passengers about the pilot-house at 8 o'clock; the weather was not thick or foggy; saw no lights. The sea was not rough. I went at once to my bunk when relieved, stripped off, and fell asleep.

"The first I heard afterwards was a crash; my bunk was forward of the steerage. The steerage was above us on the 'tween deck. I was below the 'tween deck on the starboard side. I was sleeping pretty near on a level with the water; I woke up with the crash. I heard and saw the water coming in through the bows. There was no bulkhead between me and the stern of the ship. I didn't look for the planks having parted; the water came in with a rush—flying in. There was water on the floor of the forecastle when I turned out. I put on a jacket and ran up the companionway."

Henley confirmed that there was little sign of the captain, or indeed of any sort of organized direction. He personally had to replace the plug in the bottom of one boat, without which it would have been useless:

"The first thing I did was to put the plug in the boat, which was not in when I got there; can give no reason why the plug was not in. After the boats were washed out, the officer of the watch should have seen that the plugs were put in.

"The boat tackle was loosened when I looked. I got hold of the line and tried to raise her. The blocks were hooked on the boat. No one seemed to be in command giving direction.

"We could not raise the boat because it was full of people. Don't know whether it was full when I got in to put the plug in. Tried to get the people out. Some would come out and then go back again. Don't think there were any women in this boat. Forget if there were any of the crew in it. Don't remember if there were any of the crew helping me to raise the boat.

"I left this boat and went to the port boat which I saw ladies in. Saw the purser and the chief engineer there. The stern of the boat was raised by men pulling at the rope. The davit was not swung out over the ship. Cannot tell how many ladies were in the boat. There were lights there. The boat was not lowered. It was left there so that when the ship sank it would float off. The chief engineer suggested this.

"The fires were out by this time, and the engines had stopped, but it was feared the boat would be stove on account of the heavy swell. Forget if there were children in the boat. Shortly after this the boat floated off, the water being close to the hurricane deck, and the ship going down fast.

"The chief engineer was standing in the stern of the boat, and I was alongside of him. The line was fast, and the fall was cut when the water came under the boat. The chief engineer had an ax in his hand to cut the line. It was not long that we had to wait for the water to reach the boat. Saw the stern fall cut by the chief engineer. Don't know who cut the bow fall. We floated off from the ship and were thrown back against the ship by the swell. There was a crowd of men around the boat trying to get in.

"We might have got a boat's length from the ship, but the boat was so crammed with people she could not be rowed. Think the boat was damaged by coming against the ship, as I found she was half full of water immediately afterward, and I sprang into the water. This was the last I saw of the boat."

Henley had managed to climb on board a large piece of wreckage, where he found the captain, three members of the crew and three passengers, including a woman. One by one the others had succumbed, and Henley drifted, alone and helpless, until he was picked up by the United States revenue cutter *Oliver Wolcott*, after having been in the water from Thursday night till Monday morning.

Testimony was also given by some members of the crew of the *Orpheus*. It appeared that one reason for the collision was that the captain of the *Orpheus* had been uncertain of his ship's location and had hoped to obtain it from the *Pacific*. To do this he had brought his ship very close to the steamer, and an error of judgement on someone's part had resulted in the *Pacific* striking the *Orpheus* and losing some of her rigging. At first Captain Sawyer had feared that the *Orpheus* was in danger of sinking, but when a quick examination had showed that she was not taking water, he had sailed away without waiting to inquire if the *Pacific* was in need of help. This in itself contributed greatly to the loss of life. As one crewman of the *Orpheus* declared at the Victoria inquest:

"If the ship had hove to immediately, witness thought most of the people on the steamer might have been saved, and at all events those on the raft might have been rescued, as the boat could have picked them up."

The *Orpheus* herself, a ship of 1100 tons, en route from San Francisco to Nanaimo to load coal, had eventually run ashore in Barkley Sound, apparently because her captain had confused the comparatively new light on Cape Beale at its entrance with that on Cape Flattery. This cast some doubt on his competence (and later resulted in an American inquiry into his conduct). Meanwhile testimony by other members of his crew did little to enhance his reputation:

"Had not seen the captain drinking; could not tell by his manner whether he was drunk or sober. The captain was one of the worst men witness had ever sailed with. Did not hoist any signal of distress.

"I thought something must be wrong with the steamer and reported so to the captain.

"The officers drank as much as they could get hold of. There was plenty of liquor after the ship went ashore, but could not say if they could get at it while she was afloat."

Another member of the *Orpheus*' crew agreed that "the

captain drank pretty hard sometimes."

The inquest soon focussed attention on the *Pacific*'s sea-worthiness. The ship was about 25 years old and had passed through numerous hands before being bought with 5 others for the total sum of $230,000—a sign that none of them was considered very valuable. A sinister light on the standards of inspection was shed by one member of the *Orpheus*, who said that at San Francisco the inspector "walks through a ship, looks at the fire hose, counts the buckets and goes away again. At the same time I have seen the fire hose and buckets borrowed from one ship to lend to another that was being inspected. I have seen good lifeboats borrowed for the purpose of inspection, and after the inspection hung up on the wharf under a shed because hanging on the davits is liable to spoil a good boat, and we get our own boats back again after the inspection while the inspector was down in the cabin getting a champagne lunch."

While the inquest was proceeding, ships continued to arrive at Victoria with bodies recovered from the ocean. Many of them were wearing life-preservers, but all had perished from the cold. Other bodies were brought in by Indians, or were washed ashore on the beaches of Victoria. Moody's body was never found, but a beachcomber strolling along the southern tip of Vancouver Island (not far from Moody's home) picked up a board on the beach on which was written

S.P. MOODY

ALL LOST

At first this was suspected of being a hoax, but the hand-writing was identified. British Columbia had received its last message from one who had done much to bring it into a new economic era.

For weeks funerals and memorial services were almost daily occurrences in Victoria, as well as in other centers on the Pacific coast where bodies had been returned to relatives. Yet, even when these visible reminders of the tragedy were no longer before the public, the feeling remained that drastic changes were needed to prevent another such disaster. It was recalled that at least four other ships—the *Northerner, Brother Jonathan, Active* and *Prince Alfred*—had gone down under similar circumstances in recent years. The *Brother Jonathan*, incidentally, had been the ship which had brought Douglas' successor, Governor Kennedy, to Victoria in 1864. The Governor had noticed its poor condition at the time, and when it was lost the following year he reported to his superiors in London that "The reckless-ness with which these scarcely seaworthy vessels are over-loaded and navigated renders it a matter of surprise that disasters do not more frequently occur.

"I was compelled to take passage in this unfortunate vessel when proceeding to this colony last year, after being detained at San Francisco for 17 days for want of other conveyance. On that occasion she was dangerously overloaded, and had 1100 souls on board, being licensed to carry 450 only. The American law is quite sufficient to prevent such doings, but there was not an attempt made to enforce it. We struck the bar on entering the Columbia river, and a seafaring passenger assured me that 'a few more bumps would have sent her in pieces like an old band box,' which appears to have actually taken place on her last disastrous voyage."

The *Colonist* summed up the general feeling of the community in a forceful editorial:

"We earnestly hope that as this terrible visitation has sealed the doom of nearly 300 human beings, it will also mark the close of the era of floating coffins and rotten tubs in the North Pacific. It is appalling to reflect that between a passenger and instant destruction there is but a thin plank.

"All the facts connected with this disaster will never be known, but enough has come to hand to show that there was culpable carelessness on one side or the other; that on the part of the steamship there was a lack of discipline and a want of speedy and safe methods for launching the boats; and that on the part of the ship there was an apparent indifference to the cries of distress which arose from the sinking people. We trust this matter will be sifted to the bottom, and that the brand of responsibility for the loss of life and property will be indelibly affixed to the guilty parties—to be worn upon their brows as a mark of Cain—to designate them as murderers!"

As more details were uncovered regarding the tragedy, it became clear that the *Colonist's* wrath was justified. The coroner's jury in Victoria formally concluded that "The collision between the *Pacific* and the *Orpheus* was caused by the *Orpheus* not keeping the *Pacific*'s lights on her port bow as when first seen, but putting the helm to starboard and unjustifiably crossing the *Pacific*'s bow. The watch on the deck of the *Pacific* at the time of the collision was not sufficient in number to keep the proper lookout. The said watch consisted of only three men, namely, one at the wheel, one supposed to be on the lookout, and the third a young man of doubtful experience.

"The *Pacific* had about 238 persons on board at the time of the collision. The *Pacific* had five boats whose utmost carrying capacity did not exceed 160 persons. The boats were not and could not be lowered by the undisciplined and insufficient crew. The captain of the *Orpheus* sailed away after the collision and did not remain by the *Pacific* to ascertain the amount of damage she had sustained."

Meanwhile, pieces of the *Pacific* kept drifting ashore near Victoria, and were found to be "affected by dry rot to such an extent that they fall to pieces upon being handled. In one instance a timber has been found with a piece of sound wood bolted to a piece of rotten wood, and the bolt itself quite eaten away with rust."

The *Colonist* undoubtedly spoke for the whole community when it declared:

"We can call to mind no more appalling instance of a wanton waste of human life than this calamity presents. The evidence taken before the coroner's jury as to the unseaworthiness of the steamer leads irresistibly to the conclusion that had she not collided with the *Orpheus* she must soon have fallen to pieces from a sheer inability to hold together. One skilled witness swore that 'her timbers could be shovelled out of her.'

"To sum up, these points present themselves to the writer. First, that the *Pacific* was rotten and unseaworthy, and known to be such by her owners. Second, that she was not properly equipped for a voyage to sea. Third, that twice as many passengers were taken as she had boat accomodation for. Fourth, that none of her officers were to be relied on in an emergency. Fifth, that her crew were weak, inefficient and over-worked. Sixth, that the watch on deck at the time of the collision was insufficient. Seventh, that censurable as the *Orpheus* clearly was, the disaster was avoidable by the exercise of ordinary care on the part of the steamship."

Captain Sawyer of the *Orpheus* was later arrested in California, after six of his crew accused him of having deliberately run his ship ashore in Barkley Sound. At his trial he testified that "Cape Beale light had only been lighted for four or five months then, and I had no record of it. My sailing directions gave Cape Flattery as the most northern light, and the negligence of the second mate in not calling me when he found he could not steer the courses given him caused the loss of the *Orpheus*."

Captain Sawyer had his own version of the collision with the *Pacific*:

"When, after I found I was not seriously damaged, I looked for the steamer, I just saw a light on our starboard quarter, and when I looked again it was gone. There has been a great deal said about the crying and screaming of the women and children on the steamer. Not one sound was heard from her by any one on my ship, neither was anyone seen on board of her. Neither did anyone on my ship think for a moment that any injury of any kind had happened to the steamer, for at 1.30 that night as the sailors were furling the spanker, they commenced to growl, as

sailors will, about the steamer, after running us down, to go off
and leave us in that shape, without stopping to inquire whether
we were injured or not."

The captain's testimony was not, however, supported by his
crew:

"The sailors on the *Orpheus* afterwards testified that they
begged Captain Sawyer to bring his ship round and lower a boat
and attempt to save some of the drowning passengers. He
would not listen to their appeals but headed his vessel toward the
Vancouver (sic) shore, and ran her on the beach."

The American board investigating the loss of the *Orpheus*,
meeting behind closed doors, eventually exonerated her
captain, blaming instead poor steering by his officers. It found no
fault attaching to Captain Sawyer for the loss of the *Pacific*,
declaring (in apparent contradiction to Sawyer's own testimony
that he had seen no one on board her) that "it was impossible to
take steps for the preservation of life after the collision on
account of the panic among the passengers."

Despite his acquittal, Captain Sawyer soon afterwards retired
from the sea, living out his days at Port Townsend, where he
died in 1894.

The *Colonist* unhesitatingly called the American inquiry a
complete whitewash. It noted that as both ships were American,
they were not subject to Canadian inspection, but the paper
recommended that use should be made of the Canadian regu-
lation by which the Postmaster-General had the right to inspect
any ship seeking a contract to carry mail. It also urged the signing
of an international agreement covering all matters connected
with the safety of ships on the Pacific coast.

But all this would not bring back the dead, and in the wake of
the disaster there were many sad hearts and darkened homes.
The burden of grief can hardly have been lightened by the
knowledge that with proper precautions the tragedy might well
have been avoided.   ●

1886

The Great Vancouver Fire

"The city did not burn; it was consumed by flame. The buildings simply melt before the fiery blast."

IT was now over 20 years since the first lumber mills had appeared on the shores of Burrard Inlet. During that time the industry had developed to such a degree that it was already plain that the successor to fur and gold as British Columbia's main source of employment had been found. The pioneers, such men as Stamp and Moody, had passed from the scene; but their successors had ably carried on their work. More modern machinery had been installed, and countries as distant as China and Peru were now regular customers for the tall timbers which lined the inlet.

In some respects, however, the area was still isolated. The telegraph had connected it with San Francisco, and ships travelled regularly down the coast to the California metropolis; but no railroad connected British Columbia with eastern Canada, despite the fact that one had been promised as long ago as 1870.

Its construction was well advanced, however, and, in November of 1885, the two ends of the long line were joined at Craigellachie. Port Moody, at the eastern end of Burrard Inlet, had originally been chosen as the western terminus of the railway, but the fateful decision had subsequently been taken to extend it westward another dozen miles to Coal Harbour, near the little logging community known officially as Granville, and unofficially as Gastown.

This was already a lively little place, kept prosperous by the export of lumber and the construction of the railway. In the spring of 1886 its population was barely a thousand, but already it boasted some of the features of a modern city, such as schools, churches, a police department and a post office. One lumber executive even had a croquet lawn. Saloons and temperance societies competed for attention, and to speed work on the railway the telephone was extended from New Westminster to Granville. Significantly, this was the first community on the Canadian west coast which had not begun life as an outpost of the Hudson's Bay Company—a sign that a new economic era had indeed begun.

In January of 1886 the local citizens petitioned the provincial legislature to become a city, and on the sixth of April a bill to this effect became law. Henceforth Granville was Vancouver. In the interval the city's first newspaper had appeared, and, as spring advanced, the CPR began selling lots to would-be residents. On May 3 the first civic election was held. Malcolm Maclean, a comparative newcomer to the area, defeated Richard Alexander, manager of the Hastings Mill and a long-time resident. Ten aldermen were also chosen, of whom two, L. A. Hamilton and Harry Hemlow, would live to see the icy winds of the Great Depression blow through the city's concrete canyons.

As spring advanced toward summer, more signs of progress appeared on every side. The city's first white baby, Margaret Florence McNeil, was born on April 27 (she was to die on the same day in 1972); a second newspaper, the daily *Advertiser*, joined the weekly *Herald*; plans were put forward for an imposing "Hotel Vancouver." As a sign that urban sophistication was rolling relentlessly over the primitive simplicities, it was announced that Granville, Hastings, Cordova and Water streets would soon be "planked in the middle and have sidewalks on each side."

The sound of hammers and saws was now continuous. Vancouver was still much smaller than New Westminster, but some bold spirits were already declaring that "Vancouver must succeed Victoria as the commercial metropolis of the province." In June the roadbed of the railway (but not the rails) was extended to Coal Harbour, and it was announced that within a year there would be steamship service to the Far East. The one-time lumber camp's future seemed to be very bright.

A few, however, suspected that the future also held serious dangers. The city was clustered along the southern shore of the inlet, although a large area designed for its future expansion southward had been surveyed, and the task of clearing space for future homes and businesses had begun. Every tree on the high ground about the city was being cut down and dragged down "skid-roads" to the mills by oxen; but great piles of brush were left where they were. Some attempts had been made to burn them, and the air was often filled with smoke; but, in general, it was felt that other things must come first.

As spring yielded to summer, the mounds of slash grew larger and the sun shone down more fiercely. Soon the brush was tinder-dry. Yet the newly-born city, which had no fire engines, was heedless, caught up in the feverish vision which was turning to reality before its very eyes. All else would have to wait.

On Saturday, June 12, 1886 the last deal was closed, the last saloon shut its doors, and the city went to bed. On Sunday morning most of its residents trooped off to the churches of their choice. After that came Sunday dinner and then the afternoon was free. Business transactions were frowned on, but there was nothing to stop people from strolling about the townsite and estimating its possibilities. Others merely slept the sleep of the just (fed).

A few went on picnics. A favorite spot was Stanley Park, not yet so-named, but set aside some years before as a military reserve by Colonel R. C. Moody. There was no bridge into the park, only a long log at its entrance, along which people carefully made their way; yet this merely added to the charm of the as yet unspoiled wilderness. Many families were thus separated at the moment of disaster.

It was about ten minutes past two when the shout went up: "Fire!" A glance was sufficient to show that the entire hillside above the city had caught fire, and that a wall of flames was sweeping down toward the inlet. There was no hope of extinguishing it; the only chance of safety lay in flight.

There was a wild stampede toward the waterfront. Boats and hastily improvised rafts were pressed into service in a desperate effort to escape. Some lost their lives even after they were in the water, so fierce were the flames that they swept across the inlet.

Some who saw no chance of reaching the water jumped into their wells. This would have saved them from any normal fire; but this fire was so intense that it sucked up all the available oxygen, and those who imagined they were safe died of suffocation. As one survivor afterwards recalled, "The city did not burn; it was consumed by flame. The buildings simply melted before the fiery blast."

For many who survived that day the experience was vividly etched upon their memories half a century later. One woman's recollections were typical of many:

"I had just entered a bedroom, and was standing momentarily, when with astonishing suddenness a great sheet of flame swept before my eyes down the narrow passageway between our home and the next house.

"For a moment I was bewildered, it was so startlingly sudden, and more or less mechanically, I suppose, I grasped my husband's hat which lay on the dressing-table, and as I slipped out of the room I had but a few seconds earlier entered, the windows crashed in.

"Almost simultaneously I heard my husband calling from below 'Come quick, come quick!' and then adding 'Don't waste any time!' I rushed downstairs and he told me to dash straight across the street. Upstairs was a trunk, it contained fine clothes, some jewellery and treasures, some my husband's, some my own; we kept them in the trunk for the reason that they were quite unsuitable for wear in rough and ready old Granville. He bolted upstairs, got the trunk and dragged it across the street to where I was waiting on the shore, then over the bank, and out onto the wet beach where he deposited the trunk on two good-sized boulders.

"We were cut off by the fire. There was no escape, neither to the eastward nor to the westward. One thing alone remained: take to the water, and we were not long about it either.

"On the shore were a number of people, including two lumberjacks, and those two lumberjacks certainly were wonderful men, in their great big gum boots up to their hips. Out of the loose lumber near at hand, ready for building a store for a tailor, they and others made a clumsy raft by placing beams and planks criss-cross one upon another, and onto this rickety pile of lumber —no nails or fastenings—15 men and two women scrambled as we pushed it into deeper water.

"The fire was all around us, and the flame was coming right over. Once aboard there was nothing to do but stay there. My possessions consisted of my print dress and slippers I stood in, and my husband's hat; my husband lacked a coat. In time the fire dwindled; the excitement calmed down; all that was left of Vancouver was the soil."

Many others had close encounters with death that afternoon. Charles Gardiner Johnson, the city's first poll clerk, and John Boultbee, its first police magistrate, were cut off by the fire and took shelter with a local bartender named Bailey in a big hole that marked where the roots of a giant tree had torn up the earth when it had been blown down by a wind. They covered themselves as best they could with dirt, and two of them managed to survive as the flames passed over. Bailey, however, decided to make a run for it:

"Our clothes were burning on us as we lay. Bailey could not stand this, and said that he was going to get through at any cost;

but he could not penetrate a foot in the flames, and after running
round a few seconds, he dropped and was burned up before our
eyes."

Nor was this the full extent of their trials. As the tremendous
wave of heat passed over them, a pouch of live cartridges which
happened to be in the hole suddenly exploded, and might easily
have fatally injured one or both of them. As it was, Boultbee
ever afterwards bore the scars of his nightmare: three bald spots
where live coals had landed in his hair and singed his scalp.

Another Vancouver citizen, Mrs. Duncan Roderick Reid, was
in her home when a stranger banged on the door and told her
she had but a few minutes to escape. Hastily summoning her
husband, who was having his Sunday nap upstairs, the three
adults and the Reid's little girl took shelter in a ditch. Here they
found a little water, and by constantly dipping blankets in it and
then covering themselves, they were able to save their lives.
Even so, it was a terrifying experience:

"The fire passed over us, and great holes the size of a dish-
pan were burned in those blankets as we lay in the ditch under
them. My daughter's hair was partly burned from her head; she
was just a child then; about 18 months old. Mr. Reid's hat and
coat were burned off him. Men were actually burned to death
within a few yards of where we lay."

Many of those who failed to respond at once to the emergency paid the supreme penalty:

"I saw a child at the window of a cabin. I stopped and gave the
alarm. I said to the mother, 'Come quick, the fire is coming this
way, you have no time to spare,' and I took the child by the
hand. The woman said 'Wait until I put on his boots.' I told her
there was no time—the fire was coming. I took the child by the
hand and ran; the woman waited. I looked back and the smoke
had gathered around the cabin. I did not see her any more."

Several with positions of responsibility in the community
sought to save not only themselves but records entrusted to their
care. Jonathan Miller, the city's first postmaster of only a few
weeks, was able to get across the inlet to Moodyville with some
of his department's papers; his wife saved only her prayer-book.
T. F. McGuigan, the city clerk, gathered up what documents he
could and carried them to safety. Walter Graveley, one of the
city's first real estate brokers, managed to reach his office and
salvage its ledgers. He conscientiously locked the door of the
little building before abandoning it to the flames.

Responses to the disaster were as varied as human nature
itself. Bartender Joe Fortes, later famous as the city's best-loved
lifeguard, did yeoman service by rescuing a woman and her
child from the flames. Father Fay, who had celebrated mass that

morning and at the time told his congregation of his plans for
building a church on a piece of land he had been granted, did all
he could to cheer the homeless and bereft. One eccentric citizen,
whose house had been directly in the path of the fire, had sat
placidly on its roof. While his Japanese houseboy and a friend
had passed him wet blankets from below, he had repeatedly
fired his pistol into the raging sky. This, he had explained to
passing inquirers, had created air currents favorable to the survival of his dwelling. Few must have lingered to debate this
interesting theory, but subsequent events did nothing to dis-
credit it, as his house was one of the few still standing the next
day! The darker side of human nature had also been in
evidence, when some of those seeking the safety of rafts in the
harbor had been beaten off with sticks by those already on board
them.

Most people had simply fled as fast as they could from the all-
devouring tornado of flame. As night fell, some were in the
comparative safety of ships in the harbor; others were lying on
the cold boards of the floating fish reduction plant called
"Spratt's Ark." From there, while the night wind whistled round
them, they watched the remnants of the fire still glowing angrily
in the darkness. Another group of refugees huddled together
near the False Creek bridge.

This was Vancouver's darkest hour; yet already aid was on
the way. News of the disaster had quickly been carried by telegraph and telephone to the surrounding districts, while, according to one pioneer, a more dramatic signal was written in the
heavens:

"I was walking somewhere in New Westminster and looked
up. I saw a great column of black smoke ascending to the sky;
then it mushroomed out at the top. It was the most remarkable
column of black smoke I ever saw. Then after a short while the
carriages and wagons began to arrive with the refugees seeking
food and shelter in New Westminster."

Another old-timer, John Murray, who had come out as a
child on the *Thames City* in 1859, recalled in 1938 how he was
in church at Port Moody that day "and the ashes fell on the
hymn books as we were standing up singing the hymns."

The Rev. C. M. Tate, a Methodist minister, remembered
cinders dropping on Chilliwack that day. Fifty miles away at
Mission, John Morton, the earliest settler in the Vancouver area,
had watched from his farm as the black column rose over the
spot where, a quarter of a century before, he had lived alone.

Soon other lower mainland communities were rallying to the
aid of the stricken city, and a convoy of supplies began moving
from New Westminster toward the disaster area. As night

descended, it had reached the False Creek bridge on West-minster Avenue (now Main Street) where many refugees had collected and where a few houses were still standing. Here a group of Vancouver women, most of whom were without possessions themselves, organized a "coffee brigade" and dispensed food and encouragement to their fellow victims.

Destruction was almost total. Only about half a dozen houses and the Regina Hotel were left. Most of the city's records and the wooden stakes marking property lines had disappeared. Live-stock and gardens, the city's main sources of food, had vanished in the flames. Scattered among the ruins were the remains of those who had failed to flee in time. One survivor later recalled finding against the wall of a ruined factory "six or seven persons beside the building in a sitting posture—I could see their watch chains dangling, but quite dead. I believe they were afterwards identified by their watch chains."

Another, returning to the townsite after the flames had died down, noted "three or four dead bodies under the Burrard Hotel; they had evidently crawled under the hotel to save themselves and had been burned to death."

The first task of the survivors was perhaps the most gruesome:

"We gathered together some bits of board and built a table about three feet high, five feet wide, and thirty feet long; and as each body, or part of body, was brought in, it was reverently laid upon that table.

"Some bodies had not an arm nor foot nor head left; some of the poor remains would not hold together; some weighed a few pounds, perhaps 20 or thereabouts; all had so suffered by fire that they were not recognizable. The Bridge Hotel gave us their blankets, and in these were wrapped such remains as were found, with a little note attached to each parcel saying where the contents were picked up.

"Altogether there were 21 parcels and I know of others, those which were not discovered until the work of clearing away the debris of the burned buildings began."

The exact number who died that Sunday afternoon will never be known; it may have been no more than 30 or 40. On the other hand, the city undoubtedly held many newcomers, single men whose relatives would be unaware of their whereabouts or their fate. Some were no doubt buried where they lay, and the corpses of the remainder—Vancouver had as yet neither a coroner nor a cemetery—were taken by wagons on their last long journey to New Westminster.

Although Vancouver might now be merely "a dismal black waste in the woods" where curious Indians searched for nails, its spirits had been raised too high before the fire for it to lose heart now; and even the day after the disaster, there were signs of returning life and confidence. Food, shelter and medicine are, perhaps, the basic necessities of existence, and in a rough and ready fashion they were soon provided. Contractor George Keefer set up an outdoor restaurant and dispensed meals at 25 cents each for some weeks; he later recalled others who were also serving the public—in their own way:

"The day after the fire, I saw a burned-out hotel keeper selling whisky from a bottle on his hip pocket and a glass in his hand, his counter being a sack of potatoes."

Meanwhile Dr. Beckingsale, who had managed to salvage only a couple of small hatchets from his elegant new home, opened a pharmacy and first aid station on Andy Linton's wharf, which had escaped destruction.

Fortunately the Hastings Mill had also survived, as had the Brunette Mill in Burnaby. Thus lumber was readily available for reconstruction, and reconstruction got under way almost before the ground was completely cooled. Two enterprising hardware merchants obtained fresh supplies from Victoria, and, within 24 hours of the fire, were again in business. Already, Walter Graveley, the real estate broker, was on the lookout for clients, having been aided by an extraordinary piece of luck. Many important documents, such as deeds and leases, had been in his trunk in the Sunnyside Hotel, which had been destroyed. To his amazement, the papers had been restored to him. Apparently they had been sucked up into the heavens by the tremendous wind which accompanied the fire, and later had come down, still tied together and relatively unharmed, on the beach. The bundle included the deed to the first lot sold by the CPR in Vancouver, which he himself had bought earlier in the year and which he was to retain to his dying day.

Others were also recovering rapidly from their misfortunes. James Ross, editor of the *News*, crossed the strait to Victoria, bought a press, took it back to New Westminster, and had a paper, consisting of a single small sheet, on sale on June 17. Considering the circumstances, its leading editorial struck a truly amazing note; Ross, like nearly every businessman in the city, had had his premises totally destroyed, yet he had no hesitation in declaring:

"We perceive that the fire, whatever may be its effect upon individuals, is to the city as a whole not a very serious matter. In fact, it can scarcely impede the progress of Vancouver at all. A few months or even a few weeks will restore the city to as good a basis as it was on before the fire. We have, therefore, determined to continue the publication of the *News*."

The next day the weekly *Herald*, also printed in New Westminster, was on sale, while the first issue of the *Advertiser* to appear after the fire went on sale on June 29.

The columns of these newspapers reflect the indomitable spirit of Vancouver's citizens. Within a week of the fire, the *News* had the following announcements:

"Mr. S. T. Tilley, proprietor of the post office stationery store, who was amongst the heavier losers, was the first to commence rebuilding. He was at work before breakfast on Monday morning.

"Mr. F. W. Hart lost heavily in the fire, but is not the one to give up. He is already selling goods from a temporary building, and will rebuild his store and also his manufactory on a larger scale than before.

"Messrs. Graveley and Spinks, real estate brokers, are doing business in a tent on the site of their late office, pending the erection of their building."

So many firms, indeed, were operating from tents in this period that the *News* ventured the remark that "Some of our businessmen are particularly at-tent-tive at present."

It was usual in the city's early days for convicted drunks to be tied to a convenient tree. Fortunately, even in Vancouver's most desperate hour, they had been remembered:

"When the great fire of June 13th broke out, Chief of Police Stewart had the prisoners in a tent tied to stakes. Clough was ordered to cut them loose, which he did, as the fire was driving down on them."

One of the earliest items carried by the *News* after the fire told how the needs of the sinful had been among the first to be provided for:

"Arrested individuals are for the present handcuffed to a chain attached to a telegraph pole on Water street."

Homes might be lost, records destroyed, corner-posts obliterated; but hope and courage had come in to fill the void; and few showed more of them than the city's indomitable Mayor Maclean. He telegraphed to the Dominion Government: "Our city is ashes. Three thousand people homeless. Can you send us any government aid?" He received a prompt reply from the prime minister, who promised to send $5,000. In the meantime, Maclean was hard at work in an emergency "city hall" (actually a tent), where he allocated resources and directed Vancouver's recovery. He even found time to write a letter to a friend in Montreal:

"Come along here. It will do you good. We are wiped out since the fire, but in the space of two weeks two hundred houses are under way. Our people have energy enough for anything; they are a live people, they have a live mayor, they work together for the common good. We have had a terrible clean-out, but before the end of the year we will have 10,000 people here."

Indeed, there was to be no turning back. Homes, hotels and saloons began to rise again; a fire engine (which cost a little under $7,000) arrived from Ontario, was christened the "M. A. Maclean," and underwent tests. It showed its freedom from any effete ideas it might have picked up in the east by liberally dousing the assembled civic officials. Impressed by this and other demonstrations of public spirit, the Bank of British Columbia lent the city $10,000 to erect new buildings.

Thus Vancouver recovered from its greatest disaster. On May 23, 1887, its faith in itself was justified when the first trans-continental train, bedecked with flowers and bearing a portrait of Queen Victoria, steamed proudly into the city. The steady march toward a metropolis of a million souls had begun.   ●

1887
The Nanaimo Mine Disaster

THE first half of the 19th century saw a change so great that it might well be called a revolution. Machines replaced muscles as the main force used to move things; the steady migration of working people from the farm to the factory began; and sail gave way to steam.

To drive the new wheels of industry, fuel was needed, and though wood was used when nothing else was available, the superiority of coal was plain from the beginning. Even on the west coast of North America it was in use whenever possible, despite the fact that almost all of it had to be brought around Cape Horn from Wales.

The bulky cargo made the long journey expensive, and those on the Pacific coast who needed coal kept their eyes open for a source nearer home. Even in the days when fur was king, there was a need for coal, as the Hudson's Bay Company's blacksmiths in the larger posts used it to heat their forges. The company had a small fleet of sailing vessels which transported men and supplies between its posts and picked up the annual harvest of furs; repairs to these vessels also required coal. The arrival on the coast of the S. S. *Beaver* in 1836 heralded the age of steam. Other steamships joined the company's service; although at first their boilers were fired with wood, it was realized that coal would be more efficient.

The first discovery of coal by white men on Vancouver Island

occurred about 1835. Some Kwakiutl Indians visiting Fort
McLoughlin on Milbanke Sound were watching the HBC blacksmith at his forge. When they inquired where he obtained his
"black stones," he replied that they came from far across the sea.
They thereupon told him that the stones were available much
nearer home.

He' was naturally interested, and, on asking a few questions,
learned that there was a good supply on the northeastern coast
of Vancouver Island. Senior officials of the company were
informed, and in 1836 the *Beaver* was sent to investigate. The
reports proved true: there was a considerable amount of coal
near the surface. The location was named Beaver Harbour, and
thereafter ships in the vicinity traded coal from the Indians.
There were also occasional visits by ships of the Royal Navy,
including H.M.S. *Cormorant*, which called there in 1846, and
H.M.S. *Constance* in 1848.

Before long, the company decided that the production of this
valuable commodity must be put on a more organized basis.
Accordingly in 1849 a new post was established at Beaver
Harbour and named Fort Rupert, in honor of the company's first
governor, Prince Rupert. A stockade was built around it, and
Captain William McNeill, at one time captain of the *Beaver*, was
put in charge of it. By using what labor he could get—local
natives or "Kanakas" from the Hawaiian Islands—a fair amount
of coal was produced.

It soon became evident that more elaborate operations
including the sinking of shafts, would be necessary. The
company decided that skilled workmen must be brought from
the British Isles. The Muirs, a family of Scottish coal miners from
Ayrshire, agreed to work for the HBC for three years, and left in
the *Harpooner* in late 1848. The long voyage around the Horn
did not end until June 1, 1849, when the ship reached Victoria.
After remaining in the area for part of the summer, the Muirs
were taken by another ship to Fort Rupert.

Operations soon encountered difficulties. The natives were
sometimes hostile, and the coal was of poorer quality than had
been hoped. There was a steady loss of workmen, as men
slipped away to the gold fields of California. The Muirs, as skilled
workers, resented being asked to do common labor and staged a
strike. The autocratic Captain McNeill locked them up and fed
them on bread and water. Some sort of compromise was
eventually reached, but as soon as they were legally entitled to
do so, the Muirs migrated to Sooke, where they built up a
prosperous lumber business.

Fortunately, at this juncture a new and better source of coal
was discovered. Once again, an Indian was responsible. Late in

1849, a native came to Victoria to have his musket repaired. While watching the HBC blacksmith at work, he remarked that there were plenty of "black stones" where he lived. The Indian was told that if he would bring some to Victoria, he would not only have his gun fixed without charge, but receive a bottle of rum. In due course he returned with his canoe full of coal, which proved to be of excellent quality. In 1852 Governor Douglas sent a party headed by Joseph McKay to take possession of the deposits for the HBC. At this time the location was known as "Wentuhuysen Inlet."

As it happened, the demand for coal on the Pacific coast had recently increased. The Oregon Treaty had established that the area containing the present states of Washington and Oregon was a possession of the United States, and the American government had thus become obligated to extend mail service to that region. In November of 1847 its representatives signed a contract with the Pacific Mail Steamship Company for the carrying of mail along the coast from Panama to Puget Sound. Although the company had originally envisioned using Welsh coal, Fort Rupert supplied some coal to the company's ships.

Douglas thus foresaw a steady demand for Vancouver Island coal, and decided that the new deposits, which seemed to be of excellent quality, should be developed without delay. The miners at Fort Rupert were transferred to the new location, and soon a small settlement developed around it. The famous bastion, still standing today, was begun in 1852 and finished the following year, the work being done by French-Canadian woodsmen. Almost 500 barrels of coal were shipped to Victoria in 1852, and a few months later the first shipment was made to San Francisco. By the summer of 1853, when Douglas visited the workings, the settlement contained 12 houses, a forge and a lumber store. it was a modest beginning, but an important one; not only had a new community been born, but a new industry had been put on firm foundations.

The new location, although officially known as Colville Town until about 1860, soon came to be known as Nanaimo. The word was derived by J. D. Pemberton, Vancouver Island's surveyor-general, from the local Indian dialect.

Among those transferred to the new center of activity was a young man named Robert Dunsmuir. Born in humble circumstances in Ayrshire in 1825, he had been left an orphan at an early age. He was brought up by an uncle, Boyd Gilmour, and in 1847 married Joanna White. When Gilmour accepted a post with the Fort Rupert coal mines, Dunsmuir was eager to accompany him to the New World. His wife, who had two small children, was more doubtful, but Robert promised her that if she

would agree, she would one day live in a castle. She evidently
believed him, for, in 1850, they left Scotland, and after the long
voyage around the Horn arrived on the west coast of North
America the following year.

During a temporary stop at Fort Vancouver on the Columbia
River, Mrs. Dunsmuir gave birth to a son, whom she named
James. Little could she have foreseen that he would live to
become not only premier of the province of British Columbia (a
name still unknown), but later its lieutenant-governor.

After they arrived at Fort Rupert in 1851, Gilmour was placed
in charge of prospecting operations for the HBC, with Dunsmuir
as his assistant. Mrs. Dunsmuir was unhappy. Her surroundings
were primitive and isolated, and the natives were not altogether
trustworthy; on one occasion they "borrowed" her baby, and
then attempted to buy him as a great curiosity. She was
doubtless glad when the Fort Rupert workings were abandoned
and her husband was transferred to Nanaimo.

Gilmour returned to Scotland in 1854, and Dunsmuir became
superintendent of HBC coal operations on Vancouver Island.
More workmen arrived from the British Isles, the most important
group being that brought by the *Princess Royal*, which arrived on
November 27, 1854. The voyage had been long and arduous,
lasting nearly half a year; at one time the crew had come close to
mutiny as a protest against their poor food. There were
numerous deaths among the 83 passengers; these included one
prospective coal miner, one young mother, and no fewer than
seven children. The mate, Charles Gale, wrote in his journal that
one of the latter "was thrown overboard, and no more notice
taken of it than if it had been a dead cat."

Despite these rough beginnings, some of the amenities of
19th century civilization were gradually reproduced on this
distant shore. When Douglas visited the first settlers in 1853,
they asked that a school be established. He transferred a
teacher, Charles Baillie, or Bayley, from Victoria, and each
family henceforth paid one pound a year toward his support.
Douglas, who also promised to see that a minister was provided
to direct the community's religious life, informed his superiors in
the company that "the party selected for that office should be a
member of the Free Kirk of Scotland, the miners being generally
of that persuasion, and not disposed to receive instructions from
the clergy of any other denomination."

When Vancouver Island's first legislature was elected in 1856,
Nanaimo became represented by John F. Kennedy. Missionaries appeared in 1859, and the first church was opened in 1861
by the Methodist minister, Ebenezer Robson. A literary institute,
a temperance society and a cricket club were formed, and a bank

was opened; while July 10, 1865 saw the appearance of the first Nanaimo newspaper, the *Gazette*. A fire brigade was formed the same year, and in 1866 a volunteer militia was established in case of trouble with the natives. By this time, several stores competed with the HBC for the consumer's attention.

The population, about 125 in 1853, slowly grew. A census of Vancouver Island, which recorded its affairs as of the last day of 1854 in great detail, gave Nanaimo's population as 151. By 1863 there were estimated to be 400 whites in the community, and in 1869 about 650. By 1874 the population was close to 1,000, of whom 400 were men employed in the coal mines.

The output of coal also steadily increased, as the world moved from sail to steam. Between 1852 and 1859, 25,000 tons were shipped from Nanaimo, mostly to California. By 1862, when the HBC sold its coal interests to an English firm called the Vancouver Coal Mining and Land Company, 55,000 tons had been produced. In 1863, output reached 100 tons a day, and, by 1866, nearly twice that. In 1864 a new company called the Harewood Coal Company was established at Departure Bay, and Robert Dunsmuir worked for it for a time. Its operation did not, however, prove commercially feasible.

Dunsmuir still had hopes of making the fortune which would make possible the castle he had promised his wife. Accordingly, he devoted much of his time to searching for a new coal-bearing property which he could control himself. In October 1869, his diligence was finally rewarded when he stumbled on a rich seam at Wellington, a few miles northwest of Nanaimo.

He knew that he could make a considerable sum of money from exploiting it, but he lacked the necessary capital. Once again, he had a remarkable piece of luck, when he managed to persuade three British naval officers who were visiting the area in H.M.S. *Grappler* to invest in his project. They were not to regret their decision; when, years later, Dunsmuir bought them out, they received many times their original investment.

He was now able to begin the development of the rich deposits, and with the aid of his son, James, built up a prosperous operation. The promised castle no longer seemed beyond the bounds of possibility. New methods and machinery were introduced, and output steadily climbed. At first coal was hauled in wagons by horses from the mine to the wharf; later a primitive railway was constructed. The telephone, only invented by Alexander Graham Bell in 1876, was in use between the mine and the wharf by 1880.

Dunsmuir also entered politics, apparently so that the coal industry should have a voice in the councils of the province. He was elected for Nanaimo in 1882 and again in 1886. In one way this was a remarkable achievement, as he was hostile to unions, and not at all averse to hiring Chinese to replace white men if he could get them cheaper.

Another remarkable accomplishment of Dunsmuir was the construction of the Esquimalt and Nanaimo Railway. Begun in 1883 and finished in 1886, it was a kind of extension of the main transcontinental railway, completed in the same period. Much of the capital to build the island line came from American railroad kings, but Dunsmuir retained complete personal control of operations. During this period he also bought some coal deposits near Comox, which he brought into production in 1888.

Nanaimo had boomed into a prosperous little community, and by no means as gray and grimy as one might imagine. Visitors to the city frequently remarked on its neat appearance and well-tended back gardens. Many of the miners also had their own family cow.

In some ways the life of the community had not always been harmonious. The Dunsmuirs held the gospel of "Social Darwinism" in its extreme form; those who had done best financially had proved that, as the end-product of "The survival of the fittest," they were entitled to rule, and the Nanaimo mines were run on this basis. Wages varied from $2 to $4 per day for white men, and were about half as much for Chinese. The Dunsmuirs naturally (from their point of view) used a considerable number of Orientals in their mines, which caused ill-will among whites looking for work. There was no effective union, and attempts by the men to bring pressure to bear on management by withdrawing their services were met by the importation of strikebreakers. Ugly situations developed several times, notably in 1877, when troops had to be brought in to maintain order.

Despite this dark side to the development of the industry, the completion of the railways on the mainland and on the island brought considerable prosperity. By 1887 Nanaimo was enjoying a boom. Coal was still the basic fuel of industry and the demand for it seemed unlimited. The main market continued to be San Francisco, where Robert Dunsmuir's other son, Alexander, was in charge of sales. The output of the Nanaimo mines, which had been 80,000 tons in 1874, rose in the next 10 years to 5 times that figure.

The naval officers who had invested some capital in the Dunsmuir enterprises had meanwhile been bought out, with highly satisfactory rewards for their economic courage. One of them, Lieutenant Diggle, who had invested $5,000, is believed to have received in the neighborhood of $750,000 for his shares 10 years later.

Even after such disbursements, the Dunsmuirs were, by

1887, the richest family in British Columbia—possibly the richest in Canada. The senior Dunsmuir had two sons and eight daughters, and had moved from "Ardoon," his Nanaimo house, to Victoria, where he and his wife lived in a somewhat more elegant mansion called "Fairview." James Dunsmuir remained in charge of day-to-day operations at Nanaimo.

In the Nanaimo area three collieries were in operation in 1887: the Wellington mines, a few miles from the city, owned by the Dunsmuirs; the Vancouver Coal Mining and Land Company's mine, much of it underneath Nanaimo and the adjacent inlet; and the East Wellington colliery, controlled by R. D. Chandler, a San Francisco man. Between them they produced more than 400,000 tons of coal annually.

However, accidents in the mines, some of them fatal, were frequent. Eleven men were killed by an explosion in 1879 and 23 in 1884. A constant danger was that of an explosion of coal dust; this produced a deadly gas, largely carbon monoxide, called "after-damp." The safety lamp, invented by Humphrey Davy in the early years of the century, had long been in use, its distinguishing feature being the avoidance of an open flame. Nevertheless, despite strict orders to the contrary, some men occasionally carried and lit matches, and some accidents were probably attributable to this fact.

In spite of these dangers, Tuesday, May 3, 1887, began like any other working day. The Vancouver Coal Mining Company was working two day shifts, and one shift went on duty at 2 o'clock in the afternoon. There were about 160 men, white and Chinese, deep beneath the city (some of the workings extended a mile out under the sea), when, at 5:55 p.m., disaster struck. A sharp tremor shook the whole Nanaimo area. A few moments later, black smoke began pouring from the Number One shaft of the Vancouver Coal Company. It was immediately realized that a calamity had occurred, and everyone in the city rushed to the pit-head.

As flames poured from the shaft and rose high into the sky, some suggested cutting a channel from the sea and flooding the mine. This drastic course was rejected as, not only would it extinguish the fire, but it probably would cost lives which might yet be saved, and destroy the livelihood of many families for as much as a year. Instead, men worked valiantly at pumps and formed a bucket brigade. But it was plain that the fire had spread throughout the workings and that no rescue work could yet be attempted.

It took 24 long, agonizing hours before the flames near the main shaft were extinguished, and it became possible to penetrate a short distance into the mine. An exploring party

found that the giant fan which had circulated fresh air throughout the mine had been demolished. The *Colonist* reported that it
had been the finest on the Pacific coast, having cost close to
$30,000, and noted that "The heat of the fire must have been
intense. The immense machinery is curled and twisted into all
conceivable shapes, and practically useless."

The bodies of five white men and six Chinese were found
near the main shaft, and Samuel Hudson later died from the
effects of gas after participating in the first rescue operation.

About noon of May 5, another body was found 750 yards
from the hoisting shaft. It was identified as that of Michael Lyons,
and the *Colonist* printed some further details:

"He is a mule-driver, about 18 years old, and was found at his
station near his dead mule. Lyons was taken to the school-
house, where he lies terribly burned about the face and breast.
The former is as black as a coal from the effect of the gas."

Altogether, about a dozen bodies, divided equally between
whites and Chinese, were recovered that day, and preparations
for the first of many funerals were begun. It was feared that close
to 50 women had been widowed, many of them with sizable
families. All the schools and most businesses in Nanaimo were
closed, flags flew at half-mast, a special train carrying medical
supplies and mining experts arrived from Victoria, and sailors
from ships in the harbor gave what assistance they could.

All day an anxious and sometimes hysterical crowd surrounded the mine shaft. The *Colonist* portrayed the tragic scene:

"As each cage comes up, anxious hearts look for the glad
tidings that never come. Women tear their hair in the agony of
their sorrow, and with babes to their bosoms continue to walk up
and down mourning their loss. Many are determined that they
should go into the cage to find their loved ones. The entrance to
the main shaft is being fenced, to prevent a rush when the bodies
are being brought up. Most of the men are from Cornwall, York-
shire and Wales, with a few from Nova Scotia."

A heavy rain in the evening of May 5 drove most people
indoors, but, next morning, they resumed their vigil. Early on
May 6 another penetration of the workings was made by a group
which included men of some importance in the area. Among
them were John Bryden, manager of the Wellington mine,
Archibald Dick, provincial inspector of mines, and E. G. Prior,
who had at one time held this post but was now a member of
parliament for Victoria. Prior was to have a remarkable career as
inspector of mines, MP, prominent hardware merchant, premier
of the province, and, finally, its lieutenant-governor. The group,
carrying safety lamps, descended the shaft about 6 a.m., and
soon came upon grim evidence of the disaster:

"The first man found was Andrew Muir, foreman, and just behind him 22 white men and 12 Chinese, all lying between five or ten yards of each other. Muir had evidently been guiding the way out, the men following his lead. He evidently tried to get into the slope, but found it was caved in and had to retrace his steps to the air course. Just as they had come into the slope of the air course, the after-damp struck them and all succumbed. The Davey brothers were found kneeling down, their arms around each other, and had pulled their coats over their heads to shield themselves. There were no signs of burning. They had simply been killed by the after-damp.

"As soon as the bodies were found, word was sent for the relief party, who bore the bodies to the shaft, where they were wrapped in canvas and sent up in the cage. Two others, Woobank, father and son, were a few yards behind the others and could not be got at. They could see them, six or eight feet around the corner, but the wall of damp was between. The men rushed in, however, and secured them. The lights would not live in the damp."

Another party which entered the mine on Sunday, May 8, made equally tragic discoveries:

"Sunday morning opened gloomily, and no news came from the mine of the finding of bodies until about 11 o'clock, when it was stated that 25 white men and 10 Chinese working in No. 1 level had been found. The exploring party found the gate barricaded, evidencing hard work on the part of the imprisoned men. They had evidently come out of the level, and reaching a cave-in through which they could not pass, had retraced their steps and made the barricade, hoping that assistance would soon arrive.

"One young fellow, a general favorite about the mine, had written in white chalk on his shovel, 'Thirteen hours after explosion, in deepest misery, John Stevens.' On one of the timbers was '1,2,3, o'clock"; and again, 'William Bone, 5 o'clock.'

"The Chinese had also inscribed their hieroglyphics on the timbers, but no Chinaman would venture down the shaft to decipher them."

A reporter who accompanied the party gave readers of the *Colonist* some idea of the conditions under which others had spent their entire working lives:

"The trip down into the mine was quite an experience. Darkness reigns supreme, and except for the safety lamps in hand there was not the faintest ray of light. The solid walls of coal through which runs the slope is all there is to be seen, except for the far-away twinkle of the miners' lamps. After living in the bowels of the earth, one fully appreciates God's sunlight when he emerges."

Only seven men who were in the mine when the explosion occurred escaped with their lives. One of them was foreman Richard Gibson, who was also mayor of Nanaimo. He had managed to make his way through an air shaft to the stables where the mules were kept, where he and six companions were found by one of the first rescue parties.

"He was very much dazed from the effect of the after-damp, and was not able to give a connected account of the explosion, no more than when the mine fired, he was knocked down by the force of the explosion and can hardly say how he managed to reach a place of safety.

"The first intimation he had of the explosion was when a tremendous blast knocked him down, rolling him over three or four times and bruising his body. He felt no gas or flames, and it took him three long hours to get to the shaft where, insensible, he was found by the exploring party and saved."

A coroner's inquest was opened on May 10 by Dr. Walkem, but adjourned for two weeks to enable experts to examine the mine and for survivors of the explosion to recall their experiences more clearly. Most of the miners who eventually testified at the inquest said that the ventilation of the mine had been good. After a wide variety of witnesses had been heard, the jury brought in its verdict. The *Colonist* commented on it in its editorial of June 26:

"The verdict of the coroner's jury in the Nanaimo disaster is one which will be read with a great degree of interest. They find that the explosion was caused by the firing of an unprepared and badly planted shot in the face of the diagonal slope, causing the ignition of whatever gas had accumulated or was circulating in the air in its immediate vicinity, intensified by the addition of coal dust. The jury submit that in view of the fact that the mine is an acknowledged dry and dusty one, and that coal dust is a recognized factor in colliery explosions, proper precautions were not taken for minimizing the probabilities of a catastrophe. Criminal negligence is not, however, attributed to any one."

Gradually the community recovered. Money was collected by public subscription for the widows and children of the dead, while the living continued to descend deep into the earth each day to earn their daily bread.

More bodies were recovered from time to time: one in June, one in July, two in October, and two in December. In late July it was discovered that part of the mine was becoming hotter, and might break out into a fresh fire at any time. Accordingly it was filled with water and not pumped out again for many months.

Altogether 148 men (including Samuel Hudson) lost their lives, of whom the bodies of five whites and two Chinese were never recovered.

The survivors and their companions continued to labor in the shadow of instant death; less than a year later, on January 24, 1888, 77 men lost their lives in an explosion in the No. 5 pit in the Wellington colliery, and lesser disasters occurred from time to time. Non-fatal accidents were much more frequent, as the annual report of the Department of Mines makes clear.

For the Dunsmuirs, however, things went rather better. Robert Dunsmuir had never forgotten the promise made to his wife that one day she would live in a castle. By 1888 he was well able to build one, and a firm of architects in Portland, Oregon, drew up plans. Skilled craftsmen and artists, many of them from San Francisco, were brought to Victoria, and, on 20 acres of high ground overlooking the city, "Craigdarroch" began to rise. No expense was spared, as the finest of materials began arriving on the site from the four corners of the globe. The castle contained a billiard room, a ballroom, a library, 35 fireplaces and a living-room 63 feet long. The exterior was of sandstone quarried in the Duncan area, but such items as the leaded glass windows came from Italy. The Dunsmuirs released no details to inquisitive reporters, but the castle likely cost about $650,000, the dollar of the day being worth many times its present value.

Interestingly enough, a minimum of space was devoted by the Victoria newspapers to the grandest residence yet erected in the province (and only to be outshone in later years by "Hatley Park," the even more imposing mansion erected by James Dunsmuir near Victoria shortly after the turn of the century). It would appear that the elder Dunsmuir persuaded the editors of the local papers that too much publicity would serve ill the cause of labor relations. There was always a danger that a cynic lurking in the ranks of the miners, or even of the general public, might point out the contrast in lifestyles between the Dunsmuirs and the employees without whom "Craigdarroch" would never have been built.

Yet the castle itself could hardly be concealed, and by early 1889 its construction was well advanced. It seemed likely that British Columbia's leading industrialist would be able to move into it before the year was out. But fate had other plans; in April he was taken ill and died a few days later, apparently of blood poisoning caused by kidney failure.

Yet the promise he had made to his wife was fulfilled, and within a year of his elaborate funeral his widow moved from "Fairview" to "Craigdarroch," where she lived until her death in 1908. She seldom went out, although occasionally she was taken for a drive in her carriage (complete with both coachman and footman), when she was regarded with some awe by passers-by.

Today Dunsmuir is no longer a name of importance in the affairs of the province. Some of the descendants of the founders of the dynasty proved unequal to the responsibilities entailed by the possession of great wealth. Once the original Dunsmuirs had passed from the scene (James died in 1920 and his widow in 1937), no private individual could afford to maintain either "Craigdarroch" or "Hatley Park." The former now houses a conservatory of music, while the latter is a tri-services military college. The coal fields at Nanaimo reached their peak production in 1922, when more than 1,400,000 tons were produced. After that there was a steady decline, caused partly by the change by many industries from coal to oil. The last mine at Comox closed in 1966 and at Nanaimo in 1968. With them closed an era.   ●

1894

The Fraser Valley Flood

"The whole country gives one the idea of a vast graveyard, where the toil of years, the hopes for the future, and all that makes life worth living of an entire people lie buried."

AS the 19th century drew toward its close, the main outlines of modern British Columbia had already taken shape. The provincial capital, with its nearby naval base of Esquimalt, was a center of sophistication which would soon be symbolized by imposing new legislative buildings to replace the familiar but outmoded "birdcages." On the mainland, the young city of Vancouver was still something of a frontier town, but it was plainly destined to become the commercial center of the province. New Westminster, near the mouth of the Fraser, was a thriving if smaller city, while Nanaimo on Vancouver Island was the center of the coal mining industry on which all others depended for their motive power. Outside these four, there were no other communities of any size in the province.

All its inhabitants, whether they lived in towns or in the country, naturally required food, and two areas in the province supplied most of it. One was the Saanich Peninsula just north of Victoria; the other was the lower Fraser Valley.

The valley had first been seen by white men in 1808, when Simon Fraser had descended the river which now bears his name. Later, when the entire Pacific Northwest became part of the commercial empire of the Hudson's Bay Company, the river attracted the attention of its management. The Columbia River, farther south, had a dangerous bar off its entrance, and numerous company ships attempting to reach Fort Vancouver,

just up-river, had suffered shipwreck. Fort Vancouver, established in 1825, was headquarters of all company operations west
of the Rockies, but if the Fraser could be used as the main
channel of commerce between the interior and the coast, then
perhaps a new post near its mouth could become the company's
main depot on the Pacific.

So reasoned George Simpson, virtual dictator of the North
American fur trade in the first half of the 19th century, and in
1824 he despatched a party from the Columbia to the Fraser,
with instructions to determine if the river was navigable. The
members of the party ascended the Nicomekl River to its source,
then proceeded overland till they reached the Fraser, which they
descended to its mouth. The results were sufficiently
encouraging for Simpson to decide that a new fur trading post
should be built on the lower Fraser, and, accordingly, the
summer of 1827 saw the construction of Fort Langley.

The post was built on the model of all important HBC posts,
with a high picket fence to protect it from sudden attack by the
natives, and bastions at each corner to give it added strength.
Soon the fort was doing a lively trade with the local Indians,
more than a thousand pelts being secured each year in exchange
for goods found either useful or ornamental by the natives. As
the fort was expected to be as self-sufficient as possible, large
fields of potatoes were planted around it, cattle were imported
from Fort Vancouver, and a good export trade in salmon was
developed. Then, with the discovery that the higher reaches of
the Fraser were impassable, the far western headquarters of the
fur trade were transferred from Fort Vancouver to a new post
built in 1843 on the southern tip of Vancouver Island, and
named after Queen Victoria.

For several decades after the founding of Fort Langley, the
remainder of the valley saw little settlement. The gold rush of
1858, however, brought large numbers of prospectors to the
area, as well as government officials sent out from the British
Isles to maintain order and develop communications. Among
them were the Royal Engineers under Colonel Moody, who
arrived in 1859. Some of the men, who, on completion of their
terms of service, decided to settle in the valley and devote
themselves to farming, were granted land for their past services.
The last survivor of these pioneers, one might note, was Philip
Jackman, who died in 1927.

The gold rush had ended the days when fur was king, and in
due course the gold rush also subsided. In its wake the valley
gradually developed as a major agricultural area. Captain Louis
Agassiz, a distant relative of the famous naturalist, became, in
1858, the first settler in the area which has since received his

name; Mission City, on the north bank of the river, was founded by Father Leon Fouquet in 1860; Chilliwack was the Indian name given by the first settlers in that area in 1862; the Vedder family arrived from New York in the early 1860s, and within a few years had 200 acres under cultivation near "Vedder's Creek." They were a highly religious family, and named Sardis after one of the seven churches of Asia mentioned in Revelations. The first settlers at Matsqui in 1867 named their home after the local Indian tribe, as did those in the Sumas region. Within a decade, the southern Fraser Valley, which held only about 300 white people in 1861, had 10 times that number. In 1870 a Farmers' Association was formed and in 1873, Chilliwack and Langley acquired local government. In 1879 Delta and Richmond did the same.

As the banks of the great river became lined with farms, one problem became steadily more urgent. Every spring, as the snow melted in the interior, the level of the Fraser rose sharply, and often overflowed its banks. In 1876 a serious flood did considerable damage to crops, especially in the area between Chilliwack and the point where the Sumas River entered the Fraser. The provincial government instructed a skilled engineer, Edgar Dewdney (a future lieutenant-governor of the province), to report on what measures should be taken to prevent a repetition. Dewdney's report, dated November 27, 1876, was a model of orderly reasoning, being based on a first-hand examination of the region most frequently flooded, and on interviews with longtime residents of the area, both white and Indian. Dewdney was anxious to discover if there had been any important geographical changes in recent years which might have rendered the river a greater danger to the local farm lands.

Dewdney soon learned that the recent flood had been mainly caused by the waters of the swollen Fraser forcing their way up one of its tributaries, the Sumas, instead of the Sumas feeding the Fraser, as was the case during the rest of the year. At the head of the Sumas River was Sumas Lake, and as the water of the Fraser was forced up its tributary, it greatly increased the area of the lake, so that it inundated the surrounding low-lying land. There was some evidence that the problem had become more acute in recent years.

"The district has been flooded more or less every year since its settlement. It is only, however, within the last two years that the entire farming portion has been inundated. This summer's flood has left but one or two houses which are built on the highest ground. The others had from a few inches to three or four feet in them.

"Some seasons this district has suffered only from the rise of the Fraser River forcing its way up the Sumas River and sloughs, high water not having reached the top of the banks of the Fraser between the Chilliwack and Sumas mountains. In that case the district did not appear to suffer very much, and if the difficulty stopped there, a gate at the Sumas River, with a short dam in a few places, would be all that would be required, provided the mountain or back water was not too great.

"The last few seasons, however, have shown that Fraser River has risen three to four feet over the highest point between these two mountains. When that is the case, the whole force of the Fraser rushes over the bank toward Sumas Lake, where it meets the water already backed up the Sumas River, forming a vast lake, the deepest part of which, last summer, was 26.93 feet, while at the present time it is only 4 feet.

"I may here state that this summer the amount of water was considerably increased by reason of the Chilliwack River being at its height at the same time as the Fraser freshet. This is not usually the case, the former river subsiding before the latter rises."

Dewdney learned from conversations with old-timers that there had recently been an important change in the system of waterways in the area. At one time all the water of the Chilliwack River had been carried north into the Fraser; in recent years, however, the original channel of the river had become choked with rocks and brushwood, so that much of its flow was diverted westward into "Vedder's Creek," which in turn flowed into Sumas Lake. Thus, in flood-time, the lake received water from two sources, which greatly increased the amount of flooding in its vicinity.

Dewdney uncovered some evidence that the damming of the normal channel of the Chilliwack was not entirely accidental, but had been deliberately brought about by farmers along its lower reaches who were anxious to divert the river from their land. Testimony on this point was, however, contradictory.

Dewdney informed his superiors that if levees were constructed at strategic locations, the danger of flooding could be much reduced. One levee should be built along the south bank of the Fraser between Sumas Mountain and Chilliwack Mountain, a distance of over two miles. It should be about 15 feet high and, at its western end where the Sumas River entered the Fraser, a strong gate would have to be constructed, which in early summer would be closed to keep out the waters of the great river.

A second levee, also about two miles long, but only six feet high, would run north and south to the immediate west of the Chilliwack River, thus preventing its waters from pouring westward toward Sumas Lake. The channel of the Chilliwack should also be deepened, so that it would carry more water directly into the Fraser, although Dewdney realized that this would be "a very expensive undertaking." Altogether he recommended the installation of five flood-gates, and estimated that 227,000 yards of material would be necessary to build the levees. He also gave advice regarding their construction:

"The dimensions of the levees will vary with the inequalities of the ground. I should recommend that the slopes on the side exposed to the water should be two feet of base to one of height, and a slope to the land of one and half of base to one of height. The slope to the water should be covered with turf, the grass from the prairie would answer admirably, and is the best of all materials on which waters roll without doing damage.

"The points where the levees butt on the mountains would require to be constructed with great care, and their junctions protected with brush and rocks or some other artificial defence.

"The levees should be commenced as soon as the Fraser falls, and completed before the succeeding freshet. This would probably be a difficulty here, where labour is so scarce, but a half-finished work having to face high water would certainly be greatly injured, possibly swept away.

"Every care should be taken to guard against the possibility of future breaks from defective work or the want of close watching for a time after the completion of the levees.

"Settlers would crowd into this district if the land was reclaimed, and where one home now stands, covering in some instances 1200 acres, there would possibly be a dozen, making it one of the most valuable and thriving in the province. A break then in the levee would cause universal ruin and destruction."

Dewdney had thus analyzed the situation, shown what was necessary, and warned of the consequences if his advice was disregarded. He had not, however, estimated its cost, and the Chief Commissioner of Lands and Works, Forbes George Vernon, decided that it would be excessive and chose the alternative policy, that of trusting to luck and letting farmers build their own dykes.

Another serious flood occurred in 1882, but for some years after that conditions were more tranquil. The area to the south of the Fraser continued to attract more settlers, nearly all of whom engaged in farming. When the CPR finally decided that the route of the railway to the Pacific should pass through the Fraser Valley, much construction took place in the area, which benefitted from the resulting prosperity. It also made it easier for farm produce to reach the growing Vancouver market.

After a hard winter, when large amounts of snow had

accumulated in the mountains of the interior, the spring of 1894 seemed full of promise for British Columbians. Work had begun on the stately new parliament buildings in Victoria, good mining deposits had been discovered in the Kootenays, and the lumber and fishing industries were steadily expanding. The Queen's birthday was celebrated with enthusiasm throughout the province on May 24.

Less than a week later, however, the first ominous reports began appearing in the newspapers. The Fraser had been rising for some time, as was customary at this season but, in the last few days of May, it began to look as if a serious flood might occur. The *Colonist* reported on May 29 that in the largely uninhabited area above Yale, where the river flowed through a rocky gorge, several bridges and fillings had been washed out and barred trains from reaching the coast. The paper warned its readers that it might be "a day or two yet" before a train would reach Vancouver.

Before long the crest of the river reached the lower Fraser Valley, and an important dyke at Hatzic was breached by the rising water. The *Colonist* reported that "the water was 18 feet outside the dyke when the earth gave way, and the great wave rolled in over the prairie, sweeping everything before it. No lives were lost, but many cattle were drowned.

"The rush of water was so great that the river fell temporarily about 10 inches. Early yesterday morning the CPR had a force of men at work erecting a trestle to cross the breach. All Saturday night and yesterday the settlers in the flooded district were busy removing their furniture, household goods and livestock to higher ground. In some cases the cattle could not be got out of the marshes and had to be abandoned to their fate. Haystacks, sheds and implements were carried away."

The Indian reserve on an island in the Fraser at old Fort Langley was also inundated, and the natives were forced to evacuate. Shortly afterwards an important dyke in the vicinity "succumbed to the tremendous pressure against it, and in five minutes a thousand acres of pasture and cropped lands were covered. Precautions had been taken to drive the cattle to higher ranges and none were lost, but the crops were a total loss."

By this time not merely crops but lives were being lost:

"The Langley Hotel (Peter Brown, proprietor) is completely surrounded by water to a depth of several feet. At two o'clock yesterday afternoon Brown's little son fell from the hotel verandah into the water and was drowned. The body was recovered."

A few hours later the dyke at Matsqui, built in 1889, also collapsed, and another large section of the valley was flooded.

BRITISH COLUMBIA
DISASTERS

PHOTO SECTION

(Below) Few Indian villages escaped the plague; many similar to this Quamichan encampment were left distorted, their enhabitants wiped out to the last soul. (Inset) With beautiful carved rattles like this Indian shamans, or medicine men, attempted to ward off the scourge of smallpox.

A Songhees Indian village near Victoria. Many of the Indians encamped near the fort in 1862 were from up the coast and carried the "seeds of a loathsome disease" to their homes.

"How the mighty have fallen," reported a Victoria newspaper. But four years earlier warriors such as these had been the terror of the coast; smallpox reduced them to a corporals' guard and broke the native civilization forever. (Left) Thousands of Indian children like this Quilcene lad were doomed when Indians fleeing Fort Victoria carried deadly smallpox virus the length of the British Columbia coast.

(Top) Governor Frederick Seymour led his expedition inland and found the remains of McDonald's road gang.
(Above) Chartres Brew led a 28-man expedition after the murderers.
(Right) A deceptively peaceful shot of Waddington Canyon. Sheer cliffs such as these made Waddington's "wagon road" an engineering nightmare.

Waddington's "trail" alongside the Homathko River. Along this great track blasted from the rocky cliffs, thousands of adventurers headed for the goldfields were supposed to travel after paying a toll.

Ho! for the Cariboo. Colonel Moody's engineers built the famous Cariboo wagon road, but Alfred Waddington envisioned a shortcut by way of Bute Inlet.

H.M.S. Sutley was dispatched to Benthick Arm under the personal command of Governor Seymour.

(Above) the famous Sheepshead mine on Williams Creek. Most laughed at Billy Barker when he began to dig a shaft on the lower creek.
(Below) The Neversweat mine on Williams Creek, 1868. Millions of dollars were recovered from this stretch of water. Billy Barker , the man who started it all, died a pauper.

(Opposite page, top) *The Burns Hydraulic Co. at work on the Old Black Jack Claim, Williams Creek, 1868.*
(Above) *Long after Barkerville's golden boom had peaked, mining operations continued in the area, as shown by this dredge.*
(Below) *Barkerville, the morning after the fire. The surprise was not that the town had burned, but that it had taken so long.*

(Below) The tragic steamer Pacific. Among her victims was Sewell Prescott Moody who, as he calmly waited for death, pencilled a brief message on a length of beam. Days later, his message from the dead drifted ashore in Victoria, 100 miles from the scene of the Pacific's foundering, and "within sight of the deceased gentleman's home."

(Opposite page, left) Captain Jefferson D. Howell, a brother-in-law of Confederate President Jefferson Davis and a naval hero of the Civil War, went down with his ship. (Opposite page, right) Captain Charles Sawyer, master of the Orpheus, sailed on and left the Pacific's hundreds to their fate.

(Top) Sewell Prescott Moody, saw-mill owner and founder of Moody-ville who went down with the Pacific.
(Center)Heil Henley, quartermaster of the steamer Pacific and one of her two survivors.
(Bottom) The only other survivor of the sinking of the Pacific on November 4, 1875, was F.H. Jelly.
(Left) Ships waiting to load British Columbia lumber at Burrard Inlet.

(Above) Vancouver's Georgia Street, 1896. Logging put the future metropolis on the map and caused its original destruction.
(Below) Pioneer logging operations such as this gave the future city of Vancouver the appropriate nickname, "Stumptown."

(Top) Granville Street, Vancouver, shown from the Hotel Vancouver in 1886.
(Left) A refugee's bivouac the morning after the holocaust. This view shows Westminster Avenue near Front Street.
(Below) Vancouver after the great fire of 1886. Overnight the growing city became a tent-town in a sea of ashes.

(Right) Robert Dunsmuir's castle, Craigdarroch. His miners worked for notoriously poor wages, but Dunsmuir had promised his wife a castle. (Below) Fairview, the beautiful Dunsmuir mansion in Victoria's James Bay, at the corner of Quebec and Menzie. (Inset) Coal baren Robert Dunsmuir, 1889. Time and again his mines were struck by tragedy.

(Above) Western Fuel Company's No. 1 Mine at Nanaimo. Most Vancouver Island coal mines experienced explosions and cave-ins at the cost of hundreds of lives. (Below) Miners' families and friends wait at the pit-head for news of their loved ones. About 160 men were on shift on May 3, 1887 when an explosion caved the No. 1 shaft.

(Opposite page) Two views of dredges at work during the Sumas reclamation project after the 1894 flood.
(Above) Chilliwack lies under water during the great flood. Half a century after history would repeat itself.

(Below) Mission City during the flood of 1894.

Flood at Chilliwack in 1894.

(Top) Ill-fated Car No. 6 which plunged off Point Ellice bridge May 29, 1896. Fifty-five holiday-goers lost their lives when the center span collapsed.
(Bottom) Spectators and rescuers congregate around the scene of the Point Ellice Bridge disaster.

Columbia Street, New Westminster after the fire of 1898.

(Above) The burned-out shell of the Baptist Church.
(Below) Even the Royal City's courthouse fell to the flames.

(Above left) The David Spencer residence at Belleville and Government Streets, Victoria.
(Above right) Department store owner David Spencer poses with his family. The great fire of 1910 started in his store, which was a total loss.
(Below) Looking through the ruins of the Colonist building.

(Above) A view of the Five Sisters block (foreground) after the great fire.
(Below) Although damaged, Victoria's leading hostlry, the Driard Hotel, escaped the flames and was immediately bought by David Spencer to replace his department store.

(Left) John Pease Babcock hastened to the scene, then urged the provincial government to clear the rockslide and save the salmon.
(Top) Hell's Gate, Fraser Canyon. Always a hazard to spawning salmon, in 1913 it became a death trap.
(Below) A close-up of the rock slide at Hell's Gate. Crews worked around the clock to clear the obstruction in an attempt to prevent one of the greatest ecological disasters in provincial history.

(Above) **Princess Sophia** *leaving Victoria on August 26, 1914.* *(Right) A photo of the* **Princess Sophia** *foundering on Vanderbilt Reef in the Lynn Canal on Oct. 24, 1918. All aboard perished.*

*(Above) Two views of
unemployed men in a
False Creek "jungle,"
1931. This camp was
later destroyed by the city.
(Right) A plain-clothes
Vancouver policeman
uses a rubber hose on
strikers during the
occupation of the main
Vancouver post office.*

Evacuation of unemployed demonstrators during a "sit down" in June 1938.

The post office riot. More than once the frustrations of being unemployed led to violence.

(Above) Vancouver city policemen march past a damaged department store after the rioting of June 20, 1938.
(Below) Premier T.D. Pattulo meets with spokesmen for the unemployed, June 20, 1938, after the post office riot.

The rescue of marooned chickens during the 1948 Fraser River flood.

The *Colonist* declared that "it is impossible yet to estimate the total loss along the river, but it will be immense."

Not only was the CPR unable to bring trains into Vancouver or New Westminster, or send them from the coast more than a short distance up the valley, but the Great Northern line from Seattle was also blocked. Heavy floods were now occurring throughout the entire Pacific Northwest, the Columbia, like the Fraser, having overflowed its banks. Portland, Oregon had water flowing in its streets.

Communication with the interior of the province was almost impossible, and the assizes at Clinton and Kamloops were postponed. One man who made his way down the river from Yale on a raft described the entire area he had passed through as "one immense lake, with roofs of ranches, barns and dwellings studding the surface of the water, and general effects, fence rails, implements and the bodies of cattle floating in all directions."

A day later the *Colonist* reported that "The river is still rising and is now two feet above the highest mark known in the history of the country. The breaches in dykes which have been constructed at immense cost are widening, and it will be a work of years to repair the damage.

"Evidences of the flood are presented to travellers by every vessel entering the Straits of Georgia, and hundreds of miles from the flooded district the waters of this arm of the sea are a deep mud color, and littered with debris. All railway trains arriving from the east during the past week are now being held at Kamloops."

By this time the provincial government headed by Premier Theodore Davie had realized the seriousness of the situation, and had sent a steamship into the stricken area to remove people to higher ground at provincial expense. New Westminster was partly flooded, and goods in warehouses along the riverbank were being removed. Farther up the valley, "The flood gates in the dyke at Riverside, opposite Mission, gave way this morning, and the water is pouring through the gap with tremendous velocity."

Annacis Island in the Fraser was several feet under water, and both lumbering and fishing in the vicinity had ceased. Another steamer, the *Transfer*, was sent up the river to evacuate stranded passengers and mail to the coast. On its return, those on board reported "The whole settlement of Matsqui is now under water to the foothills. Dykes and bridges are gone, and the people are living in the upper stories of their desolated homes, stepping from second floor windows into their rowboats when it is necessary to move about."

An important railway bridge connecting the valley with the

United States crossed the river at Mission City. The approaches
to the bridge were either washed away or under water, and a
locomotive was left stranded on the bridge. Two hundred head
of cattle were reported marooned on Barnston Island, and a ship
was sent to rescue them. Three vessels were now engaged in this
work: the *Transfer, Gladys* and *Courser*. At Hatzic, "The
Transfer sailed up over farms and fences, across the slough,
Hatzic bridge and the dyke, and tied up to the rails of the CPR
track."

The flood had not yet reached its crest, but already public
discussion had begun as to how to prevent another such disaster
in the future. The *Colonist* declared that the government must
spend large sums on an elaborate dyking system to protect the
entire lower Fraser Valley, pointing out that this would really be
a sound investment:

"The flooded lands, if properly drained and made safe from
inundation by scientifically constructed dykes, would be very
valuable indeed, and could soon be made to pay the full cost of
all improvements."

But this was largely hindsight; in the meantime makeshift
efforts were all that could be made. A form of communication
was established with the interior and trains from the coast still
reached Mission, even though considerable stretches of the track
were underwater. From there a steamer took passengers to
Ruby Creek, above the worst-hit area, at which point another
train was available to carry them eastward.

It was now clear that the province had suffered a major
economic disaster. The CPR estimated damage to its properties
at a million dollars (an even larger sum in those days), and losses
by farmers in the valley were reckoned to be at least as great.
The railway had 2,000 men at work repairing damage, but the
water was still relentlessly rising. One traveller who reached the
coast declared:

"I can't begin to describe the tremendous effects of the flood.
Right back to the hills there is only a mass of water to be seen,
with the tops of the trees raising their heads above it. Everything
else has disappeared. Sumas, Stave river district, and Nicomen
are a veritable waste of water. I was informed that from Chilliwack clear to the American boundary one could navigate in a
rowboat."

Another who passed through the valley said:

"The whole country gives one the idea of a vast graveyard,
where the toil of years, the hopes for the future, and all that
makes life worth living of an entire people lie buried."

Even in the mountain passes far to the east, the situation was
serious:

"At Craigellachie, the bridge and five hundred feet of track have water washing over them six feet deep. At these breaks the CPR has a thousand men employed, who when the train left had been working five days and nights without sleep up to their waists in water. Some three hundred worked until they dropped down in the water and had to be carried to the high ground, falling asleep before they were laid down."

The famous suspension bridge across the Fraser at Spuzzum, rightly thought to be an engineering marvel when it was built 30 years before, was washed away. At Yale the river was two feet above the high water mark of 1882. Many tragic sights were witnessed in this period:

"Floating on the Fraser at Ruby Creek workmen found a small raft, its sole cargo being the dead bodies of an entire family— mother, father and three little ones. The only supposition is that they had been floating at the mercy of the flood for several days, until after a season of terrible suffering they entered upon their eternal rest. The bodies were found securely tied together. There were no papers by which to identify them. They were buried in a common grave."

Many unusual sights were noted at this time:

"A little girl was seen struggling in the water in a big boat, and holding a pet lamb that persisted foolishly in attempting to get away and plunge into the water. It seemed miraculous that the child could save herself and rescue her pet in that awful hour; all she thought of apparently was the safety of her little lamb.

"Chilliwack people sailed to church in canoes yesterday, anchored them to their pews, and prayed God to deliver them from further distress from the flood and to 'give them this day their daily bread.'"

At Delta, church services were cancelled and the clergy toiled alongside their parishioners to strengthen dykes and save livestock, although this area was not seriously damaged by the flood. Most industry in the valley had come to a standstill; at New Westminster the water reached the power-house and the entire city was plunged into darkness. At nearby Sapperton the river was flowing through the Brunette sawmill.

The transfer of cattle to higher ground continued, those on Nicomen Island being removed to Sumas Mountain by the *Gladys*. One curious feature of the flood was that the rats of the area had taken refuge in those treetops still above water. By contrast, a few sturdy farmers were standing their ground:

"At Riverside, opposite Mission, William Elliott had an incubator in full blast in his dwelling, when the flood swept through the Matsqui dyke, and rapidly rose around the hatching machine. Mr. Elliott thereupon bored holes through the floor

above, and passing a stout rope under either end of the
incubator, hoisted it up to the ceiling, where it is still two or three
feet out of the reach of the water. Several duck eggs have been
hatched out since the flood commenced. The upper verandah of
his house, which is surrounded by 10 feet of water, constitutes Mr.
Elliott's poultry yard for the present, and here several broods are
disporting themselves."

The provincial government, anxious to obtain an official first-
hand report on the situation, sent Colonel James Baker, the
provincial secretary, up the Fraser in the *Gladys*. He reported
that "the wharf at Mission was so deep under water that it was
impossible to land. At Nicomen all the farms are deeply inundated, many up to the eaves of the houses, but wherever there
was an upper story the inhabitants were still remaining in the
building. In all instances the settlers, including women and
children, manifested a cheerful and brave spirit under their misfortunes."

The Colonel also learned that some residents of the Sumas
area, in hopes of diverting the flood from their farms, were
considering drastic action:

"On arriving at Chilliwack I was informed by a deputation of
the inhabitants that some of the Sumas people were determined
to blow up with dynamite the timber jam which prevented the
waters from Vedder Creek flowing into the Luk-a-kuk, and that
if this was permitted it would completely destroy some of the
most valuable lands in Chilliwack; that the Chilliwack people
were determined to resist it with force, if driven to do so, while
the Sumas people were equally determined on the other side, as
they suffered from the overflowing waters of Vedder Creek. I
was informed that immediate action was imperative, as rifles
were threatened to be used.

"I therefore called the magistrates together, instructed them to
swear in special constables, appoint a government engineer to
look into the rights of the case, and that I would see that justice
should be done. This was carried out and I am happy to state
that it prevented any disturbances."

The Colonel had not only analyzed the situation but had
taken steps to deal with it. The disaster area he described as
"about 100 by 15 miles, the greater part of which was under
water, with bridges gone and communication by rail, telegraph
and ordinary steamer traffic stopped." Two things were needed
immediately, he reported on his return to New Westminster:
fodder for starving cattle and seed to resow the fields as soon as
the flood subsided. Old-timers furnished him with estimates of
the amount of seed required, and when Baker returned to New
Westminster he placed orders for 500 tons with three firms,

including the Brackman-Ker feed company. The companies estimated that they could secure this amount within three weeks from other parts of the continent.

Baker appointed the reeve of each district as the official distributor of the seed among the farmers of that area, giving instructions that each must sign a receipt for the amount of seed obtained, and agree to repay the government at some future date, if at all possible. The Colonel noted in passing that "numerous and urgent applications for food, fodder and seed were made by people who did not really require assistance, but they were always refused." He later estimated that he had spent $20,000 on feed and $1,250 on fodder, helped 666 settlers to begin life again, and in return had received promises to repay the government to the amount of $5,375.

Having done his duty to the general public, Colonel Baker made his way by what means he could find to the Kootenays, the district he represented in the legislature. There he set about mending his own political dykes with a view to the election which Premier Davie had called for later in the summer. There is little doubt that the prompt response of the provincial government to the emergency made the general public inclined to regard it favorably, a fact that sat sourly with the opposition. One newspaper declared that "certain people are urging the government should take into its own hands the dyking of the Fraser, and the electors are invited to send down representatives who will be ready to approve the program. How much money are the electors willing to see squandered to provide for a Davie carnival?"

Election day would show that the voters approved of Premier Davie, but in the meantime the flood continued. Matsqui and Sumas were still the worst-hit areas, while Nicomen Island in the Fraser, some eight miles long, was entirely under water, Brodie's cannery on Deas Island was washed away. As the temperature at some points in the interior soared to 100 degrees Fahrenheit, more of the snows which capped the mountains lining the valley melted and fed the floodwaters. For all that, on June 10, the *Colonist* was able to report that the waters were receding.

One sidelight on the flood came when two farmers were charged with attempting to divert the Chilliwack River into the Luk-a-kuk, a stream running north into the Fraser, and away from Vedder Creek and the Sumas area. They were really only attempting to restore the Chilliwack to its original course, but those earning their living on the land below the log-jam which had diverted the river for some years were uninterested in historical arguments. The *Colonist* reported that "there has been trouble for years over this log jam. One section of the community is anxious to see it removed, and the other is equally anxious to keep it there."

This quarrel was soon overshadowed by the arrival, on June 28, of the promised new seed. The task of distributing it to local farmers began at once, the government's prompt action making it possible for many of them to reseed their fields in early summer and harvest a crop in the fall.

There still remained the larger question of preventing a recurrence of the disaster. Premier Davie informed Prime Minister Sir John Thompson that "plainly the lesson of the floods is the necessity of a comprehensive system of dyking, which will include the whole inundated area of the Fraser valley." Davie suggested a joint effort in this regard, beginning with a detailed survey of the Fraser River. In the fall the federal government agreed to pay half the cost of such a survey.

In 1896 a careful examination of the area was made by a competent engineer, Frederick Tytler. He was critical of many of the dykes thrown up in the wake of the flood by local farmers. The numerous sticks and stumps which they contained would constitute weak places that another flood would soon find and take advantage of; moreover the earth for the dykes had been dug from directly behind them, thus creating an area into which flood water would be sure to seep.

Tytler recommended an elaborate system of dykes, dams and pumps, all of the work to be of the best quality. The dykes should be of solid earth and covered with grass, while consideration should be given to building banks of stone along the river. He also recommended deepening and dredging the channel of the river, and estimated that the entire project might well cost a million dollars.

These plans were approved, and after some delay the work began. The first dyke at Maple Ridge was completed in 1898, that at Matsqui in 1900, and the two dykes in the Chilliwack area in 1901. Much of the work was done by local farmers, who were paid wages for their efforts. There were no bulldozers in those days, and teams of horses dragged the earth to the riverbank. The circulation of money in the valley doubtless did much to put it back on its feet.

For many years the dyking system held against all pressure, and after the First World War a more ambitious project was begun. This was the reclamation of a large area in the Sumas district, and its conversion to good farm land. More than 30,000 acres were protected by new dykes and giant pumps, and the area soon became an important new source of food for the growing metropolis of Vancouver.

Before long the British Columbia Electric Railway had a line running over land which had often been many feet under water, and eventually the wide Trans-Canada highway was built through the same area.

For many years the valley seemed to be safe from the annual fury of the mighty Fraser, as the spring run-off came and went and the dykes held. Then came June, 1948, when all these calculations were proved false and the disaster of 1894 was repeated, this time on a still greater scale. But that is another story.   ●

1896

The Collapse of the
Point Ellice Bridge

THE last decade of the 19th century was a time of transition for British Columbia and its capital city. Although these years were later to be called "the gay 90s" they were actually a period of depressed economic activity throughout North America. Nevertheless, there were many signs that, although the pace of progress had slackened, it had by no means come to a halt. Toward the middle of the decade, the stately new legislative buildings began rising on the shores of James Bay; a railway line was completed from Victoria to the tip of the Saanich Peninsula, and though automobiles had not yet appeared in Victoria, they were the subject of frequent articles in the newspapers.

While they waited to move into their spacious new quarters, members of the legislature and the civil service went about their duties in the old "birdcages," first opened in 1860. Some who could recall those distant days had only recently passed from the scene. J.D. Pemberton, who had arrived in the gold rush days and surveyed much of the island for the government, had died a true Victorian death in 1893, collapsing when he was riding in a paper chase. The stern Judge Begbie had died in harness in 1894. Amor de Cosmos, who had founded the *Colonist* in 1858, was still alive, but had been officially declared of unsound mind and would die in 1897. By contrast, some of the pioneer generation were still hale and hearty and had already become legends in their own lifetime. Among these were Dr. Helmcken, who had arrived in 1850, and Dean Cridge, spiritual adviser to many Victorians since 1855.

Moreover, a new generation with new ideas was rapidly coming to the fore. The place of women in society was beginning to change. Physical education for girls began in the Victoria schools in 1894, even though one school trustee "objected to great big girls going round climbing ropes and doing acrobatic feats." The following year saw Mrs. Gordon Grant elected the first female school trustee, while the *Colonist* for May 28, 1895, was produced almost entirely by women. They were also beginning to smoke cigarettes in public, while at a slightly lower level the police "notified a number of women of questionable character that they must cease parading on bicycles or be prosecuted under the vagrancy act." Meanwhile people were beginning to take notice of a rising young artist named Emily Carr.

Victoria was by now well known to the rest of the world. It had recently been visited by poet Pauline Johnson, Sir Wilfrid Laurier, General Booth of the Salvation Army, and Winston Churchill's parents. New inventions and pastimes continued to make daily life more interesting and enjoyable. The first "kineto-scope" (i.e. moving picture) appeared in Victoria in 1895, the yacht and polo clubs were active, while the city was about to see its first soda fountain and bicycle built for two.

In the spring of 1896 the gilded statue of Captain George Vancouver, on this coast a century before, was put in place atop the new legislative buildings. The action seemed to symbolize both Victoria's attachment to its romantic past and its belief that it was entering a new era full of promise. As spring gave way to summer, a variety of matters were in the news. In South Africa, the British were having trouble with what the *Colonist* termed "the ignorant and brutal Boers," although the situation was yet three years short of war. The Spanish were finding it hard to keep their Cuban subjects in line, while in Russia a new tsar, destined to be the last of the Romanovs, was about to be crowned amid scenes of barbaric splendor.

To most Victorians, the high point of every year was the Queen's birthday. Celebrations had grown steadily more elaborate in recent years, as an increasingly affluent and sophisticated society felt an even greater pride in the accomplish-ments of the empire of which it was an outpost. This time there would be something for everybody: bicycle races, a regatta, cricket and baseball matches and, as the grand climax, a military parade and sham battle at Macaulay Point, a mile or two west of the city. Imperial forces were still stationed in the Victoria area, and among those taking part were to be the Royal Marines.

In 1896, the Queen's 77th birthday fell on a Sunday, so
events were divided between Saturday, Monday and Tuesday.
Those of Saturday were highly successful, and the next day
everyone went sedately to church. Monday saw boat races on
the Gorge, the waterway that divided Victoria from the nearby
district of Esquimalt. These and other events went off well, and
Victorians turned their attention toward the great military display
to be held at Macaulay Point on Tuesday afternoon.

To reach this location, they would have to cross the harbor by
one of the bridges which spanned it. As the morning advanced,
some set out in their carriages or on bicycles toward the parade
ground, while others began travelling in that direction by
streetcar, an invention which had first made its appearance in
Victoria in 1890. The line led westward from the city center by
way of the Point Ellice bridge, named for an early magnifico of
the Hudson's Bay Company, and numerous Victorians took
advantage of its services.

The bridge was the latest of several which had spanned the
harbor at the same point. The first, built in 1861, had been
replaced in 1872. The third had been opened to the public in
August 1885. It had been built by the San Francisco Bridge
Company of California, its metal parts having been supplied by
the long-established Albion Iron Works of Victoria. Four spans,
two of 150 feet and two of 120 feet, were set on concrete piers.
Approaches added 105 feet, so that the total length of the bridge
was 645 feet. Its cost had been a modest $11,827.

No thought had been given to streetcars when the bridge was
built, but when they made their appearance in Victoria in 1890,
one of the earliest lines crossed it en route to the naval base of
Esquimalt, about three miles west of the city. The city limits of
Victoria were extended in 1891, and as a result included an area
on the western side of the harbor. The city thus became
responsible for the upkeep and regular inspection of the bridge.

How frequently or thoroughly the bridge was inspected would
later be a matter of much controversy. Beyond dispute,
however, was the fact that on May 24, 1893, while a streetcar
was crossing it, the roadway of the bridge had suddenly sagged
an alarming three feet. However, the car, under the guidance of
Jabez Talbot (usually called Harry) successfully reached the
other side, without casualty. Not surprisingly, suspicions about
the bridge's safety had been aroused, and as a result the city
council spent a thousand dollars on strengthening it. It was then
pronounced to be as good as new, although those taking horse-
drawn vehicles over it were advised to go slowly, lest vibration
undo all the repair work.

So matters stood at mid-day on Tuesday, May 26, 1896.

Holiday crowds were beginning to converge on the parade ground, all looking forward to seeing the military perform their intricate manoeuvers. The troops themselves had not had to march to Esquimalt from their Victoria barracks; their commanding officer, Colonel Prior, anxious to have them appear as smart as possible, had brought them round to Macaulay Point by sea. Thus they made no use of the Point Ellice bridge on this occasion, which may have altered the course of subsequent events.

The company had a variety of cars in service, and on this particular day there were two quite different models on the Victoria-Esquimalt run. Number Six was quite a light car, while Number Sixteen was considerable larger and heavier. It also had platforms at the front and rear on which, although it was against regulations, many passengers were clustered. Indeed, on this holiday every car was carrying its maximum load, and Number Sixteen considerably more. Exactly how many it was carrying as it began its last journey is not known, but it was close to 150.

The two cars made their way from the center of Victoria toward the bridge, stopping once for a change of crew. This resulted in Harry Talbot becoming the conductor of Car Sixteen. He was thus in charge of the same car which, while under his direction, had almost suffered a serious accident on the same bridge on the same holiday occasion three years before.

Whether this coincidence occurred to him as the car approached the bridge we shall never know, as he was not to reach the other side. Car Six was on the line just ahead of him, and as it moved onto the bridge, a passenger in Talbot's car suggested to its motorman, George Farr, that it might be advisable if both cars were not on the bridge at once as it was known to be shaky. Accordingly he reduced speed, and as Car Six safely reached the far end of the bridge, Car Sixteen began to cross.

At this fateful moment there were others on the bridge: a two-horse carriage, two one-horse carriages, a bicyclist, and several pedestrians. It was a hot day, and most of the windows of Car Sixteen had been opened. Those on board were anxious to arrive at the parade ground on time; the military manoeuvers began at 2 o'clock, and it was now 10 minutes to the hour.

The car began crossing the bridge, idly watched by numerous holiday-makers in boats on the water below. It had travelled some 30 or 40 feet when there was a loud crack. The car dropped about 18 inches, but continued to go forward. Then came another, louder crackling sound, and an entire span of the bridge collapsed. The car tipped over on its right side and fell into the water, while parts of the bridge came down on top of it in a mass of timbers.

The disaster had occurred before the very eyes of pleasure-seekers on the waters of the Gorge. It had also been witnessed from the nearby residence of Captain William Grant, a director of a company engaged in the sealing industry. This handsome house, built in 1886 and not demolished until 1958, stood near the eastern end of the bridge. A friend of Captain Grant, Captain H.R. Foote, was looking out of the window at the holiday scene. When he saw the bridge collapse, he rushed to his friend's boat-house, cast off a skiff, and began rescuing those struggling in the water.

These included most of those who had been standing on the outside platforms of the streetcar, although some of them had been stunned or crushed by falling timbers and were still somewhere beneath the water. Others had escaped through the open windows of the car and were clinging to pieces of wreckage.

They were hastily dragged into rowboats and other craft and brought to shore. Two young women, daughters of Judge Drake, were active in this work, pulling no fewer than seven people from the water. Many others joined in the rescue work, and the *Colonist* thought it worthwhile to record in its account of the disaster that "class distinctions were forgotten."

Divers were hastily summoned to the scene, and before long bodies were being taken from the car. It was only a short distance beneath the surface of the water, being partly supported by the wreckage of the bridge. There was still a chance that some of those recovered by the divers might still be alive, and as the bodies were laid on the lawn which led down from Captain Grant's house to the water, doctors worked feverishly to restore their breathing. One of the numerous eye-witnesses of the disaster later recalled the scene:

"Delicate ladies whom one might expect to shrink from scenes of horror aided in the work of resuscitating the unfortunate victims as one by one they were brought ashore and laid on the lawn of Captain Grant's house. It was an awful sight as one motionless form after another was brought up the steep bank and placed upon the grass. Mrs. Grant without a moment's hesitation threw open her house as a receiving hospital, and the neighbors from round about brought blankets, brandy and restoratives and people eagerly offered their services."

Despite the best efforts of everyone, there were soon several rows of corpses lying on the grass in the bright sunshine. "It was a pitiful sight to see some poor little child, who had gone out a short time before with its parents to enjoy a happy afternoon, laid out still in death on the grass. There seemed to be so many little ones among the victims. One pretty little girl with golden hair lay with a peaceful look on her face, while close by was a gray-haired old man, his hands clenched and a set face as if he had fought hard against death."

Meanwhile inside the Grant house there were many tragic scenes:

"Downstairs in the drawing-room of the Grant house, poor Mrs. Bowers, who had just been rescued, thought not of herself but of her two daughters, begging someone to tell her of their fate. Poor woman, one of her girls was at that moment lying dead outside, while the body of the other was still at the bottom of the arm.

"A few feet away Dr. Frank Hall and a number of ladies were trying ineffectually to bring back to life Miss Sophie Smith, daughter of Captain H. Smith of Menzies street. Beside her, half crazed with grief and utterly unmindful of her soaking clothes, stood her sister who had fortunately escaped unhurt. She could not believe that her sister was dead, and implored in agonized words the workers not to give up their efforts. For two hours and a half everything possible was done to resuscitate Sophie Smith, but all to no purpose. One young lady at last coaxed her sister to allow her clothes to be changed and took her to her home in a hack, where the news was broken as gently as possible to her invalid mother."

Altogether, 48 bodies were recovered by the end of the day, and seven more the next morning. A total of 55 men, women and children had been suddenly taken while around them the city celebrated its principal holiday. The conductor, who was among those killed, had been collecting fares when the bridge collapsed, and his papers showed that 98 people had paid when the disaster occurred. It was estimated that there were 50 more on board, so that the number of survivors was about 90.

Among those who perished was the lone bicyclist on the bridge, later identified as Frank James, one-time gardener to Sir James Douglas. Conductor Talbot was drowned, leaving a widow and four children, one of them less than two weeks old, to mourn his loss. The motorman, George Farr, was also drowned. The two horse-drawn vehicles on the bridge were thrown into the water; the horses, caught in their harnesses, perished, but the passengers survived. The third vehicle on the bridge was saved by the instincts of its horse. The animal was already on the doomed structure when it sensed that something was wrong and, wheeling about, raced back to the safety of shore.

Among the last to hear of the disaster were the troops drawn up at Macaulay Point. As news of what had happened spread through the crowd of spectators, which included Mayor Beaven, they hurriedly left the scene, and fearing for friends and relatives, made their way to the scene of the tragedy. The troops remained in their appointed places, but when word was brought to their commanding officer of what had happened, he gave the order "Cease fire," and before long the parade ground was deserted.

All other events planned for the holiday, such as dances, were cancelled, and the next day all schools were closed. Some of the bodies were taken to Hayward's funeral parlor, and the rest to the city market, which became a temporary morgue. Some of them were still wrapped in the curtains of the Grant house, which had been used for shrouds. Relatives sought out loved ones, and a coroner's jury identified some of the corpses.

Meanwhile, already looming up behind the disaster, was the question: how had it been possible? Was someone to blame for it, and if so, who?

The coroner's jury visited the scene of the tragedy and spent several hours examining the remains of the bridge. What they discovered, as reported in the *Colonist*, was highly disquieting:

"It was found that at least one of the floor beams had broken across, the break showing it to have been so thoroughly rotten that the wonder is that it did not give way long months ago . . . It was found that the end beam nearest town was so rotten that a juror pushed his knife into it up to the hilt without any difficulty."

Soon afterwards, a public inquiry was held into the tragedy in an effort to determine responsibility. Several civic officials, as well as survivors of the accident, were closely questioned; the official record fills two large volumes. Edward Ashley Wilmot, the city engineer, testified that he had been supervisor of public works for the city for the previous four years. He said that the bridge had been examined by the city carpenter in December 1895, and pronounced by him to be in good shape.

The man directly responsible for examining bridges and side-walks was his subordinate, James Wilson. Wilson told the inquiry that he had only been responsible for the city's bridges since April 25, 1896, a month before the disaster; before that he had been superintendent of streets. The economic background of the period was a factor in this situation; times were not unduly prosperous, and the city, hard-pressed for money, kept as small a staff as possible. Wilson testified that he and Wilmot had recently inspected, as they termed it, the bridge. Some of the questions put to him and the answers he gave to them were both illuminating and disquieting:

Q: "Will you tell us how you inspected the bridge?"
A: "We watched the vibration of the cars and horses upon it."

Q: "Where were you?"

A: "We were on the water in a boat underneath it, backwards and forwards."

Q: "And you watched the cars going?"

A: "Yes."

Q: "Is that the only inspection you made?"

A: "We came up and looked over it. That is all we could do, you know."

Q: "Walked over it?"

A: "Yes."

Q: "Did you take up and examine any of the timbers?"

A: "No, sir."

Q: "Examined nothing?"

A: "Examined nothing as far as that."

It also came to light that, although the maximum weight which the bridge could be expected to bear was 10 tons, the large, overcrowded streetcar had weighed 21 tons.

Before long, numerous lawsuits were launched against the city by survivors of the 55 victims. Because of the state of public feeling, the trials were held in Vancouver. Two test cases were held, those of Mrs. J.B. Gordon and Mrs. J.T. Patterson, who had lost their husbands. In both trials the city was found responsible. It appeared that Victoria would have to pay a large sum of money in compensation to the others, and in an effort to avoid this, it launched numerous appeals which eventually reached the Privy Council in London. The highest court in the Empire was as unsympathetic to the city as the lowest. Its spokesman, Lord Halsbury, declared that the occasional test boring of beams in past years had merely increased the dangers to the bridge:

"The boring of the holes and leaving them so as to collect water was calculated to rot this beam, that for a period of four years this beam was left in that condition collecting water; and if the evidence is to be believed, diffusing a state of rottenness all through the beam. That act was done by an officer of the corporation (the city engineer), upon their direction and paid for by them. This would, under ordinary circumstances, be ample evidence to justify the verdict which was ultimately found against the corporation."

Eventually, after several years of litigation, the city was forced to pay more than $150,000 in claims. For some months after the disaster, a ferry service was in operation across the harbor, and the public was allowed to use the Esquimalt and Nanaimo Railway bridge farther south. A temporary bridge was later erected across the waterway, and the remains of the old one were dynamited in July 1900. In November of 1901 a contract to build a new bridge was awarded to the Puget Sound Bridge and Dredge Company of Seattle. This aroused a widespread public protest against not giving the contract to a Canadian firm, and the contract was cancelled. In 1902 a bid from the Victoria Machinery Depot was accepted, and a four-span bridge on concrete piers was built at the original location and opened in April 1904. It served until its replacement by the present span in November 1957.

The Point Ellice bridge disaster was the worst streetcar accident ever to occur in North America. Fifty-five people had lost their lives, and many families which had looked forward eagerly to Victoria's annual celebration would long remember it with heavy hearts. Their grief would not be lessened by the knowledge that if the bridge had been inspected regularly and thoroughly, the disaster which struck Victoria on May 26, 1896 might well have been avoided.   ●

1898
The New Westminster Fire

AFTER the first permanent white settlement on or near the
coast of British Columbia, Fort Langley, was founded in 1827
by the Hudson's Bay Company for the purpose of trading with the
natives for furs, the company built small posts at other places
along the coast. These included Fort Simpson, a little north of
the present city of Prince Rupert; Fort McLoughlin on Milbanke
Sound, near Bella Bella; and Fort Durham (sometimes called
Fort Taku) on the Taku River. All these were mere pinpoints on
the map of an almost unknown wilderness; even Fort Langley,
though it developed extensive fields of potatoes, and built up an
export trade in salmon, was a comparatively modest place.

The gold rush which developed on the lower Fraser River in
1858 changed all this forever. Thousands of miners swarmed up
the Pacific coast from California to Fort Victoria, where they
obtained supplies and then crossed the Gulf of Georgia to seek
their fortunes on the mainland. This totally unexpected development caught both the British government and its chief lieutenant
in the Pacific Northwest, James Douglas, by surprise, but they
quickly responded to the challenge.

A new British colony was established on the mainland and
named British Columbia; Douglas, while remaining governor of
the quite separate colony of Vancouver Island, was appointed its
governor. The energetic Scot was informed, however, that this
was contingent on his severing all connections with the fur trade.

He accepted this condition, and on November 19, 1858 was sworn in by Judge Begbie in the main hall of the HBC post at Fort Langley as first governor of British Columbia.

The fur trade continued active for some time yet, but a new era had begun. Government had come to the wilderness, and this meant that schools, churches, hospitals, prisons and roads would have to follow. A capital city would also have to be chosen from which law and order would radiate. Douglas favored Derby, a small settlement on the south bank of the Fraser near Fort Langley, but to assist him in making a final decision he had been ordered to give careful consideration to the views of his principal subordinate in the new colony, Colonel Richard Moody of the Royal Engineers.

Moody, a man of much ability and experience, had been specially chosen by the British government to develop communications in the new colony. He had arrived in Victoria on Christmas Day, 1858, and a week later had set out for the Fraser River, being much impressed by the scenery:

"The entrance to the Fraser is very striking; extending miles to the right and left are low marsh lands, apparently of very rich qualities, and yet from the background of superb mountains— Swiss in outline, dark in woods, grandly towering into the clouds —there is a sublimity that deeply impresses you. Everything is large and magnificent, worthy of the entrance to the Queen of England's dominions on the Pacific mainland. I scarcely ever enjoyed a scene so much in my life."

Before long, the Colonel had decided on the best site for the new colonial capital:

"It is the right place in all respects. Commercially for the good of the whole community, politically for imperial interests, and militarily for the protection of and to hold the country against our neighbours at some future day. Also for all purposes of convenience to the local government in connection with Vancouver Island, at the same time as with the back country. It is a most important spot."

The site selected by Moody was about 10 miles below Fort Langley, on the north bank of the Fraser at the point where it divides into two channels, each of which then makes its separate way to the sea. It was accessible to deepsea shipping, and more easily defended against a possible American invasion than any site on the southern side of the river. Moody also believed that it would make a good terminus for a transcontinental railway—a remarkable thought to have crossed his mind, as not until 1870 would one be promised to British Columbia, and not until 1886 would it reach the Pacific coast.

Governor Douglas was by no means pleased by Moody's

recommendation. It cast doubt on his own judgement, and meant that his survey of the Derby area and the subsequent sale of lots there to the general public had been largely wasted effort. He felt bound, however, to yield to the professional advice of his subordinate; accordingly on February 14, 1859, Douglas proclaimed "Queensborough," as he called it, the capital of British Columbia.

There was some controversy about this name, and the question was referred to Queen Victoria. In accordance with her wishes, in July 1859 it was renamed New Westminster.

The carving of a capital city from primeval wilderness had already begun. The area was surveyed by the engineers, and a city of some size and distinction was envisioned in Moody's plans. Those who had hopefully bought lots at Derby were allowed to exchange them for ones in the new capital which, in July 1860, received the right to elect its own municipal officials.

Colonel Moody and many of his men returned to the British Isles in 1863, but some of the engineers, having completed their terms of service, settled down either in New Westminster or on the surrounding farm land. Governor Douglas retired from public life in 1864, and not one but two men were appointed to succeed him: Governor Arthur Kennedy in Victoria, and Governor Frederick Seymour in New Westminster.

Seymour was an affable, bald-headed bachelor who took an intelligent interest in the young mainland colony. Unfortunately the period was not a prosperous one; when the gold rush peaked, economic growth became sluggish. Few gave much thought as yet to the beginnings of an export lumber industry along nearby Burrard Inlet, and the three New Westminster men —the famous "three greenhorns"—who in 1862 became the first settlers in the Vancouver area were thought to be eccentrics.

In an effort to reduce expenses and co-ordinate policies, the two Pacific colonies were united under the leadership of Governor Seymour in November 1866, and New Westminster became the capital of the entire area between the Rockies and the Pacific Ocean. Governor Kennedy returned to England, Vancouver Island ceased to exist as a separate colony, and henceforth the name British Columbia was applied to it as well.

Two years later New Westminster suffered a shattering blow, when the capital was moved to Victoria. Most government officials were transferred to Vancouver Island, and a major source of employment was lost. The population rapidly declined, and at one time there were only some 500 souls remaining in the once-proud "Royal City."

But slowly hope revived. New Westminster had had its first church since 1860, its Royal Columbian Hospital since 1862,

and its first public school since 1863. The telegraph reached the
city from the United States in 1865, in time to bring word of the
death of President Lincoln. The following year the line was
extended into the interior as far as Quesnel, at that time still the
scene of a lively gold rush. The city's "Hyack" fire brigade,
founded in 1861, was a source of pride to the community. Its
unusual name was derived from the Indian word for "quick,"
and the force prided itself on the speed with which its horse-
drawn vehicles could reach the scene of a fire.

When the colony entered Confederation in 1871, it was on
the understanding that a railway would connect it to the east.
Poor economic conditions delayed the commencement of this
great project for a long time. However, once the final decision
had been made that the line should reach the coast by way of the
Fraser, there was increased activity, and the 1880s saw a revival
of confidence in New Westminster. Traffic at the city's wharves
increased, as rails and machinery were unloaded, and an ever
greater amount of forest products left the port for the four
quarters of the globe. In 1887 the first train reached New
Westminster from the east, and in 1891 the Great Northern
connected the city with the United States. The following year
an interurban electric railway joined New Westminster to the
rapidly growing young city of Vancouver.

Thus as the century neared its end, the community had
digested, if not forgotten, its great disappointment, and was
enjoying a fair share of the economic activity of the province. It
had numerous fine buildings—some of them reminders of the
days when Colonel Moody had envisioned it as a future
metropolis—a good public library, numerous churches, two fire
halls, and an opera house. It had celebrated the Queen's
Diamond Jubilee in 1897 with enthusiasm, although it was
realized that her long and glorious reign was drawing to a close.
Other world figures were to disappear into the shades before
her; both Bismarck and Gladstone died in the summer of 1898.

The city had planned an elaborate exposition for the autumn
of 1898. Both industrial and agricultural products were to be
displayed, and the main feature of the celebration would be "a
pyrotechnic display surpassing in magnitude anything heretofore
seen in the province of British Columbia."

Preparations for this were well advanced when the city went
to bed on Saturday, September 10, 1898. Many residents were
no doubt already asleep when, about 11 o'clock, they were
roused by the sound of fire alarms. As the city was built on the
side of a steep hill rising from the north bank of the river, anyone
looking from his window could see that a serious fire had broken
out along the waterfront.

It had started on Front Street in a large hay-filled warehouse owned by the Brackman-Ker feed company. It was never determined whether the cause was spontaneous combustion or whether sparks from a passing steamer had fallen on the roof of the building. At all events the warehouse was soon a mass of flames, which also destroyed the nearby city market where both the fruit exchange and the creamery had their headquarters. From there the fire spread rapidly in several directions, and was soon sweeping up the hillside.

The first area to be severely damaged was the business and government section of the city, which was concentrated near the river. This was about six blocks square, and contained most of the city's finest structures. Three steamers, the *Gladys*, *Edgar* and *Bon Accord*, which were tied up at their wharves, caught on fire, and as their mooring ropes parted, began drifting down the river, spreading the fire as they went. The *Gladys* and *Edgar* soon sank, but the *Bon Accord* was scuttled as it approached an important lumber mill.

Soon the entire area from the Telegraph Hotel to the CPR station, a distance of six blocks along the river, was in flames, and the fire was sweeping up the hillside as far as Royal Avenue in the residential section. As one observer later recalled, "Columbia street looked a mass of flames right across the roadway, and every now and then the fire would zigzag over from one side of the street to the other, and in a few moments more another building would vanish as if dissolved into the air. The fine public library was so completely burned that its brick walls collapsed into the cellar.

"Attempts were made in many instances to remove goods in drays, but so quickly did the fire spread that the drays caught fire, and the horses had to be cut loose to save their lives."

By this time the fire department had gone into action, under the command of the deputy chief, as Chief Ackerman was away on vacation. It was soon apparent that, as in the case of so many other British Columbia disasters, the forces assigned to deal with it were not in a state of readiness. Both fire halls caught fire and were destroyed; the city reservoir had been allowed to fall to a very low level; horses were not immediately available for the fire engines; and a fire boat stationed on the river was not ready for action. Meanwhile terrified householders were pouring water from garden hoses on their homes, further reducing the available amount of water. Some hydrants had been opened and hoses attached, but the flames had advanced so rapidly that they had to be abandoned even before they could be turned off. Thus in the hour of its greatest need, the city found itself virtually defenceless, and suffered accordingly.

Even so, its firemen showed a high sense of duty. One heard a child crying in a burning building and crawled into the smoke until a jet of flame blinded him in one eye. In spite of this, he persevered until he had located the child and carried it to safety. Another fireman fell from a roof and sustained severe injuries. As he was being carried away, he broke loose from those assisting him, and, with the cry, "My duty is there!" plunged back into the flames. In a few minutes he fell unconscious and was again dragged to safety.

One woman asked bystanders to save her three children from their burning home. When they refused, she rushed inside and saved them all, although her dress was enveloped in flames. She eventually recovered from her injuries. Two other children were placed in a building believed to be a safe distance from the fire, and were forgotten until almost too late. When rescued, they were still alive, but badly burned about the hands and feet.

As soon as it was obvious that the city was facing a major disaster, Mayor Thomas Ovens telegraphed Vancouver for assistance. In a remarkably short time Chief Carlisle's horse-drawn engines had arrived and were assisting the Hyack company. By tearing down small buildings which might spread the blaze and pumping water directly from the river, they were eventually able to confine the fire to an area about seven blocks square. Nevertheless at the height of the blaze, about 3 o'clock in the morning, the center of the city was an inferno: "House after house was falling victim to the raging element. Myriads of sparks were falling, and on every roof were seen people with pails and ladders, endeavoring to prevent their homes from catching fire. All around, in every open space on every street and in nearly all the gardens were strewn furniture, bedding, clothing and numerous household effects, all of which had frequently to be saturated with water to prevent the sparks from setting fire to them.

"Men were busy with picks and axes cutting away the sidewalks, which were carrying the fire along the roads. Telephone and electric light wires were falling in every direction. From sewer traps, columns of smoke were pouring hundreds of feet into the air, and every few minutes a whirlwind would tear along the street, collecting smoke, sparks, ashes and dust in its course and whirling it all around with tremendous force. In the midst of all this chaos, men and women were carrying their goods and chattels out of the reach of the fire. Wagons and express carts were carrying furniture, safes, etc. up the hill. On the right a man was seen dipping a cloth into an open drain and sprinkling the water over a collection of goods covered with a carpet. Other men were carrying pails of water to shower over their goods. Many were quietly stamping out the larger sparks and lighted pieces of wood that were falling on the sidewalks all around."

By dawn, the flames had been extinguished, but a large part of a once-proud city was a wasteland. "The sidewalks were literally licked up, and where they had been, in the light of morning were seen paths of greyish brown dust, exactly as though a long strip of carpet had been rolled up after long service. This was as much a sight for early risers as were the fantastically twisted telegraph and telephone wires festooning the grey-black streets, or pendant like giant cobwebs from the scarred shell of some once stately structure of brick and stone."

It had been the most serious fire in British Columbia to date, and in many ways worse than others which followed. The Vancouver fire of 1886 had been sudden and violent, but the wooden buildings of a considerably smaller and more primitive community were quickly rebuilt. The loss of life was undoubtedly greater in the earlier disaster; perhaps 30 had been lost when Gastown went up in smoke, whereas the only death in New Westminster was that of a Chinese merchant who dropped dead from a heart attack. His loss was perhaps compensated for when three children were born prematurely. Several horses used by the Brackman-Ker Company to deliver feed were burned to death.

A mere catalogue of New Westminster's losses shows the magnitude of the disaster: the CPR station, all the major hotels, every church but one, the city hall, the court house, the offices of the *Daily Columbian*, two canneries—one containing a whole season's pack, a warehouse full of coal, and another full of feed for livestock, the public library, both fire halls, the opera house, two banks and the post office, many business firms and private residences, numbering about 300 in all. Few property owners, it transpired, had carried fire insurance.

Only one important building was saved—the city jail. When the fire broke out, the prisoners were released, and under the supervision of their guards succeeded in saving their temporary home. After the fire, it was used as the city hall until another one could be built. Some valuable papers were lost in the fire. These included the maps of the Fraser River being prepared as part of the plan to prevent any recurrence of the great flood of 1894. Relics connected with Captain George Vancouver and Sir John Franklin were lost when the public library was destroyed. Not, perhaps, as regrettable was the loss of $20,000 worth of opium, then legally available for sale in the province.

Reaction to the disaster was rapid. Mayor Ovens sent a wire to Premier Semlin in Victoria: "All hotels and places of business

and many residences have been wiped out by fire, and several
thousands of people are homeless. Please come here without
delay." The reference to "thousands of people" was perhaps an
exaggeration, but pardonable in the circumstances, and the premier ordered tents and blankets to be sent at once to the stricken
city. Coal baron James Dunsmuir ordered a special train load of
relief supplies to be sent north from Victoria to Nanaimo, where
his company's steamer, *Joan*, waited to cast off for New Westminster immediately upon its arrival. Altogether 664 pairs of
blankets and 83 tents reached the mainland city in a short time.

The commanding officer of military forces in Victoria, Lt-Col.
Peters, also gave assistance. Requisitioning 800 blankets and
100 tents from army stores, he had them despatched to New
Westminster, as several high government officials rushed to the
scene of disaster. These included Mayor Redfern of Victoria, as
well as Fire Chief Deasy of the capital city, who planned to
investigate the cause of the fire and determine how such
disasters could be prevented in the future. Relief committees
were set up in both Victoria and Vancouver, and money and
supplies were collected for the victims of the fire.

Though the loss of life had been negligible, what once had
been the center of a thriving community was now 20 acres of
ashes. Over a thousand people, after one or more nights
between blankets in the open air, were living in tents or billeted
in homes which had escaped the fire. A visitor from Victoria
painted a picture of the desolation for the *Colonist*:

"When he reached New Westminster he seemed to be in a
strange city. Although he had known New Westminster well, the
fire had obliterated the buildings, and it was impossible to tell in
the confusion of ruins where any particular structure had stood.
The sidewalks were smouldering, the box drains on fire, and the
water had given out. Furniture and other household effects lined
the streets, and people exhausted by the excitement of the night
lay sleeping in chairs or on bundles of the few effects they had
managed to carry to vacant lots."

Yet, like Vancouver a decade earlier, the city began returning
to life almost immediately. Within a few days there were signs
that hope had survived the flames:

"On the city hall square there have now appeared half a score
of makeshift shacks in which the representative merchants of the
town are offering new stocks to the impoverished citizens. The
city hall is represented by a 12 x 10 tent, from which the
municipal officers direct the allotment of space, for the square
resembles nothing so much as a typical boom city, and is staked
by the business community in much the same manner as mining
ground."

Meanwhile the CPR had contributed $5,000, James Dunsmuir $3,000, to aid the victims and, little by little, recovery began. The dominion government announced that it would rebuild its buildings in the city. Provincial officials conducted their business from the city jail. The banks of British Columbia and Montreal opened their vaults and found that their contents were still intact. It was announced that the great exposition scheduled for October would not be cancelled, even though visitors would have to find lodgings in Vancouver.

There was only one sour note in this period. There had long been keen rivalry between New Westminster and Vancouver, and no doubt a few on the shores of Burrard Inlet rejoiced in the troubles of those on the shore of the Fraser. Only one public figure, however, dared to exult openly; this was Walter Nichol, editor of the Vancouver *Province* and a generation later to be Lieutenant-Governor of British Columbia. In an editorial soon after the fire he declared:

"It can probably be said that the fire determines the fate of New Westminster. Its dreams of greatness have been scattered to the wandering winds of heaven. It is inevitable that the population should rapidly decrease, and that most of those who formerly claimed New Westminster as their home should now locate in Vancouver or some other equally advantageous point. New Westminster is a city of yesterday."

Few citizens of New Westminster agreed with this verdict, and some dissented forcibly. A group of them journeyed to Vancouver and invaded the editorial sanctum of the offending newspaper, where their leader beat up its editor. In sedate Victoria the *Colonist* commented that "he should have gone this far, few will approve, although the people of Vancouver and New Westminster alike are agreed that the provocation was great."

By this time Victoria's fire chief, having made an unofficial investigation of the disaster, had drawn up a list of reasons why it had reached such proportions so quickly:

"Taking circumstances under consideration, the firemen of New Westminster worked as hard as men could work with the limited apparatus and water service at their disposal. At the start of the fire, the firemen coupled two lengths of hose to a hydrant and were compelled to leave them, which left five inches of water to run waste. People were using water on their residences and buildings throughout the whole city, reducing the pressure in the streams in the hands of firemen, and all that was available was a mere dribble.

"The fireboat was not ready, and would have been the only means of stopping the blaze in the large shed of hay belonging to

Brackman and Ker, deriving its supply as it would from the Fraser.

"The steam fire engine which had been kept in reserve was not provided with horses, and therefore was some time preparing for active service. Vancouver firemen were working at both ends of the city and the Westminster firemen in the heart of the city, and this system reduced the pressure at all points. If all forces were concentrated, there is no doubt stronger and heavier streams would have been obtained."

The failure to keep firefighting forces in a state of complete readiness for any emergency had caused New Westminster to suffer the worst setback in its history. Nevertheless its citizens did not lose heart. The great exposition was held on schedule only a month after the fire; some surrounding municipalities cancelled their own fall fairs in order to contribute to the success of New Westminster. Lumber companies and canneries did not have exhibits, however; the former were too busy producing material for reconstruction, and the latter had been almost completely destroyed.

As the year ended, the *Daily Columbian* declared, "In less than four months we have made almost phenomenal and certainly most creditable progress in recovering from that blow. Ere another year has rolled by, it will be very difficult to believe that the Royal City had a fiery visitation so lately."

One storekeeper, a few days after the fire, had summed it up more briefly but just as accurately. His advertisement was headed BLISTERED BUT NOT BUSTED.   ●

1910
The Great Victoria Fire

VICTORIA in 1910 was a happy and prosperous place. Favored from its very beginning with pleasant climate and scenic surroundings, as the fur trade days steadily gave way to the age of science and industry, it acquired more of the blessings of 19th century civilization. The telegraph had arrived in the 1860s, the telephone in the 1880s; 1890 saw the first streetcar run in the city, while five years later the first moving picture was on display. The dawning of a new century and the beginning of a new reign merely accelerated the pace of progress. The first automobile appeared in Victoria in 1902; university work was begun; the cornerstone of the Carnegie library was laid in 1904; and there were many elaborate social functions. In the early years of the century the CPR announced that a large modern hotel would be built on the Inner Harbour, and on January 20, 1908, the Empress opened its doors.

By this time the city, and indeed the entire western world, was in the midst of an economic boom. Fine private residences and handsome public and commercial buildings were rising on all sides. The youthful premier, Richard McBride, announced his intention of covering Vancouver Island with a network of railways, and the grateful voters renewed his mandate. A stock exchange was opened in the city, a local merchant declared himself "ready with another lot of men's good serviceable suits at $6.75," and even the death of King Edward cast only a temporary pall over the city. Houses (and even streetcars) were shrouded for a time in black and purple, but work continued on the Dunsmuir's imposing mansion "Hatley Park."

The *Colonist* (50 cents a month, delivered) continued to be the mirror of the passing scene. The tobacconist E.A. Morris took space in its pages to proclaim that "I am the man who imports cigarettes for ladies," while W. and J. Wilson, the clothiers, were advertising what they were pleased to term "sox" at 50 cents a pair. The appropriately named "Ideal Provision Company" advertised sirloin of beef at 12½ cents a pound; for those who thought this price excessive, they had pot roasts at 9 cents.

A *Colonist* editorial predicted that Winston Churchill was "almost certain to become an exceedingly formidable factor in the public life of the empire"; another opined that women would receive the vote by 1920. The paper declared that all motorcars should carry lights after dark, but that "by and by we won't glance upward at flying machines unless something is dropped on our heads." It also predicted that "there will at a very early date be such an upheaval in Russia as will put to the blush all records of previous revolts of the masses." In the meantime the paper printed a long article asking "Can England be invaded by airships?" It reached the mildly reassuring conclusion: not yet.

On the local scene, perhaps the most noteworthy event in Victoria as the autumn of 1910 approached was the conclusion of a financial agreement with the residents of the local Songhees Indian reserve, comprising 115 acres just across the harbor to the west of the city. In return for a payment of $10,000 to the head of each of the 43 families on the reserve, they agreed to cede the area to the white man and move to a new location.

One of Victoria's leading citizens in this period was David Spencer, born in Glamorganshire in 1837, the year Queen Victoria came to the throne. Upon emigrating to British Columbia in the gold rush days, he had opened a stationery store in Victoria. Later he had gone into the drygoods business, and his store on Government Street had become a formidable rival to that of the Hudson's Bay Company. His wife had arrived on the "bride ship" *Robert Lowe* in 1863.

On the evening of October 26, 1910, one of Spencer's employees, an auditor named Monteith, was working late in the store and did not leave until 10 o'clock. At that time all seemed well, and in any case two watchmen remained in the building as a precaution against fire and burglars.

About 10:45 the proprietor of the Army and Navy cigar store was leaving his premises on Government Street when he saw a small blaze in the center of the main aisle of the Spencer store. A moment later the two watchmen, named Luscombe and Gale, rushed from the store, crying, "Call the firemen!"

The tobacconist ran back into his shop and phoned the fire department. Then he hastened toward the Five Sisters Block at the corner of Fort and Government, where he lived with his wife and child. When he had roused his own family, he went from door to door waking others, who began carrying their most precious belongings to safety.

By this time the fire department had reached the scene of the fire, while Chief Davis, who was not at the hall, was en route by automobile. He and his men entered the ground floor of the store, but so much glass and debris was falling from the floors above that they had to retreat into the street and play their hoses on the second story. However the flames had already swept up the elevator shaft and were visible on the roof. It appeared that the store and all its contents were doomed.

This soon proved to be the case, and the labors of the firemen were applied to preventing the loss of adjoining buildings. Despite their heroic efforts, the Five Sisters Block (named for the five daughters of Sir James Douglas) was ablaze by midnight and was soon a total loss. The same fate befell the Victoria Book and Stationery Company and Henry Young's drygoods store. The offices of the *Times*, the *Colonist*'s afternoon rival since 1884, were damaged but not destroyed. For a time it looked as if the imposing new Pemberton Building (now the Yarrow Building) at the corner of Fort and Broad might catch fire, but it was saved.

By midnight the business area of the city was crowded with spectators. Some of them had been attending the theatre and were in evening dress. Most of them were content to watch the blaze, but a few helped firemen to haul hoses. Useful assistance was also given by 150 members of the garrison at Work Point Barracks in Esquimalt. An effort had been made to reach them by telephone, but the wires were down. Accordingly a motorcar was sent racing to the barracks for help.

Victoria was well-supplied with telephones in this period, but the wires were all of the overhead type. Even at the best of times this made the business district an unsightly jungle, and many citizens had been urging for some time that they be placed underground. The fire destroyed a great many wires and poles, impeding communications in the city. All electric current in the affected area had been deliberately cut off by the authorities in case firemen were electrocuted by falling wires. Nevertheless the absence of electricity was hardly felt, as the blaze lit up a large area as though it were daylight.

At this time the most prestigious hotel in Victoria was the

Driard, located between Broad and Douglas streets. The hotel had been opened in 1872 by a Frenchman, Sosthenes Driard. It had passed through a variety of hands, and in 1892 had been completely rebuilt. It soon became famous far beyond Victoria, as the quality of its food, drink and service was perhaps the best on the Pacific coast. In 1910, a few weeks before the fire, a Mr. Weldon became its latest proprietor.

The fire, several times spurting across Broad Street, came close enough to the hotel to damage it considerably, but the building did not actually catch fire. Guests were advised to leave, however, and many carried their belongings into the nearby streets. Their rooms subsequently suffered water damage from fire hoses.

Many valuable documents and records were lost in the fire. Among these were those of the celebrated architect Samuel Maclure, whose office was in the Five Sisters Block. Savannah's photo studio in the same building was also destroyed, and more than 50,000 negatives, which had formed a unique record of the city's early days, went up in smoke. Lowe's photographic supply firm was also destroyed, and six small ships in the nearby harbor were damaged by falling sparks.

By 3 o'clock in the morning the fire was under control; by dawn all flames had been extinguished. Nevertheless the new day revealed a sad sight. The entire area bounded by Government, Fort, Broad, and Trounce streets had been destroyed, with an estimated loss of property and merchandise of $1,500,000, and the streetcar line along Government Street was blocked by debris. Only one death had occurred, however, that of Mrs. Samuel Shore, wife of the proprietor of the Bismarck Hotel, who died of shock.

Some blackened walls which continued to stand presented a further danger to the public and in the next few days the Government Street wall of the Spencer store was brought to the ground by dynamite, and other ruined buildings were dismantled and cleared away.

Christopher and Victor Spencer, sons of the founder of the family business, were in Vancouver at the time of the fire. They promptly announced that their Victoria store would be rebuilt on a larger scale. A few days later they informed the public that they had bought the Driard Hotel, as well as the nearby Victoria Theatre, for $370,000, and would soon be carrying on their business from this new location. So ended the career of the famous hostelry; and so began the Empress's undisputed leadership as the premier hotel of Victoria.

Another result of the fire was that View Street, which previously had come to an awkward end at Broad Street, was extended one block farther west to Government Street, thus improving the flow of traffic. This also made possible the erection of two handsome new office blocks, the Central Building and the Union (now the Royal Trust) Building.

Indeed, Victoria recovered with remarkable speed from the most serious fire in its history. The great boom which had set in at the turn of the century ran for several years more, and general optimism ran high. The rubble was cleared away, Luney brothers, the contractors, having advertised for a hundred laborers, and before long newer and finer buildings were rising from the ruins. As well, many of the unsightly telephone wires in the business district were put underground.

One thing the fire had shown was that even in the center of a modern city sudden devastation could occur. Was the same true of western civilization as a whole? A few may have pondered this question; the newspapers carried many accounts in this period of the accelerating arms race between the great powers. Before many years had elapsed this question would receive its tragic answer; but in the meantime, despite occasional setbacks such as the 1910 fire, life in Victoria in the last of the golden years before 1914 was very good indeed. ●

1913 & 1914
The Fraser River Slides

THE river had from the beginning been British Columbia's main artery. Down it Simon Fraser had travelled to the Pacific in 1808. Later George Simpson, chief officer of the Hudson's Bay Company in North America, had travelled this way to estimate the possibilities of the fur trade in the far west. When the age of fur gave way to the age of gold, the treasure seekers headed up the river toward the rich creeks of the Cariboo. A generation later the transcontinental railway found a way through these rocky gorges to the ocean.

No one had found the journey easy. For a considerable distance between Hope and Lytton, the river had forced its passage through the "sea of mountains" by cutting a deep but narrow channel through the bare rock. Here were numerous rapids and whirlpools; jagged rocks raised themselves intermittently above the surface; iron cliffs frowned down on the traveller. In early summer, when the snows in the mountains melted, the river became a torrent, and its level in the narrow gorges often rose in a few weeks by as much as 80 feet.

None dared to challenge it at such times. Fraser had been forced to abandon his canoes and make his way along the cliffs by clinging to precarious handholds, a terrifying experience he never wished to repeat. As he wrote afterwards, "I have been for a long period among the Rocky Mountains, but have never seen anything equal to this country, for I cannot find words to describe our situation at times. We had to pass where no human being should venture."

Simpson had actually conquered the Fraser. With seven companions in two canoes, he had successfully descended the river in the fall of 1828. Even though the Fraser was comparatively quiet at that time of year, he had realized that precious cargoes of furs could never be entrusted to its middle reaches, and when the fur brigades began to travel from the interior to the coast, they took other routes. At first they came down the side of Okanagan Lake to the upper Columbia, and later, after the Oregon Treaty of 1846, in a southwesterly direction from Kamloops to a point on the Fraser well below the rapids.

The gold miners who worked their way up the river in 1858 also found it a stern challenge. In some places they used canoes or rafts, but often they retreated to the shore and followed paths worn by the sure-footed Indians. Sometimes, when pausing for a moment to look down at the river below, they saw washing past them toward the sea the canoes and bodies of those who had gone before them.

Not all the bodies had been the victims of the rapids. Many of the native inhabitants resented the appearance of strange white newcomers in their midst, and attempted to drive them out. Numerous minor skirmishes took place in the first year of the gold rush, and on one occasion in July of 1858, a small battle was fought between the two races. The last white survivor of this fighting, it might be mentioned, was Ned Stout, who died in 1924.

One motive behind the Indian resistance to the newcomers was doubtless the desire to preserve undisturbed their age-old fishing grounds. The Indian civilization of the Pacific Northwest had long been based on the salmon and the cedar. Between them, these two natural products, both very easily obtained, supplied nearly every need from food and shelter to clothing and oil. Their availability was the main factor in producing a society comparatively rich in material goods, and with the leisure to become highly skilled in many arts and crafts.

The white man was also quick to realize the wealth the river could be made to yield. As early as 1830 Fort Langley was exporting barrels of salmon, packed in salt, as far as Hawaii, and after 1870 modern canneries began to appear at New Westminster. By-products were also developed: inferior or rotten fish was made into fertilizer, and grease was used as a lubricant, notably on the "skid-roads" down which mighty logs were dragged to the water's edge by the rapidly expanding lumber industry.

By the early years of the 20th century, the Fraser River and

the waters near its mouth were a major source of employment,
both to those who toiled in the canneries and to the fishermen
who cast their lines and nets into the open sea. Some thought
had been given to protecting this valuable source of income from
depletion. Negotiations had been under way for some years
between Canada and the United States, with a view to restricting
the annual catch of fish to the amount which would keep their
numbers undiminished. Agreement had proved impossible,
however, as each side perceived some temporary advantage,
and fishermen of both countries remained free to catch as many
fish as they could. Many Indians were still to be seen along the
river, assembling each year at strategic points as the salmon
came up in summer to spawn, and spearing them from platforms
built on the edge of the turbulent torrent. White men, however,
were forbidden to catch fish in this manner.

The province was in the midst of an economic boom when,
early in 1909, Premier Richard McBride announced that a new
railway would soon be crossing the province. This was the
Canadian Northern Pacific Railway (later to become part of the
CNR), and its route to the coast would be by way of the Fraser.
Contracts were signed with William Mackenzie and Donald
Mann, the promoters of the railway, and work on it soon
commenced. As the Grand Trunk Pacific was meanwhile
making its way across the northern part of the province toward
Prince Rupert, railways were very much in the news, and there
seemed to be no limit to the benefits which they might bring to
the province.

It was plain from the beginning that the most difficult part of
the new project would be the cutting of a right-of-way into the
cliffs along the east bank of the middle reaches of the Fraser.
However, few doubted that what the CPR had done in an earlier
age along the west bank might be done in the burgeoning new
century, and dynamite, picks and shovels, and sweating backs
were applied to the task. There was one notable difference from
the days of John A. Macdonald: no Asiatics were employed in
constructing the line. This clause in the agreement was the result
of pressure by members of the white working class, who feared
that their places might be taken by cheaper labor.

The worst stretch of the river, as far as the promoters of the
railway were concerned, was the "Great Canyon." This reached
from Yale to Cisco, south of Lytton. Here the river was compressed between high rocky cliffs, as the Coast Range on the west and
the Cascade Range on the east confined the river in a narrow
channel. The most striking feature of this part of the Fraser was
"Hell's Gate," between Boston Bar and Spuzzum, where great
masses of rock thrust out into the river from either bank.

Between these promontories the river had to pass. Even at low water in wintertime it ran swiftly here; in early summer it became a raging torrent. The Fraser drained a watershed of 84,000 square miles, and when the snow on the mountain peaks melted in early summer, all the water so formed ran first into the great river's tributaries and then into the Fraser itself. All the river system above Hell's Gate had to pass through this narrow gorge, forming in early summer an almost impassable barrier to man or fish.

Even so, each year thousands of salmon successfully negotiated it. Urged by some deep instinct, after four years in the open sea they made their way back to the stream where they had been spawned, there to spawn in turn and die.

When they came to Hell's Gate, they often had to make many attempts before getting through it, and the weaker members of the species frequently failed. Fortunately the two great jutting rocks which formed the gate were not directly opposite each other, and this created a back eddy near that on the right bank where fish could rest before returning to the fray.

As 1913 arrived, British Columbians had enjoyed a decade of uninterrupted prosperity and looked forward to another buoyant year. The three basic export industries of the province— lumbering, mining and fishing—were constantly setting new records. Between 1910 and 1913 more than 40 million sockeye salmon had been caught in British Columbia waters, and in the best year better than 2 million cases of fish had been packed for shipment abroad.

There was a noticeable tendency for every fourth year to produce an unusually heavy salmon run, and 1913 was a year in which a record harvest could be expected. Meanwhile the new railway was steadily making its way along the east bank of the Fraser. Progress was slow, as the roadbed often had to be cut from the solid rock, but the contractors were confident that, before long, another "last spike" would be driven.

When the earlier railroad came down the Fraser Canyon, rock removed from the right-of-way had simply been dumped into the river. The builders of the new line saw no reason to adopt any other procedure. Accordingly, as the work progressed, large quantities of rock were blasted from the cliffs, then unceremoniously pushed over the edge of the roadbed and into the river.

When a considerable amount of blasting directly above Hell's Gate had the effect of further narrowing the river at what was already its narrowest part, the velocity of the water pouring through this gap was greatly increased. Moreover, some of the rock had come to rest in the back eddy near Hell's Gate, where fish had once been able to rest after their journey from the sea. This made it harder than ever for them to fight against the torrents which poured through the narrow passage during the early summer run-off.

Unfortunately, as in the case of nearly all the other disasters which had struck British Columbia in the previous 50 years, little thought was given to the dangers of this situation until too late. As the spring of 1913 gave way to summer, the salmon began their long journey from the sea toward the creeks where their life had begun four years before, and where nature had decreed that it should end.

At the same time the river, fed by the melting winter snows, began rising; nowhere was it more turbulent than at Hell's Gate. Meanwhile, work on the railroad continued. Man's work and nature's purposes were about to clash, and out of this clash would come disaster.

Up from the open sea through the Strait of Juan de Fuca came the salmon, travelling in great schools and from time to time leaping out of the water, a habit which made their progress easy for fishermen to follow. It also fitted them for negotiating the difficult parts of the river. Each fish knew on which tributary of the river, indeed on which small creek, it had been spawned, and unerringly made its way toward it. Although this might mean a journey of as much as 600 miles, the salmon did not eat, living instead on the stores of fat and oil which it had accumulated in its years in the sea.

As the fish made their way up the Fraser, some turned off and ascended the tributaries along its lower reaches. These found the place of their origin from four years before, and there renewed the life cycle before dying. For those which had come originally from the upper reaches of the river, however, it was a different story. When they reached the narrow gorge at Hell's Gate, they flung themselves at it in vain. Time after time each fish would make a rush at the raging torrent; time after time the river would prove too strong, and it would fall back exhausted.

A few did finally get through; of these, most were too weak to negotiate a lesser obstacle at Scuzzy Rapids, three miles above Hell's Gate. Soon the water was choked for several miles below the canyon with salmon about to die without renewing themselves. Before long every sandbar below the canyon was covered with rotting salmon and the air was thick with their smell.

However, the harvest from the waters off the mouth of the Fraser had been a record one, and at first not many realized that a major ecological disaster had occurred. Then reports of very few fish being seen on the upper reaches of the river led W.J.

Bowser, Provincial Commissioner of Fisheries, to instruct his assistant, John Pease Babcock, to make a report on the situation.

Babcock, born in Minnesota in 1855, had worked as a young man for the California State Fish Commission. In 1901 he had come north at the invitation of Premier McBride to advise the British Columbia government on important questions regarding the fishing industry. Later, having become a Canadian citizen, he was charged with the task of determining why there were such wide variations in the annual salmon run. For example, in 1897 the two countries had packed in excess of a million cases of salmon, whereas in 1903 less than 400,000 cases were obtained.

With the aid of scientists who had developed a rudimentary system of tagging fish and then studying their subsequent movements, Babcock learned much about the life cycle of the five species of salmon found in provincial waters. These were the spring or tyee, coho, sockeye, humpback and chum. He learned, for example, that although the life cycle of the sockeye was almost invariably four years, the other four species had varying cycles. Moreover, they chose different months of the year to make their migrations. Commercially, the Fraser River sockeye was by far the most important, so Babcock concentrated his energies on learning all he could about both.

It was mainly through his efforts that the possibility of an eventual permanent depletion in the sockeye catch was first drawn to the attention of the provincial government. However, for a long time he was unable to persuade his superiors of the need for planned conservation of this important economic resource. They preferred to believe that the fish would always adjust their breeding habits to the needs of the consumer.

Accordingly, nothing had been done to limit the catch, and indeed, there seemed little sign in the early months of 1913 that any action was needed, as the catch in recent years had actually improved, and that of 1913 broke records.

When, that summer, reports began reaching Victoria that many salmon had been unable to ascend the river past Hell's Gate, Babcock hastened to the scene. Not much more than a glance was needed for him to realize that a major provincial industry was facing disaster. As he reported to his superiors, "Immediately below Hell's Gate, and for 10 miles downstream, sockeye were massed in incredible numbers. Vast numbers were seen approaching the Gate on both sides of the channel. They filled every inch of space where they could make headway against the stream, and even in the most rapid parts of the channel fish were seen struggling to advance.

"In attempting the passage at the left bank of Hell's Gate, only those hugging close to the rock wall appeared to be successful, the others being swept violently outward and downstream. The number of fish being swept downward at Hell's Gate was, at this time, and almost to the end of the season, pronounced.

"Previous to the construction of the Canadian Northern Railway a bay of some considerable extent existed on the left bank immediately above the Gate. Here such fish as succeeded in passing on that side found shelter. That bay has now been filled with immense masses of granite, and but little space remains in which salmon can maintain themselves. The filling of this bay has also greatly altered the currents through the Gate. Formerly the waters from the left bank were forced across toward the right bank, so that along that bank, and close to it, a back-eddy was formed, which enabled the fish attempting to pass on that side to reach the smoother water above.

"In former years the main portion of the ascending fish passed through on the right side. Now the currents have been so changed that no fish were seen passing through, although many thousands were constantly attempting to do so.

"No sockeye were observed in the eddies immediately above. Many of those which had passed through the Gate and gained shelter immediately above, on attempting further ascent were swept into the channel and downstream. It became apparent that the number passing was limited to those which could find resting-places in the pockets and eddies just above the Gate, and that those attempting the passage greatly exceeded the capacity of the passage-way."

The lower reaches of the Fraser confirmed the extent of the disaster:

"Few of the bars in the river channel between Yale and Hope showed above water at this time, where dead and dying sockeye would ordinarily be stranded, but such as were exposed were covered with sockeye which had died without spawning.

"Many dead sockeye were lodged along the shelving shores wherever the water was at all slack, and their dead bodies were also seen hanging from every snag. There were many shelving gravel-bars in the numerous channels of the Fraser between Hope and Agassiz Landing on which vast numbers of dead sockeye were found. It was a condition commonly witnessed in the extreme upper stretches of the Fraser following the spawning in the years of a big run, except that all of the many dead fish examined were found to have died without spawning. Their fins were not worn, the jaws of the males were less distorted, their bodies had not taken on the deep red color that characterizes their maturity, and there were no marks to indicate the cause of their death.

"In addition to the dead which covered the bars and those found in the slack water along the shore, a considerable number of living sockeye were seen drifting downstream which made no effort to stem the current, and were apparently helpless. Many were not even headed upstream, but were drifting down broadside on. Some were so near to the boat they could be touched with a pole, and few of these had energy enough to move away from it.

"From Hope to Ruby Creek, and for some miles below the latter, the air was foul with the stench arising from the dead fish that covered the exposed parts of the river. The shelving bars and banks were covered with great numbers of sea-gulls and crows feeding on the eyes of the dead sockeye, which rose lazily upon our approach. There was no evidence to show that they were eating any other part of the fish, and in many cases we observed that only one eye had been taken. The dead sockeye were so numerous that the appetite of the birds, numerous as they were, was satisfied without turning over the bodies to obtain the other eye.

"I again visited this section two weeks later. The lowering of the water had exposed additional bars. I found even greater numbers of dead sockeye than before, and further examination showed that all had died without spawning. In fact, in no instance was a dead sockeye found that had spawned."

Immediately grasping the magnitude of the disaster, Babcock did not wait for instructions from his superiors before taking action. He and an assistant obtained dynamite from the local railway gangs, and blew a small passage through the rubble in the river. This temporarily eased the situation while the river was still in flood. But, once its level subsided, the fish again had great difficulty in getting upstream.

Babcock next sought help from the New Westminster office of the Dominion Department of Marine and Fisheries, but the response was perfunctory. An urgent appeal was then made to Ottawa, and J.D. Hazen, Dominion Minister of Marine and Fisheries, told his subordinates to bestir themselves.

Accordingly on September 27, 1913, a conference was held at North Bend, some 140 miles from the river's mouth, attended by both federal and provincial officials. The former included F.H. Cunningham, Chief Inspector of Fisheries in British Columbia and the department's resident engineer, Mr. Wilby. The latter were represented by Babcock and G.P. Napier, assistant engineer in the Department of Public Works. As a result of their investigations and discussions, men, tools and dynamite were obtained from the CPR and further blasting was done.

More fish were able to get through, but the level of the river was steadily falling and the situation again became serious. However, after blasting was done later in the year, it was believed that the emergency had been successfully overcome.

This would, in any case, have proved a false diagnosis, as countless thousands of salmon had failed to reproduce themselves, and their descendants would not be appearing in the river four years later. But now a second blow was about to strike the industry, once again at its most vulnerable point. In the words of a subsequent government report, on February 23, 1914, "Residents of Camp 16, the quarry site on the Canadian Pacific Railway at Hell's Gate, had observed during the day a continual rain of small rock from the shattered cliffs immediately above the Canadian Northern Railway track on the opposite side of the river. The day had been very mild, with a light rain falling, and it was assumed that possibly a few groups of disintegrated rock had detached themselves away from the main cliff after being frozen there during the winter. Later on in the evening, however, the fall of rock became greater, and at about 10 p.m. a tremendous rumbling roar was heard, as a huge portion of the cliffs opposite detached itself and fell toward the river."

One hundred thousand tons of rock had fallen into the Fraser at its narrowest point. As a result, in the words of an official of the provincial fisheries department, "The Fraser River certainly did look like a creek from the cliffs above. It was so narrow that a stone with a line attached was thrown clear across the river at the water's edge, and the width of the river showed only 75 feet."

This time there was no delay; work was begun at once to remove this formidable new obstacle to the approaching salmon run. A contract was awarded to the Pacific Dredging Company, and the CPR co-operated in various ways with the project. One obstacle to progress was that the Canadian Northern Pacific Railway was still constructing its line through the region, and was not prepared to significantly curtail its own operations. This meant that men at work on the rockslide often had to move to a safe location while work on the railway was in progress above them. However, machinery to lift rocks from the river bed was installed, and considerable material was removed to a location some distance back from the canyon. Other rocks were drilled and blasted into smaller pieces, which the river then carried further downstream. Some details of the work, as reported by the engineer in charge, are of interest:

"It was necessary to commence work at the water's edge in order to dispose or the huge angular rocks which lay at the toe of the slope. Some of these rocks were of tremendous size, measuring over 100 cubic yards, and much drilling was necessary preparatory to blasting. Passage of men and materials was extremely difficult, and added to the already difficult conditions was the fact of similar work being done on the Canadian Northern Pacific road-bed almost immediately above.

"Meanwhile a change was beginning to take place in the river. The weather at this period was very warm and fine, and in consequence the river began slowly advancing, sometimes as much as a foot a day during the daytime, and it seemed impossible to do the clearing at the toe which seemed so necessary.

"The rock proved very hard to drill, the exposed seamy trap-rock of the canyon walls being of the hardest and most difficult nature. Holes were loaded with 60% dynamite, well tamped, and 30 or 40 holes fired by battery, this concentration of explosives doing considerably more destruction than if the holes had been fired singly. Subsequent events showed that the work done at this time was very successful."

Other parts of the canyon were also improved:

"The work at China Bar proved to be more difficult than had been expected. After the outer covering of big rocks on the face of the mass of broken material had been disposed of with 60% dynamite, it was found that the uncovered material which had been almost entirely submerged during the previous freshet had become almost solidly cemented together by the silt which comes down the river when in flood.

"The digging and scraping away of this silt preparatory to blasting proved to be both slow and expensive, and it was found necessary to adopt the method of sinking a series of holes from 6 to 10 feet deep from 6 to 10 feet back from the water. These coyote-holes were loaded with 40% dynamite and occasionally 25% stumping-powder, and a complete rim was torn off and shattered at each firing. There was also a tremendous back-break, and quantities of shattered rock and silt were carried down the river at each blast.

"The work at White Creek proved an eye-opener in many respects. I am satisfied from the exposure of fish-bones and rotting salmon that considerably more fish were destroyed here during the run of 1913 than at any other point of the river. The whole bank seemed to be a series of cul-de-sacs filled full in many cases with putrefying fish. The odor was sickening and the place altogether horrible to work in.

"Many individual rocks measuring 100 cubic yards were drilled and blasted in the endeavor to increase the stream section as much as possible and to destroy those places where fish could be washed into and stranded. This work, as at Scuzzy Rapids, was commenced at the water's edge and worked upwards in parallel lines up the bank."

So important was it considered that the obstruction should be cleared away in time for the annual salmon run that the work continued around the clock:

"From April 14th onward to the end of the month, the work of excavation was continued without interruption, the men working Sundays, and even though the actual work accomplished during that time was great, yet it was feared that unless special efforts were made to force the work, very little could be accomplished towards diminishing the current and reducing the falls in time for the first run of sockeye, which was expected in the early part of July.

"A night gang was immediately organized and acetylene lights installed, and about five weeks after the commencement of the work a night gang of about 30 men commenced work. The location was extremely dangerous even in daytime, and at night-time, even though powerfully lit up, the danger was considerably greater. Thus day and night, almost without a stop, the work continued for three weeks. It had accomplished good work, and with the rising of the river it was decided no further benefit could accrue from the continuation of the night-work."

When the summer run-off began in earnest, the level of the river quickly rose 70 feet above its winter low-point. It was noted that many fish negotiated the rapids successfully, while others were carried past them in nets by Indians hired for the purpose. Temporary restrictions were placed on the numbers of fish which the natives could take for their own use. This caused some ill-will, as it was the first time that this ancestral privilege had been in any way interfered with. However, despite strong objections from the natives, the new regulations were enforced, and it seems likely that in the end the Indians obtained sufficient fish for their needs.

As the year ended, it appeared that a large proportion of the 1914 run had successfully reached its spawning grounds and could be expected to do so in subsequent years. Despite the diversion of labor into war industries, fishing continued to be a major source of employment, and both 1915 and 1916 saw good harvests.

Then came 1917, and the full extent of the 1913 disaster became apparent. The salmon which had died in the whirlpools below Hell's Gate had left no descendants, and the catch was only a quarter of that of 1913. The loss could be reckoned in millions of dollars, and one of the province's basic sources of employment had suffered a heavy blow.

Even though the 1921 season also showed the effects of the Hell's Gate disaster, and the average catch in the post-war years was well below the pre-war average, little was done by those in authority, despite Babcock's urgent pleadings, to place the industry on a sounder basis. The province was caught up in the post-war industrial boom, and all eyes were turned to the clatter of rising skyscrapers. Meanwhile fishermen of both British Columbia and the United States remained free to catch as many salmon as they could. The results of this policy, or lack of it, eventually became so serious that in 1928 less that 100,000 cases of salmon were packed, a mere fraction of the 2 million cases packed in 1913.

Canadian-American negotiations, which had continued intermittently for 20 years without tangible results, were finally begun in earnest. But it was not until 1937 that a treaty was ratified by both countries and the International Pacific Salmon Fisheries Commission established, with power to regulate the annual catch and, if possible, restore it to what it had once been.

The industry gradually recovered, but it became apparent that even in the years when the river was least turbulent, the barrier of Hell's Gate took a heavy toll. Something more would have to be done, and merely deepening the channel seemed no solution. Accordingly, energies were concentrated on building flumes through which fish might make their way past the famous obstacle.

Both countries made contributions to solving the problem. A large model of the worst part of the river was built at the University of Washington, and prolonged studies were conducted of the effect of water pouring through it. From the observations made, plans were drawn up for the construction of two large concrete flumes, one on each side of the river, through which it was hoped that salmon in large numbers would be able to pass.

Despite the fact that another great war was raging, work began on installing the flumes in the fall of 1944. Working conditions for the men employed on the project were highly dangerous, as often they had to be lowered by ropes to the river from the cliffs above it. Here they performed such difficult tasks as blasting out a bed in which the flumes could be securely laid. All the debris was removed to a safe distance from the river.

This work occupied two winters, but when finished was a remarkable achievement. Two long concrete flumes, one 220 feet long and the other nearly 500, had been attached to the walls of the canyon. Inside each was a series of bars, or baffles, which converted the water flowing through it into a series of relatively calm pools, each slightly higher than the one below it. Fish entering these tunnels, one of them 20 feet wide and the other slightly smaller, thus had many opportunities to rest and Royal Northwest Mounted Police (not yet the RCMP) tele-

gather their energies before continuing their journey upstream. At flood-tide the tunnels are far below the surface of the river, but at low water they are usually visible.

More work was done in the next 20 years to improve the installations. Long before that it was apparent that the Hell's Gate fishways had saved a vital industry from possible destruction.

The history of the Fraser River salmon run had been a valuable illustration of the harm which man can do to nature and the possible price he might have to pay before the injury is redressed. When the disasters of 1913 and 1914 occurred, the science of ecology—the very word—was still unknown. Today, more and more attention is being paid to maintaining a proper balance between man and nature, and perhaps we may say that in this sense the sacrifice of the salmon run at Hell's Gate 60 years ago was not entirely in vain.   ●

1918
The Loss
Of The Princess Sophia

FOR more than four long years the world had been at war, and many British Columbians had spent much of them in muddy trenches in France. By 1918, the long nightmare was ending, and the province, like the rest of the world, prepared to celebrate the dawn of peace.

Thanks to the wireless telegraph, even the most northerly parts of the Pacific coast were aware of the approaching end of the war. It was 20 years since countless thousands had taken the "Trail of 98" to the Yukon and Alaska, although mining continued to attract men in search of a quick fortune. Many of them, knowing that the coldest months of the winter were just ahead, had decided to spend them in the warmer climes of Vancouver, Victoria or Seattle. Accordingly, there was a brisk demand for passages south, and on most ships every place was taken.

This was especially true of the Canadian Pacific steamship *Princess Sophia*. Built in Scotland in 1912, she was 245 feet long. Her capacity was 200, but on this occasion more than 260 tickets had been sold, and with her crew of 75, under Captain L.P. Locke, she left Skagway at 10 p.m. on Wednesday, October 23.

In order to reach the open sea at Juneau, the ship would have to pass through the narrow Lynn Canal, given that name by Captain George Vancouver, whose birthplace was King's Lynn,

Norfolk. The weather was seldom good in this area, and before long a snowstorm was blowing. This seriously reduced visibility, but Captain Locke, a sailor with long experience, did not reduce speed, and the ship surged ahead as if eager to make its rendezvous with the bright lights several hundred miles to the south.

In addition to prospectors and river pilots going south for the winter, there were a few American soldiers on board, as well as 33 women and 17 children. There were also a number of horses destined for an army camp near Victoria. From there it was planned to ship them to eastern Siberia where a detachment of Canadian soldiers was vainly endeavoring, with the aid of forces from several other countries, to break the Communist hold on Russia. The ship, of 2,320 gross tons, was also carrying five tons of general freight, including Christmas parcels for Yukon soldiers serving in France.

Captain Locke, aged 65, was within a few months of retirement. Born in Halifax, he had gone to sea at 16 in a windjammer, and later served on the New York-Liverpool run. He had come to the Pacific coast in 1891, where he commanded several ships of the CPR fleet. One of his three sons was serving in France, and another was stationed in Salonika.

The manager of the CPR fleet on the Pacific coast at this time was Captain J.W. Troup, who lived in Victoria. The recent invention of wireless had made it possible for Troup to keep in touch with the numerous vessels in the fleet.

This improvement had been welcomed by both the company and its captains, as the north Pacific coast had long been known for its treacherous storms. Countless ships had foundered on its barren and rocky shores, and many remembered the loss of the *Valencia* off Pachena Point in 1906, with 115 lives. A few could even recall when the *Pacific* had gone down in 1875 off Cape Flattery with the loss of 270 lives.

Not every accident, of course, had ended in disaster. In 1910 the *Princess May* had run onto Vanderbilt Reef in the middle of Lynn Canal, about halfway between Skagway and Juneau, but had eventually been pulled off and repaired.

Probably few were thinking of past marine disasters when the ship left her berth at Skagway at 10 p.m., October 23. Snow was falling, and an icy wind was blowing as she sped wouthward through the night. The ship was comfortably appointed, however, and one by one her passengers retired to bed. Then, at 3 o'clock in the morning, they were jolted awake as the *Sophia* shuddered to a sudden stop.

The ship had struck Vanderbilt Reef, and was now firmly stranded on a large submerged rock. An immediate examination of the hold was made by the crew, and sleepy passengers inquiring what had happened were reassured that the ship was not taking water and that there was no immediate danger.

Nevertheless, several passengers put on life preservers, and one, moved by some mysterious feminine impulse, donned a black evening dress. But as nothing further seemed to be happening, after a time they drifted back to bed.

Dawn found the ship still firmly on the reef, and high tide at 6 a.m. Thursday morning failed to float her free. There was apparently nothing to do but wait patiently for assistance. As news of the mishap had already been flashed to stations along the coast and to Victoria, Capt. Locke did not for a minute fear that help would arrive promptly.

The ship was in American territorial waters, and as the day advanced a number of small American ships appeared and surrounded the *Sophia*. These included the government lighthouse tender *Cedar*, commanded by Captain Leadbetter, a halibut schooner named *King and Winge*, and the *Estebeth*, commanded by Captain James David. Captain Leadbetter, shouting through a megaphone, asked Captain Locke if he wished to transfer passengers from the *Sophia* to the *Cedar*. Locke, evidently considering his own ship in no danger, and noting the heavy seas, replied that in his opinion his passengers were safer where they were. He then wirelessed to his superior, Captain Troup, in Victoria:

"*Sophia* still fast on reef. Resting safely, strong northerly wind. Unable to transfer passengers until wind moderates or perhaps at high water. Steamer and two gas boats standing by."

For the remainder of the the day the *Sophia* and her passengers remained where they were. The American ships retreated to the shelter of a nearby island for the night, and as midnight approached Captain Locke again signalled Victoria:

"Ship sitting firmly on reef. Unable to transfer passengers on account of strong northwest sea. Ship pounding heavily. Cannot get off without salvage gear."

At daybreak Friday, October 25, the American ships returned to the scene of the accident, but, once again, no passengers were removed from the *Sophia*. Captain Locke again reported to Victoria:

"Steamer *Cedar* and three gas boats standing by. Unable to take off passengers on account of strong northerly gale and big sea running. Ship hard and fast with bottom badly damaged, but not taking water. Unable to back off reef. Main steam pipe broken. Disposition of passengers normal."

Some of those on board found this a convenient time to record their impressions of the accident in their diaries or in letters. One young American soldier, for example, wrote to his mother:

"It's storming now, about a 50-mile wind, and we can only see a couple of hundred yards on account of the snow and spray. We were going along at full speed at 3 a.m. yesterday when she hit a rock which is submerged at high tide, and for a while there was some excitement but no panic. Two women fainted, and one of them got herself into a black evening dress and didn't worry about who saw her putting it on. Some of the men, too, kept life preservers on for an hour or so, and seemed to think there was no chance for us. But we passed through the first real danger point at high tide at 6 a.m. when it was thought she might pound her bottom out on the rock and everybody settled down to wait for help.

"We had three tug boats here in the afternoon, but the weather was too rough to transfer any passengers. The most critical time nobody except the ship's officers, we soldiers and a few sailors among the passengers were told about. That was at low tide at noon, when the captain and chief officers figured she was caught on the starboard bow and would hang there while she settled on the port side and astern. They were afraid she would turn turtle.

"But her bow pounded around and slipped until she settled into a groove well supported forward on both sides, and the wind and sea from behind pounded and pushed her until she is now, after 30 hours, on the rock clear back to the middle and can't get off.

"She is a double-bottomed boat, and her inner hull is not penetrated, so here we stick. She pounds some on this rising tide, and it's slow waiting, but our only inconvenience so far is the lack of water.

"The main steam pipe got twisted off and we were without lights last night and have run out of soft sugar. But the pipes were fixed so we are getting heat and lights now, and we still have lump sugar and water for drinking."

Another passenger, however had a premonition that this voyage might be his last. A Dawson resident named John Maskell wrote:

"We struck the reef in a blinding snowstorm during the night. A great number of passengers were thrown out of their berths and great excitement prevailed. Boats were made ready to lower when information was received that the ship was not taking water. The passengers became quiet. Owing to the storm the boats were not lowered.

"This morning we are surrounded by a number of small boats, but it is too rough to transfer the passengers. In the realization that we are surrounded by grave danger I make this, my last will."

Maskell divided his estate between his father and his fiancee, and placed the document in an inner pocket. Then, feeling that he had prepared for the worst, he waited and hoped for the best.

During the day (Friday, October 25) the weather grew steadily worse. The *Sophia* still remained fast on Vanderbilt Reef, while the boats which had been keeping an eye on her took shelter from the storm behind nearby islands. Then, at 10 minutes to 5 o'clock in the afternoon, out of the gathering dusk came an alarming message:

"Taking water and foundering. For God's sake come and save us."

The *Cedar* at once replied:

"Coming full speed, but cannot see on account of thick snow and heavy seas."

For some time communication was kept up between the two ships, but gradually the *Sophia*'s wireless became weaker. The *Cedar* advised the stricken ship to save it for extreme emergencies. For a little while there was no word from the *Sophia*; then came her final message:

"For God's sake hurry. Water coming in the room."

Then . . . .silence.

The *Cedar* was unable to locate the *Sophia* that night, but at dawn reached the scene of the tragedy. Her wirelessed report told all:

Nothing left but one mast out of water.

Soon afterwards Captain Miller of the *King and Winge* also arrived on the scene, leaving it at once to look for survivors. At 11:30 he sighted a lifeboat on the beach of nearby Shelter Island, and sent some dories to investigate. They returned with a single lifeless body. Working his way along the western side of Shelter Island, at 2 in the afternoon Captain Miller found two more bodies, after which he had to return to Juneau for fuel.

Soon several more small vessels, including the *Estebeth*, *Peterson* and *Amy* were searching for survivors. Later the salvage steamer *Tees* examined the reef and found the *Sophia*'s mast still above water, but her after-half missing. It appeared that she had broken in two under the relentless pounding of her hull on the rocks; half of her had remained on the reef, while the other half had slipped down into the deep icy water. The surrounding area was covered with oil, in which many birds were desperately struggling to fly.

In the next few days scores of bodies were found either floating in the water or washed up on nearby beaches. One boat alone picked up 30 corpses. A day or two later a member of the

graphed to his superior at Dawson:

"One hundred and seventy-nine bodies recovered. More expected tomorrow. Positively identified, 84. Bodies in horrible condition. Only two actually drowned, others suffocated in crude oil. Presume tanks burst when ship slid across rocks."

Word of the disaster had become general knowledge in the cities to the south, but its full extent only became plain when at 5 p.m. on October 26 came a brief official announcement from the CPR head office in Montreal:

"The President regrets to announce the loss of the Company's steamer *Princess Sophia,* with all passengers and crew."

It had been the worst marine disaster in the history of the Pacific coast. No fewer than 268 passengers and 75 crewmen had been lost, as well as all the horses. The sole survivor was an English setter which straggled into Juneau a few days later, covered in oil.

Some of the passengers were found to have had considerable sums of money concealed in their clothing, suggesting that they were retiring from the north with the savings of many years. The bodies were taken to Juneau, and those which were identified as belonging to residents of cities farther south were placed on board the *Princess Alice.* As the war in Europe drew to its end thousands of miles away, the ship made its way down the coast to Vancouver. The bustling young city was celebrating the Armistice with wild enthusiasm when a small group of relatives gathered at Pier D to receive the 64 coffins containing their loved ones. Later the ship went on to Victoria, tying up in the Inner Harbour, where the freight shed on Belleville Street was converted into a morgue.

An official investigation was launched, much of it centering around Captain Locke's decision not to transfer passengers from the *Sophia* to other craft nearby. As there were no survivors of the tragedy, no one who had been on board the *Sophia* could testify, and a picture of the steamer's last hours had to be pieced together from her various wireless messages, the observations of those on the other ships, and letters found on the corpses. In the end no blame was attached to anyone, and despite lawsuits launched in American courts by American citizens who had lost relatives in the disaster, no compensation was ever awarded to them.

Those lost in the Lynn Canal were only a fraction of those dying every day in France. Even the influenza epidemic then raging both in Europe and North America was taking a heavier toll. It was perhaps the suddenness and unexpectedness of the *Sophia* disaster which seemed to give it a special horror. Had she been on a slightly different course, if snow had not blinded her lookout, if her passengers had been taken off in time, many of them would no doubt have been part of the cheering crowds which gathered in the streets to salute the end of one era and the beginning of another. ●

1918-1919
The Influenza Epidemic

*And I looked, and behold a pale horse; and his name that sat on him
was Death, and Hell followed with him. And power was given unto
them over the fourth part of the earth, to kill with sword, and with
hunger, and with death, and with the beasts of the earth.*

— Revelations

THE war of 1914-1918 has long been recognized as one of
the greatest disasters in history. Deaths in battle alone were
close to 10 million, while the number of those crippled for life,
nearly all young men in the prime of life, was at least as large.
When we add to this the destruction of property and the cost in
money, we see that the total loss suffered in four years by
western civilization was almost beyond calculation. It is hardly
surprising that this catastrophe has haunted the mind of man
ever since.

It seems curious, then, that a disaster which caused losses in
human life at least as great, and compressed into a much shorter
space of time, should have largely faded from memory. This was
the great influenza epidemic of 1918-1919, which, recognizing
no battle lines or neutral states, swept across the world in a few
brief months, carrying at least 20 (perhaps 50) million human
beings of all ages to an untimely grave.

It began in Europe in the early months of 1918, and at first
attracted little attention on the western coast of North America.
In the climactic year of the war, newspapers were almost exclusively devoted to news from the battlefields. In March, the
Germans launched their final drive on Paris; later, after this had
ground to a halt, the allied armies, reinforced by growing
numbers of Americans, began advancing relentlessly toward the
soil of Germany. The speeches of public figures became in-

creasingly full of fiery descriptions of the punishment which would be meted out to the defeated Germans, especially the Kaiser. Meanwhile nearly every day the newspapers contained pictures of local men who had fallen far from home. From time to time long casualty lists took up several columns of type.

Yet as summer gave way to autumn, news of another kind began appearing in the press. It had been clear for some time that a serious influenza epidemic was sweeping across Europe, and now it became evident that it had reached North America.

It had actually appeared as early as February in a military camp in New Jersey, but the newspapers had devoted little attention to it. By early autumn, however, it could no longer be ignored, and on October 2 the Victoria *Colonist* noted that "The epidemic began in Europe last year and has crossed the Atlantic. It is very prevalent in the eastern cities, and we may expect it in the west."

Victoria's medical health officer, A.G. Price, reassured local citizens that the authorities were watching the situation closely:

"If Spanish influenza should develop in Victoria, we would be bound to use the strongest possible measures to kill the epidemic at once. It would be our duty not only from the national standpoint of public health but from the standpoint of duty to the Empire."

On October 3 the *Colonist* carried an ominous report from the American capital:

"Further spread of Spanish influenza over the country and in army camps, with an increasing death rate, was indicated today in reports received by the public health service and at the office of the Surgeon-General of the army. New cases developing in army camps totalled 12,004."

Despite such reports from other parts of the continent, in British Columbia there were still no signs of alarm, and the authorities took no visible moves to deal with a crisis should it arrive. The approaching Armistice still held first place in the public mind.

Within a few days, however, British Columbians realized that the Rocky Mountains were no barrier to germs, especially as wounded soldiers suffering from influenza were arriving daily from the east. Five cases were reported in Vancouver, then a city of 100,000, which resulted in consultations between Dr. F.T. Underhill, the city health officer, and Mayor R.H. Gale. The mayor evidently feared that the city was about to be struck by the disease, and suggested that children should be banned from attending theatres and movie houses. He also contemplated closing the schools. Dr. Underhill, however, did not yet think it necessary, and the mayor contented himself with a reassuring warning to the general public:

"The city has officially taken every possible precaution, but public co-operation is also vitally essential. I call upon the citizens to assist in warding off a threatened epidemic."

Meanwhile the newspapers gave their readers some advice as to how to recognize and deal with the disease:

"The onset is usually very sudden, being accompanied by great bodily weakness, pains in the head, eyes and muscles. There may be vomiting and dizziness, and a feeling of cold and chilliness, accompanied by shivering and sometimes by sweating, high fever and loss of appetite. The whites of the eyes are reddened, and the throat feels sore.

"Patients should be kept in a separate room and most of the relatives kept out. The nurse or mother should tie a piece of gauze or muslin over her nose and mouth. All cutlery should be boiled."

A day or two later, the provincial cabinet gave municipalities authority to close all theatres or other buildings where crowds might collect. The city of Victoria at once decided to close its schools, as there were already 50 cases in the area. In the eastern part of the country, Montreal had already closed its theatres, schools and dance halls. Other news from eastern Canada was not encouraging. By now no one could deny that a serious epidemic was sweeping North America, and the Vancouver *Province* reported:

"One of the outstanding features of the epidemic has been the enormous number of cases reported in military camps, mainly in Ontario and Quebec. In camps at Toronto, Hamilton and Montreal, scores have died, but commanding officers report that the disease is now well in hand."

This last statement by the military authorities was doubtless intended to raise public morale, but was quickly contradicted by events. In the next few days the situation in Vancouver became more serious. There were now 19 cases officially reported in the city and several more in New Westminster. Victoria, however, had 60 cases, with two deaths. All public places in the provincial capital were closed, including churches, theatres, pool rooms and schools. The *Colonist* reported that "the city streets were practically deserted during the evening hours, and the few people who populated them drifted about aimlessly and somewhat peevishly." The Victoria city council, however, decided that it was not a public assembly itself, and continued to hold regular meetings. Vancouver schools remained open, although all city streetcars were treated with formaldehyde.

October 10 saw 14 new cases in Vancouver, bringing the total in the city to 40. Movie houses remained open, and many people took advantage of the occasion to see "Her Man," which, according to the advertisements in the *Province*, displayed the heroine "defending her man as a tigress defends her cubs. This gently nurtured society girl harks back to the primeval instincts of her sex."

There were soon 200 cases in Victoria, and all public meetings were prohibited. Only the war news remained encouraging, as the papers announced the fall of Cambrai to the advancing allies.

The next day 15 deaths were reported in Seattle. Winnipeg had by now closed all its schools, theatres and churches. Nevertheless the war was rapidly drawing to its close and, looking ahead to the peace treaty, a spokesman for the British government warned against any leniency to the Germans: "They were brutes before the war and will remain brutes. The alleged change in their constitution has not changed their hearts."

In Vancouver, although there were 70 known cases and two deaths, public places remained open, and Dr. Underhill declared that, "Taking all present local conditions into consideration, the public should not be stampeded into regarding things as serious." Victoria had several hundred cases but the number of deaths was still less than those represented by the photographs in the newspapers of soldiers who would not return.

By October 12 there were a hundred cases in Vancouver, and three deaths. The sizable Japanese colony in the city was hard-hit, though its members were being treated by a doctor of Japanese ancestry named Takahara. A temporary hospital was set up on Powell Street for these cases.

Victoria, which continued to be more seriously affected than Vancouver, reported a big run on cinnamon, which was believed to be an antidote to the disease. Meanwhile, in Prince Rupert, all public buildings were closed.

The number of cases continued to increase at an alarming rate. The *Province* for October 14 reported 217 cases, with 7 deaths to date. At this time the university campus at Point Grey had not yet been completed, and classes, some conducted by the redoubtable Dr. Sedgewick, were held in some buildings adjacent to the general hospital—the "Fairview shacks." The auditorium and some classrooms were converted into a temporary hospital, and a hundred beds were installed.

Despite indications that the epidemic had not reached its peak, Vancouver schools remained open as medical authorities believed that children could be kept under more continuous observation in school than at home. Very few children had, in fact, been affected by the epidemic, which seemed to concentrate its force against the middle-aged.

By October 15 there were about 300 cases in each of the province's two main cities, and schools in North Vancouver were closed and fumigated. Two days later there were 500 cases in Vancouver, and King Edward High School was also converted into a hospital.

On October 18 Vancouver schools were closed, and the *Province* reported increasingly serious news:

"Spanish flu in Vancouver took an alarming jump this morning, no less than 139 additional cases being reported to noon, bringing the total up to 758 cases, with 17 deaths. Dr. F.T. Underhill, city medical health officer, was forced to throw up his hands. He called for an emergency meeting of the city council, and reported that the closing of the city schools and the great influx of flu patients from outside the city added so greatly to the responsibilities of his office that he would have to apply to Victoria for an order-in-council closing down the city tightly for an indefinite period.

"This action was accordingly taken, and everything in the nature of a public gathering will be definitely off on Saturday, as the entire city, barring industrial plants, will be shut down, to start tomorrow morning."

Vancouver now took on the atmosphere of a city under siege. Even churches remained closed, marriages were postponed, and funeral services took place outdoors. Businesses remained open, with the exception of laundries, whose employees were all on strike. Advertisements in the papers reflected the new conditions. A shoe store announced that it was "disinfected daily," while an insurance firm began issuing policies which, if they could neither prevent nor cure influenza, at least provided some balm for relatives of its victims. For every $24 invested, $1,000 would be disbursed to the beneficiary, and the public was told that "we are issuing dozens of policies." By contrast, a letter received by the mayor's office said that the epidemic was receiving too much publicity, and it "was not doing the cause of the allies any good."

Meanwhile the war still dominated the front pages, and there were daily reminders of events in Europe:

Berlin to be bombed by giant British airplanes"
"Ladner youth falls in action"
"Sensational jumps in peace shares"
"Must cure the Huns"
"Fought and died with Highlanders"

Many soldiers died in military camps. On October 19 the deaths of four soldiers were reported by the Coquitlam military hospital, bringing the total for the lower mainland to 17 men in uniform. Many doctors, their resistance undermined by lack of rest, were also seriously ill, and since many of the younger ones were overseas, a heavy burden fell on these overworked, often elderly men. An appeal went out for volunteer nurses, and many women in this period received their first introduction to working outside the home. One doctor who was stricken by the disease he sought to cure later recalled his experiences:

"Our house was in what is now Woodward's parking lot on the north side between Seventh Street and Ash Street, and it was in this house during the flu epidemic of 1918 that I very nearly died. In fact I was so far gone that the doctor told the nurse that it didn't make much difference, to let me have anything I wanted, so as to keep my mind at peace. However I had a nurse who was not only a practical nurse but had some common sense, and she refused to accede to my urgent cry for chicken sandwiches. At least so I was told afterwards, when I regained consciousness.

"I was still in bed convalescing when the Armistice was declared in November 1918. I still have recollections of the funerals passing along Sixth Avenue for the victims of the epidemic. Nurses were almost unobtainable, and doctors were so overworked that during the time I was ill I had five different doctors. They worked themselves into a state of exhaustion, but each one of them took over where another one had just dropped, and carried on. It was a terrible time, and many of my friends died."

Another doctor recalled the epidemic many years later:

"The disease was a virulent one. It struck rapidly and the patients developed a toxic, congestive pneumonia, that because of its appearance at autopsy was termed a 'black pneumonia.' Faces became flushed with a peculiar type of cyanosis that because of its unusual color was known as 'heliotrope cyanosis.' Nose-bleeds were common, and were so severe that they required the packing of both nasal passages.

"Due to the sudden onset of the disease, the volume of the work, and the frequency of the nasal hemorrhages, the doctors were on the go day and night, many becoming so seriously exhausted that their acquired immunity was overwhelmed and they themselves succumbed to the influenza and died. Others had to stop work, quite unable to carry on, and it was at this time that some of the few remaining shamans were reported to have taken up their art again among the Indian population in remote areas."

No effective cure was known for the disease, but it was widely believed that liquor was beneficial to its victims. This was not easy to obtain as prohibition was in force, and a doctor's prescription was necessary. Nevertheless long lines formed outside the government liquor stores, and the newspapers described the scene:

"Working women and society women stood in the queue, and became friendly over the absorbing topic of their symptoms. A dapper lawyer celebrated for his nice taste in spats was wedged in with some shipyard workers who joined the throng soon after 4 p.m. Even a uniformed policeman came along and fell in."

For those unable to obtain prescriptions for whisky, other restoratives were available. An advertisement for "Kennedy's tonic port" called it "the great South American remedy and preventative for the flu." Camphor was also believed to be valuable in this respect, and under the pressure of frantic demand its price soared from 40 cents to $6.50 a pound. Many people were now wearing makeshift masks, and such places as the "Wonder Millinery" were offering white gauze "flu veils" to prudent and fashionable stenographers.

Another enterprising shopkeeper, "Tom the Tailor," had a similar message for the public:

"BE SAFE FROM THE INFLUENZA
WEAR A MOUTH AND NOSE PROTECTOR
35¢
SEE THE GIRLS IN MY WINDOWS ADJUST THEM"

Hardier souls were working out their own salvation. For example, news arrived from Lillooet of a prospector who lay sick and alone in his cabin for five days, unable to eat and with no fire. Though sometimes delirious, at the end of the fifth day he made up his pack, walked twenty-five miles through the snow to the nearest railroad, and eventually returned to civilization, cured.

Not everyone in the interior was so fortunate. The Cranbrook *Herald* reported that "The *Herald* is being published under difficulties this week. Part of the staff is sick, the linotyper has the flu, and the paper is being set by hand."

The *Herald* also announced that "owing to the amount of sickness in town, it is forbidden for children or other persons to celebrate Hallowe'en in the street or other public places."

The Kelowna *Courier* had a similar story to tell. It reported ten deaths, nine of them Chinese and one a Hindu. All churches were closed and public meetings banned. A rather bizarre advertisement in the paper attempted to combine two contrasting threads of history:

"How to avoid the flu
1. Use Camphor, quinine and courage—buy Victory Bonds
2. Keep your feet warm. On the first sign of cold feet, buy Victory Bonds
3. Avoid worry. Think of victory and buy bonds

4. Take plenty of exercise—try selling Victory Bonds

5. Use ginger—when buying Victory Bonds."

In Prince Rupert, the *Daily News* appealed for help in delivering its papers—all seven newsboys were sick. A Hindu who died in the city was cremated by his fellow lumber workers on a funeral pyre. At nearby Metlakatla a hundred Indians were sick, of whom eight soon died. Nearly 50 natives died at Anyox and 16 at Kitwanga. The mayor of Prince Rupert appealed to private citizens to donate spare beds, which were used to set up a temporary hospital in the Salvation Army citadel.

Two nurses in charge of a boarding school for Indian children at Kitimat had a terrible few weeks. They were a long way from civilization, and lacked a doctor to treat the sick and a minister to bury the dead. Nevertheless they coped as best they could, and one of them found time to write an account of her experiences to relatives in England:

"Monday morning at seven, one girl said she was sick, and nine went to bed that day. Many more on Tuesday, and by Wednesday Miss Hartop and I, with the help of one girl, started nursing the thirty who were in bed.

"I never saw such nose-bleeding; we could not stop it. The only girl whose nose did not bleed suffered hallucinations and was out of bed, trailing bedding or clothes, and crying that she had killed herself, or asking me to cut her in pieces, or else hunting for her lungs or other parts of her body that had fallen out. Food had to be cooked and fires kept burning, and there were only two of us.

"Meantime the people in the village had begun to die, two or three at a time, so there were funerals to conduct. You can imagine us keyed up by stress of work and lack of sleep. Three or four lying sick in one room—the father or mother or child carried out by others who were more or less sick. The trail to the graveyard—two white women to conduct the services. Several times we gathered three coffins, once there were four, and read a service over them. It was heartbreaking to go out and bury the father or mother or some of the children, and come back to tend them when they were too sick to be told of their loss.

"The sickness ran a course of about 10 days. On the ninth day the patient slept hour after hour, and that indicated recovery. The toll that death has taken in Kitimat is 29; some half dozen more are not expected to live."

The epidemic peaked in Vancouver about October 22, when 500 new cases were reported in the city. There were now over 2,000 known cases (including Mayor Gale) in a population of 100,000, and a period of several days saw more than 20 deaths. The worst day was October 27, when 24 deaths were reported.

Many people kept their blinds drawn, so as to be spared the sight of constantly passing funeral processions. Despite the establishment of a round-the-clock ambulance service, which, on one day, carried over a hundred people to hospital, help often arrived too late. As Dr. Underhill reported,

"A very distressing feature of this work was the great number of people who had to be removed in a dying condition, owing to the lack of any one to give them attention."

Meanwhile, the loss of the steamship *Sophia* in the Lynn Canal with all her passengers and crew plunged many additional homes into mourning. Moreover, every day brought news of further casualties from the distant battlefields:

"Native son gives life for empire. Is killed after winning DCM."

A temporary drop in reported cases in Victoria gave some cause for hope, and the city medical officer issued what proved to be an unfortunate statement:

"I have yet to learn that Spanish influenza is a dangerous disease. If the public will only think of itself and use reasonable precautions, everything will be all right, and we will be through with the epidemic in short order."

Dr. Price also declared that masks (by this time compulsory in San Francisco) were useless against germs. Meanwhile the death toll in the capital city climbed to 15. Restaurants and soda fountains in Victoria were yet open, and as their contribution to the general welfare, the city's garbage collectors had gone on strike.

By early November the epidemic appeared to have peaked, although each day brought fresh cases and more deaths. Soon came news of a more cheerful kind: mutinies in the German fleet, the flight of the Kaiser, and, after a false alarm which set the bells ringing, the official end of the war on November 11.

The ban on public meetings remained, so no thanksgiving services could be held in Vancouver churches. Instead, the first of December was officially set as the date for such observances in British Columbia. On November 20, theatres in Vancouver reopened, and soon crowds were flocking to see the new star Charlie Chaplin. World politics were not entirely forgotten, however, and the *Province* warned its readers that "The Germans are not reformed. They are only restrained. The Kaiser has been deposed, not because he was an autocrat but because he has been beaten."

Yet even the Kaiser was rudely elbowed off the front pages. Assorted uprisings were occurring all over Europe, and few of them seemed calculated to bring much joy to middle-class hearts. The defects of the "Huns" receded with some celerity into obscurity, and soon the reading public was being informed that "Bolshevism is the great peril."

The early months of 1919 saw a final flare-up of the disease, but by the end of March the epidemic was over. Its cost had been high: about one British Columbia resident in three had been affected, and, in Vancouver alone, nearly 800 had died. This was one of the highest death rates in North America, considerably higher than that of Seattle and about the same as San Francisco. The age group most seriously affected had been those between 20 and 40.

More ominously, none of the measures taken against the epidemic had done more than alleviate it slightly, and the exact bacillus responsible remained unidentified. The possibility thus remained that at some future time it might strike with equal or greater force. As an editorial in the *Canadian Medical Association Journal* for November 1919 remarked, "A constantly increasing number of individuals become infected before any preventive sanitary regulations are put in force. By the time such regulations become operative, the epidemic has passed beyond control."

The official report of the Provincial Board of Health in Victoria was also somewhat discouraging:

"The invasion of the epidemic was sudden. It swept over the country, following the lines of travel, and in many instances found us ill-prepared to meet such an overwhelming calamity. Over 200 of our medical men and as many nurses had gone to the front.

"A supply of vaccine was received from the Connaught Laboratory, also some from Dr. Gordon Bell of Winnipeg, and distributed. The reports that we received as to the results of the use of the vaccine were very contradictory, and our experiences in this correspond with those of all other places.

"A great deal of investigation has been carried on in regard to vaccines, and the consensus of opinion is that we do not know the exact cause of the influenza, and have not been able to isolate the germ. There is no vaccine against influenza."

British Columbia's experience had been part of a world-wide disaster in which more people had died than in any epidemic since the Black Death. The casualties were certainly of the same order as those on the battlefields of France and Flanders. In the United States, for example, more than 80,000 died from the flu. It is remarkable in the circumstances how quickly it receded from memory. Few histories of the 20th century mention it, and even novelists who must have remembered it first-hand seldom referred to it in their subsequent work.

Certainly it disappeared quickly from the newspapers of the day. Perhaps one reason for this was the wide variety of other developments which were soon clamoring for public attention. The Peace Conference, inspired in its early stages by Woodrow Wilson and dominated in its latter ones by Lloyd George and Clemenceau, sputtered to an inconclusive end; the illustrious president soon afterwards had a stroke and retired from the world scene. The first transatlantic flight by Alcock and Brown was successful, primitive radios appeared in affluent homes, and the Model T Ford was soon ubiquitous. Inflation became a major topic of conversation till it gave way to deflation, and "Reds" replaced "Huns" as the source of the world's woes. Sports demanded an increasing proportion of the average citizen's attention; golf and tennis were no longer the preserve of the elite. In plain terms, the dark days of grief and sacrifice had ended; the jazz age, the whoopee years were beginning, and North America, at least, was joyfully embarking upon a spree which would last a decade.

Soon the great influenza epidemic would be laid away in the dusty storerooms of the past, and the world would move confidently into a new era which, though its outlines might be misty, at least would be rosier than the age which had preceded it. Ten years would have to pass before skies would once more become grey, and the word "disaster" was restored to the public vocabulary.   ●

1929-1939
The Great Depression

AS the golden summer of 1929 drew to its close, the dark days of 1918 seemed very far away. This was hardly surprising; the years between these two dates had seen dramatic changes, both in British Columbia and in the world at large. The sufferings of the war (more often called "the war to end war" than "World War One") had receded into the past, as had memories of the great influenza epidemic of 1918. The high-flown idealism and rhetoric of Woodrow Wilson no longer stirred the hearts of millions; instead, the voice which now charmed the multitudes was that of the advertiser.

For the great boom of the '20s, gathering force throughout the decade, was now at its glittering peak. The uncertainties of the immediate post-war years, symbolized by such social disorders as the Winnipeg general strike of 1919 and the brief but sharp depression of 1920-1921, had faded from the public memory. Almost every year, the United States and Canada had set new records for industrial production, and British Columbia had participated to the full in the bonanza. The products of its mines and forests were in keen demand throughout the world, and such harbors as Vancouver were busy places.

Social change had also been striking; women had been granted the vote, and Mary Ellen Smith had for a time been the first and only female cabinet minister in the British Empire. The University of British Columbia held its first classes on the Point

Grey campus on September 22, 1925; cocktail parties had replaced prohibition, and theatres and art galleries were attracting more patrons. Movie houses were always crowded, film stars were international celebrities, department stores had built or were planning new additions. Aeroplanes no longer attracted much attention when they passed overhead, while the steamship service to Australia had been improved.

As the end of the decade came in sight, the world of 1918 seemed very far away. Another major international war seemed unthinkable, while the average North American citizen was enjoying the highest standard of living on record. Indeed, he was often augmenting it by judicious flutters on the stock market; if by any chance he lacked sufficient cash to enter the financial arena, his broker stood ready to lend him whatever he required. At the beginning of 1929, Vancouver absorbed the adjacent municipalities of South Vancouver and Point Grey to become the third largest city in Canada, with a population of a quarter of a million. The Marine Building was almost completed, while a new, enormous Hotel Vancouver was rising. There were said to be 80 millionaires in the city; nor were they alone in their glory, the average weekly wage being close to 30 dollars. What with stocks going up, gin going down, Mackenzie King in Ottawa and the genial veterinarian Dr. Simon Fraser Tolmie presiding over the government in Victoria, life seemed very good indeed.

Few would have believed, even if someone had told them, that this pleasant landscape was about to be swept by a hurricane. It had begun as a cloud no bigger than a man's hand, when a speculative fever had set in on the New York Stock Exchange in the spring of 1928. The market had been rising for several years and many competent observers considered it fairly high, when, suddenly, from out of nowhere, had appeared thousands of average citizens, each of them anxious to make what seemed to be easy money. Their arrival in the marketplace had the effect of driving prices still higher, and this in turn confirmed the growing belief that the market was a one-way street. These developments in the New York market were reflected in Montreal, Toronto and Vancouver, and soon brokerage houses in these cities were crowded with eager speculators.

By the late summer of 1929 the general level of prices was discounting not merely the future but the hereafter. Few, however, suspected (no more than they had in the early months of 1914) that the western world was about to cross one of the great divides of the 20th century.

Yet so it was, and few decades were to present a greater contrast than the one now ending and the one about to begin.

Early in September the New York stock market fell off, and

continued to slip for the rest of the month. Then, early in October, it turned up again, and it was generally assumed that before long it would surge into a new high ground as it so often had before.

But this time things were to be different. The market indeed rallied somewhat in early October, but then it turned down again, with an ominously increasing volume. On Wednesday, October 23, selling was so heavy that the ticker tape fell far behind the transactions it was designed to report. The next day was worse; huge blocks of stock were dumped on the market for what they would bring, which was far below the prices of only a few weeks before. For the remainder of the week prices held about level, but on Monday the decline was resumed. Panic was now sweeping the marketplace, as incredulous small investors saw the savings of years—perhaps of a lifetime—evaporate.

The climax came on Tuesday, October 29. In the heaviest day's trading in the history of the New York Stock Exchange, stocks were thrown on the market in a wild scramble to get out. For the next few weeks, there were erratic rallies and declines, but, as the year ended, even the best stocks had lost half their value, and the more speculative ones far more.

Similar scenes had occurred on the Vancouver stock exchange. This had been an increasingly lively place in the closing years of the decade, and when the collapse came, the panic was equally dramatic.

What did it all mean? The conventional wisdom, reflected in soothing editorials across the continent, was that a number of foolish speculators had been badly stung, while the basic economy of the country remained sound. A few were not so sure; they recalled the famous saying of a former editor of the *Wall Street Journal*: "When coming events cast their shadows before, that shadow falls on the New York Stock Exchange." Was the market trying to tell people something?

The answer was not long in coming. Even before the year was out, there was a noticeable decline in the volume of exports shipped through Vancouver, while unemployed workmen became a common sight in the city streets. Soon there were bread-lines outside the city relief office which, in December, was raided by hungry men. The next day there were some ragged parades of unemployed men in Vancouver, which made more timorous citizens fear that an insurrection might take place.

Despite these ominous signs, the new year and the new decade were greeted by reassuring editorials and sonorous statements by financial magnificos. It was not long, however, before events began giving the lie to these pronouncements. The province's most important product, lumber, found its export

markets contracting; the United Kingdom had diverted a large
proportion of its buying orders from Canada to Russia, while the
United States was erecting the Smoot-Hawley tariff against
foreign products. The steady fall in the price of wheat caused
building construction on the prairies to grind toward a virtual
halt. Nor was lumbering the only industry to be hard hit. Within a
year of the crash, provincial fish canneries had two million cases
of salmon on hand and no markets in sight. The fruit industry of
the Okanagan valley was also in desperate straits.

For a time in the early part of 1930, it seemed possible that
things would improve; but, by the end of the year it was plain
that this was wishful thinking. Yet it was likely not until 1931 that
the great majority of British Columbians finally faced the fact that
they were in the midst of a major social and economic crisis. At
the end of 1930 Vancouver had 3,677 residents on relief; a year
later the number was 8,880; a year after that it was over 14,000.
In the nation as a whole, in mid-summer 1931 there were
2,564,000 gainfully employed and 471,000 out of work.

By this time the problem was well beyond the local authorities'
power to deal with, and the province had assumed partial
responsibility for the unemployed, with the federal government
also making a reluctant contribution.

Responses to the depression were varied, but at the bottom of
the economic heap survival was the only watchword. Here and
there, especially in the larger cities, "jungles" grew up where
single unemployed men built shelters from old lumber and lived
in them as best they could, sometimes begging, sometimes going
from door to door in search of work, sometimes, no doubt,
stealing. The jungle in Vancouver first attracted attention in the
spring of 1931, as one old-timer later recalled:

"The jungle, as it was called, was on the city dump at the
False Creek fill between Campbell Avenue and Heatley Avenue.
There was another jungle on the old Hastings sawmill site. It was
a collection of nondescript habitations made out of anything
which could be begged, borrowed or stolen, and hung together
somehow to afford shelter from the elements to a large number
of unemployed men. They were men from everywhere, all sorts
of ages, education, characters, which a common want and
misery had banded together for mutual help."

The jungle on the Hastings mill site (the mill itself had ceased
operations before the depression began) was much the same. As
one of the harbor commissioners later recalled:

"It was a shocking afternoon, the rain came down in sheets.
Through the window I saw a man disappear under some rails,
put on my coat, and went out into the storm to investigate. I
stooped down, and looked under the rails, and saw what

seemed to be several men sheltering under there. I called out to them, and finally enquired if any were returned soldiers. One replied "Yes," so I told him to come on out of there, and he came. He told me he had been a bugler in the Princess Patricia's Canadian Light Infantry. After I had fished him out I discovered there were 13 more under there, and two of them were without boots.

"I pointed out two wooden sheds on the shore, and told the bugler to take charge of the party. We had a stove down at the Lapointe pier, so I sent over and got that, and went round and bought canned milk, tea, sugar, and some bread and tobacco.

"Then we sent the men over to the fish wharf. The fishermen gave them three ten-pound salmon. We got a few potatoes, brought the cook stove up, and started housekeeping with the bugler in charge.

"The 14 men had no sooner moved out from the rail pile than more went under, and we had the whole situation duplicated again.

"Finally the thing got a little too big, so the office staff took charge, and undertook to run the show in their spare time. Some of my personal friends took an interest. I think I must have clothed 30 men with the clothes which were sent to me to distribute. Mrs. Eric W. Hamber took a very great interest and one day sent down two dozen pairs of boots, two dozen each of suits of underwear, socks, shirts, and 10 pounds of tobacco. The fishermen at the wharf were very good all through the existence of the jungle, and always gave what they could spare.

"As the thing began to get bigger, all three Harbor Commissioners began to take a private and personal interest, and one day a ton of potatoes was mysteriously found in the basement of the office, and the strange thing was that that ton of potatoes was akin to the oatmeal of the barrel in the Bible; there was always more potatoes, in fact, altogether there must have been several tons. The fishermen at the wharf sent over fish every day; P. Burns and Co. sent meat; Capt. Binks came down one day with 10 dollars worth of cigarettes; the Vancouver Club sent 10 gallons of soup every morning, Sundays included, and all the bread, rolls and buns left over from the day. Once a week, sometimes twice, and oftener, the Terminal City Club sent down hot mulligan.

"We lined up all returned men for first choice as soon as the stuff arrived; then the men who had registered came next, and the rest followed. Every morning when the soup came down we lined them up in a ragged column on the board walk. The issue was a bowl of soup, one third of a loaf of bread, a piece of soap, and some cigarettes. They were a quiet orderly lot; one was a graduate of Cambridge."

In September 1931, the civic authorities decided that the jungles were a health hazard, and they were torn down. Their former inhabitants were housed in emergency refuges dotted about Vancouver.

In the same year work camps were set up throughout the province. Here the men built roads and airfields, at first under civilian direction and later, for a time, under military control. The men were paid 20 cents a day plus room and board.

1932 and 1933 were the two worst years of the depression. By this time many men had come to the coast from the prairies, drawn by the milder climate. This placed an added burden on the province, and some maintained that men from other parts of Canada should be driven back across the Rockies. This policy, being unconstitutional, was never officially put into effect, but efforts were made to achieve the same result by denying relief to men who had recently arrived from other provinces.

In June 1932, R.W. Bruhn, provincial minister of public works, outlined his government's attitude to the crisis:

"How it will be done, I don't know. We haven't got the money to look after these outsiders. Our duty is to our own residents first. Perhaps we shall not be able to maintain even the present reduced scale of relief."

The minister also announced that the hours of work for the men in relief camps (then numbering about 4,000) had been increased from six to eight a day, with no increase in pay. A month later the newspapers gave further details of new provincial regulations:

"Further reductions in B.C.'s unemployment relief costs were ordered by the government today, as Premier Tolmie continued to press the federal government for a definite unemployment agreement.

"Under a program outlined this morning, many men now in government road camps who can maintain themselves, at least during the summer, will be eliminated."

The government estimated that this would cut 2,000 men from the rolls, at least in the sunny weather, and other economies were also in prospect:

"In future, a uniform system of allowances for destitute families will be inaugurated all over the province. This will replace the present arrangements whereby one municipality pays $30 a month in relief to a man and wife, and another $40 and a third perhaps $45. Instead, the government will authorize a fixed amount, to be calculated according to the cost of meals. It is believed that an allowance of 15 cents per meal per person will be a fair working basis, with a further fixed allowance for rent and fuel where they are required.

"This new scale will be put into almost immediate effect as part of the campaign to cut the province's relief costs almost in two."

Others somewhat higher in the economic scale were faring little better in those dark days. An item in a Vancouver paper gives some idea of what many of those who had spent their life working toward a secure old age were faced with:

"The case is drawn to the mayor's attention of a couple aged 65 who owe $600 principal on their home of 30 years, which is assessed at $1,300. The wife is unable to walk and the husband is ill and cannot work. The mortgagee has signified his intention of foreclosing on Monday unless the year's interest is paid. The man hopes to scrape together the interest but is not certain of this.

"Taxes amount to $49, but three years must elapse before the home is sold for unpaid taxes."

"This is just one case," declared the mayor. "There are hundreds like it."

It is remarkable in the circumstances that there was so little violence by victims of the depression. Yet from time to time incidents did occur which suggested that tempers were growing short. For example in Vancouver in 1933: "In a sudden raid on the unemployment relief office shortly before 11 o'clock this morning, a crowd of 150 men broke into the hall, overturned office registration files, tore out telephone connections, and fled before police could reach the scene."

Even a small rural community like Maillardville in the Fraser Valley was not exempt from such scenes:

"Pandemonium reigned here Saturday night and until 8 a.m. Sunday when a number of unemployed forced their way into the basement of the Coquitlam municipal hall and refused to leave until some arrangement had been made to supply them with food.

"Reeve McDonald who arrived on the scene at 11 p.m. was kept a prisoner in the hall, the unemployed refusing to let him leave the building.

"All members of the council were present, and endeavored to get the men and women to go to their homes, but it was not until two hours after Inspector Cruickshanks and 25 provincial officers had been summoned that the unemployed, having secured a promise that they would have a small allowance made for a meal, dispersed and went to their homes."

The lowest point of the depression was probably the spring of 1933, when about 128,000 British Columbians were receiving some sort of government assistance. There were 14,000 on relief in Vancouver at the end of 1932, and a quarter of the city's budget went to support them. The customary scale of payments to those in need was scarcely lavish: $9 dollars a month for each head of a family, $3.50 for a second adult, and $2.50 for each dependent. Those who had recently entered the province from other areas were ineligible. A pamphlet written in this period by a self-styled "hobo" gives some idea of general conditions:

"There are men working nine and ten hours a day washing dishes in cafes for the magnificent sum of three dollars a week and board.

"There are experienced gardeners working in the districts of the luxury class for 75¢ a day and two meals.

"There are store clerks employed in this city for five dollars per week.

"There are experienced mechanics working in garages and services stations for five and six dollars per week, and some of them doing a twelve-hour shift for that money.

"There are young girls employed throughout the city, earning from two to five dollars per week for an eight hour day.

"There are first-class cooks receiving the disgraceful wage of nine dollars for a seven-day week of ten hours.

"There are painters and paper-hangers free-lancing for a dollar and a half to two dollars per day, and supplying their own tools."

Like many people in this period, the author of the pamphlet had a ready cure for the depression:

"If every woman who has a male member in her family was compelled to give up her job, two-thirds of Canada's unemployed would go back to work. They in turn would take care of the women by marriage. Homes would be built, furniture bought, automobiles, radios, electrical appliances and hundreds of other items would be purchased. Trade would receive a natural stimulus. In two years the depression would be ended."

It should be noted, however, that prices had also fallen, and many items were selling at figures which would seem unbelievable a generation or two later. Stores offered 25 pounds of potatoes for 15 cents and two dozen oranges for 25 cents. Restaurants would supply liver or bacon and two eggs for 15 cents, while two doughnuts and a cup of coffee cost 5 cents.

Inevitably, the depression produced numerous plans for solving it. Newspapers and government offices received a steady stream of material, some closely argued, some illiterate, explaining how happy days could be restored. At least two political movements, the CCF (later the NDP) and Social Credit, began their march toward the seats of power in this period. Other groups such as the technocrats were at least regularly in the public eye, while communists, proclaiming grandly that "1929 had brought clarity out of existing confusion," worked and prayed for the inevitable apocalypse and the subsequent New Jerusalem.

Meanwhile, those charged with the actual responsibilities of power struggled with the crisis. Some municipalities, such as North Vancouver, themselves fell victim and went into bankruptcy. The rest, alarmed by these developments, steadily reduced their public expenditures, even if this appeared to involve increasing unemployment.

A commission set up by the provincial government to suggest ways of coping with the crisis, brought in its report in 1932. Among other things it recommended were ending all grants to the university, reducing the size of the legislature to 28 seats and the cabinet to 6, closing down the Pacific Great Eastern Railway, and reducing the period of free public education. These suggestions were never implemented, but they were an indication of what at least some level-headed people believed was the best policy.

Many politicians were driven from power as a result of the depression. These included U.S. President Herbert Hoover and Prime Minister R.B. Bennett. A more violent convulsion saw the end of democracy in Germany. In November 1933, Premier Tolmie was replaced by Duff Pattullo in an election which saw the first appearance in the British Columbia legislature of members of the CCF. The electorate was clearly ready for new experiments; Hugh Savage, editor of the *Cowichan Leader*, was elected on a platform of "absolute sincerity, absolute purity, absolute unselfishness and absolute love."

Ever so slowly, after 1933, the dark clouds grew a little brighter. Those on relief in British Columbia, who at one time had totalled 128,000, had dropped to 76,000 by the fall of 1935 and to 43,000 two years later. Governments by this time were bestirring themselves more actively. Premier Pattullo inaugurated a public works program sometimes known as the "little New Deal." He established the 48-hour week in all major industries, raised minimum wages, and at least contemplated a comprehensive health insurance scheme. Forestry training plans, set up in 1935, absorbed several hundred men; a revival of gold mining in the interior gave hope to others. Meanwhile the Ottawa trade agreements of 1932 gave British Columbia lumber a preference in the British market, and this industry began a steady revival. A fine new bridge across the Fraser at New Westminster gave employment to many, while Vancouver completed an imposing new city hall. The world-famous Lions Gate Bridge was opened in November 1938.

Even so, sporadic incidents of violence revealed that much resentment yet smouldered against the established political and economic order. In March 1934, 250 inmates of a Vancouver shelter for the unemployed went on a rampage and wrecked it. Over a hundred men were arrested, as "rushing through a barrage of broken furniture, crockery and metalware, detectives and constables forced the locked doors and entered the building."

Sometimes the confrontation of authority and despair seemed to mock the deficiencies of the former:

"Nineteen unemployed men who obtained meals without paying in a downtown cafe were sentenced by Police Magistrate J.A. Findlay to one month in jail.

"Returned to cells in the city hall after being sentenced, the men lustily sang patriotic songs and cheered the magistrate."

More serious trouble occurred in Vancouver in 1935. The city authorities had forbidden the unemployed to ask for money from passersby, but the "tin-canners" defied the ban and collected better than $4,600 in a single day. They also paraded through the streets bearing placards with slogans such as "Work and wages," and "Down with the slave camps." At one time they invaded the Hudson's Bay store and had to be driven out by the police. Mayor McGeer (who was something of a radical himself, in an erratic sort of way) then read the Riot Act in Victory Square. There were no further disturbances, but, soon afterwards, the men occupied the city museum. This time, after being granted some meal tickets, they agreed to leave peacefully.

Some of them, however, were soon involved in what perhaps was the most tragic event of the period. Moved by mingled feelings of despair, resentment and hope, large numbers of men began making their way eastward across the country in the famous "On to Ottawa" trek. They planned to lay their plight before the very seats of power, but those occupying those seats took alarm and gave orders that the marchers were to be turned back. On July 1, 1935, in Regina, bitter fighting took place between the marchers and the authorities, represented by the local police and the RCMP. Many heads were cracked; one man, a city detective, was killed, 130 men were arrested, and some were sent to jail. The defeated and dispirited marchers dispersed to their homes in various parts of Canada.

This was not the last outbreak of violence in depression Canada. In the spring of 1938, 1,600 men occupied the Vancouver art gallery, post office, and the Hotel Georgia. Those in the hotel soon evacuated peacefully, but the other groups remained defiant. On Sunday morning of June 20, after an ultimatum from the city, those occupying the art gallery left with little disturbance. Those in the post office refused to do so, and were driven out by the RCMP with considerable violence. In retaliation, as the men retreated through the streets, they broke windows of the major department stores.

The depression had a considerable effect on social attitudes and customs. Both the marriage and the birth rate declined, and many women attempted to enter the labor force. Racial resentment against Orientals increased, because of competition for the lowest paid jobs. In some cases this was also reflected in government policy; in the Cowichan district, Vancouver Island, Chinese on relief received less than white men.

Other trends were also noticeable. The wild parties and reckless behavior of the younger members of the wealthier classes which had characterized the 20s was much less in evidence in the 30s. Children stayed in school longer, and there was a growing interest in books about serious issues of the day. Unlike most major industries, motion pictures suffered no loss of patrons. Miniature golf, a sort of parody of genuine business, flourished for a time, as did such bizarre phenomena as dance marathons.

The most important change of all, however, was the near-universal recognition that the days of unrestricted *laissez-faire* must end. From this point on, governments would assume an increasing responsibility for not merely relieving distress but guiding the general course of the economy. The real division in politics occurred between those who believed this should be a gradual process and those who believed its pace should be greatly increased. As even so conservative an organ as the Vancouver *Province* declared, in a rebuke to the crusty prime minister of the country, "It is begging the question to suggest, as the Dominion suggests by its attitude to the problem, that unemployment relief is charity. It is surely unnecessary after five years of distress and efforts to meet the distress to go back to the old arguments and warm them over again. We have advanced in those five years to quite a new conception of the situation. We regard unemployment relief not as charity at all but as a crude and fumbling effort to adjust the working of an economic machine which has somehow gone wrong."

In practice, however, society had become divided into two groups—those with jobs and those without. Both sides seemed to recognize this fact, as vignettes in the newspapers from time to time revealed. For example, in April 1934, Vancouver gave two free hockey tickets to each family on relief so that the recipients could watch the Toronto Maple Leafs play the Detroit Red Wings:

"To prevent congestion at the arena tonight, a section of the gallery has been set aside for the relief tickets, but after 8:45 the relief men may transfer into seats available in the lower gallery."

On another occasion, even the humane Premier Pattullo seemed strangely insensitive. A delegation of the unemployed, in search of a better deal, were granted an interview with him. "The single men asked for three 15¢ meals a day, said W.A. Fitzger of Vancouver. Now they received only two 15¢ meals.

"I only eat two meals a day myself," the premier remarked, "but I admit they all cost more than 15¢."

It was by no means a cheerful province which saw the sad decade approach its weary end. The worst days of the depression were clearly past, but there was little sign that full employment would ever return. Whether it would have done so under normal peacetime conditions we shall never know.

For by this time the world was moving out of one era and into another. World conditions were steadily growing more dangerous; there were wars in Ethiopia and Spain, and by the time of the Munich crisis in the fall of 1938, it appeared that a general European war was inevitable.

Finally, one Sunday morning in September 1939, it arrived. Outwardly, little seemed changed at first, but as the recruiting offices opened and the war industries developed, unemployment at last disappeared. The great depression was over, but its scars would long remain. Not until at least a decade after the war would it begin to fade into memory.   ●

1948
The Fraser Valley Flood

AFTER the boom, the slump; at the end of the depression, the war. Then in 1945 came peace, and British Columbians wondered what the post-war years would bring.

Even amid the twin celebrations of victory (one in the early summer for the end of the war in Europe, one a few months later for the end of the war in Asia), the mood was not altogether hopeful. Many recalled the dark days of the 30s, and how they had ended only when the recruiting offices opened and the munition plants were built. When the soldiers and sailors returned, would the depression years be resumed?

Many feared that they would. True, the first year of peace seemed as prosperous as the last year of war, as the ex-service-men were mysteriously absorbed into the work force, but was this merely a false glow before the economic fires grew cold? The question was much debated, even as the second year of peace saw steady if unspectacular growth. Doomsday was apparently postponed.

As 1947 gave way to 1948, the general mood remained somewhat uncertain. Many recalled that the province's history had been marked every few years by some sudden, unforeseen disaster. Moreover, these often seemed to have come in pairs, the second blow of fate often resembling the first, but occurring only when the earlier one had become part of a rather dim and shadowy past. Thus the smallpox epidemic of 1862 had been paralleled by the influenza epidemic of 1918; the loss of the *Pacific* by that of the *Sophia* in 1918; the Barkerville fire of 1868 by the Vancouver fire of 1886; and the New Westminster fire of 1898 by the Victoria fire of 1910. Would one of the province's past calamities before long be re-enacted?

If so, the disaster most likely to recur was apparently the great depression, while the least likely was surely the great Fraser River flood of 1894. So much destruction had been caused by that disaster that every precaution had been taken to see that it was never repeated. At the turn of the century an elaborate dyking system had been constructed along the lower reaches of the river, to protect the valuable farm lands which every year were being more thickly settled. In the 1920s more work had been done in the area; Sumas Lake had been reclaimed for agriculture, dykes strengthened, and giant pumps installed to deal with emergencies. The results, which created the largest dyking system in Canada, seemed to justify the expenditure; the years between the wars saw no major flood, and the war years saw the river do nothing to hinder the national effort. The mighty Fraser, 850 miles long and draining 90,000 square miles, had apparently been tamed.

Meanwhile there was a continuous influx of new settlers into the valley; in 1894 there were perhaps a thousand residents in the area, but by 1948 there were 50,000. In addition, many industries had set up plants within easy reach of the Vancouver market, and municipalities along the riverbank were seeking to attract more.

So 1948 advanced from spring into summer, and the snows of the previous winter began melting in the mountains and making their way down innumerable streams into the great river and thence to the sea. This year the spring had been cold, and May was well advanced before the annual run-off began in earnest. Some of those in authority perceived the dangers in this situation; officials of the Department of Lands, for example, reported to the provincial government that "protracted warm weather or warm rains could produce a flood hazard very quickly. Flood prevention agencies, therefore, should be on the alert."

Little publicity was given to this report. For that matter, none was needed, as a sudden rise in temperature throughout the interior wrought a great change—and disaster—overnight.

Most British Columbians were preparing to celebrate the annual May 24 holiday when the first ominous reports appeared in their daily newspapers. A column on an inside page of the Vancouver *Province*, for example, noted that, "Flood hits interior centres." The accompanying story told how the temperature in the interior valleys had suddenly jumped into the 80s, and had caused the level of the Fraser to rise sharply. the gauge at Hope had passed 26 feet. Farther inland, the Shuswap River had broken a major water main and the small community of Enderby was, ironically, without water. At Prince George the Chilako River had weakened an important bridge, while the Tulameen at Princeton had risen 18 inches in 36 hours.

Despite these warnings, most British Columbians, at least those in the coastal cities, enjoyed the holiday with carefree optimism. When they opened their morning papers the next day, however, they were greeted with banner headlines across the front page:

AID TO FLOOD-STRICKEN INTERIOR CITIES

The most serious trouble was in the Kootenays. Kimberley and Grand Forks had been hard-hit by rising waters. Twenty thousand sandbags were being flown to Kimberley, as well as thirty tents to shelter people forced from their homes. In Grand Forks, some downtown streets were under three feet of water, while the town of Fernie was cut off from eastern points.

Moreover, there already were signs that the lower Fraser Valley would soon face a crisis, as the gauge at Mission registered 18.8 feet. This was below the danger point of 20 feet, but, higher up the river at Hope, the Fraser had risen three feet in three days. One of its major tributaries, the Coquihalla, was also rising rapidly, while it was reported that at Hell's Gate the river had risen no less than seven feet. Serious trouble was plainly fast approaching, and newspapers declared that "the Fraser Valley tensely awaits full flood force."

On May 26 came the first ominous signal, when the river made a small breach in the elaborate dyking system which lined its southern bank near Agassiz, some 80 miles from Vancouver. Although 25 men, who were attending a dance in the area when pressed into service, attempted to strengthen it, they toiled all night in vain; as morning arrived the dyke gave way, and 20 acres of farmland were flooded. This was not a major disaster, but, fearing that a more serious breach might occur, local residents asked for assistance from the camp of army engineers at Chilliwack. Meanwhile an inspection of the valley from the air did not prove encouraging. It was reported that "the Fraser is no longer a river; from the air it looks more like a great long muddy lake."

The situation continued to deteriorate. The gauge at Hope, which less than a week before had registered 26 feet, passed 31 feet, within four feet of the record reached in 1894. The Mission gauge had risen more than a foot in 24 hours, and was now close to 22 feet. The most critical point was still near Agassiz, where 100 farmers toiled continuously to strengthen the dykes. But their efforts proved insufficient, as the Fraser began washing over the man-made barriers onto their fields. Some of them, fearing a general disaster, began moving their cattle to higher ground. Soon over a thousand acres of arable land were underwater, and many families had to be evacuated. Meanwhile the CPR line at Harrison Mills was washed out, leaving the CNR the only remaining link with Vancouver.

Other parts of the valley did not escape. Thousands of acres around Fort Langley were soon under water, while the railway yards at Port Mann were flooded. Some industrial operations were affected, and work had to stop at the Hatzic sawmill.

Although the Fraser Valley was the worst-hit area of the province, the sudden rise in temperatures had caused trouble elsewhere. The Bulkley River overflowed its banks, there were 18 inches of water in the streets of Telkwa, and the town of Hazelton was virtually isolated from the larger world.

The Fraser Valley remained critical, however, because of its heavy concentration of population. By May 28 most of Agassiz, a town of 2,000, was under three feet of water. All women and children were evacuated from the area to the nearby Mount View cemetery, where a makeshift refugee camp was established. Orders were given that all drinking water must be chlorinated. The CNR line had also become impassable, and an aerial observer reported:

"Agassiz today is a ghost town. There is no land to see. Only the railway station, on slightly higher ground, shows any signs of life. Groups of huddled people stared up as we flew over. Most of them didn't even bother to wave."

Other parts of the valley were also hard-hit. The Trans-Canada highway west of Chilliwack was under water, as was most of the town of Harrison Mills. Hatzic was partially flooded, and news arrived in Vancouver that "Dewdney was abandoned to the flood at 11 p.m. Thursday." A small break had occurred in the dykes at Fort Langley, though those at Matsqui were still holding. By this time tugboats and naval craft were cruising about the flooded areas, rescuing stranded families and live-stock. There were still 400 familes on Nicomen Island, which covered an area of 14 square miles some 55 miles east of Vancouver; some still had hopes of remaining there, but many were abandoning their houses and farms. In the meantime Premier Byron Johnson arrived in the stricken area, quickly realized the magnitude of the disaster, and after a few days hastened to Ottawa to seek financial assistance from the federal government.

On May 28 the gauge at Mission read 23.4 feet, compared

with the 1894 peak of 25.5. Nine hundred cattle were evacuated from Barnston Island; two-thirds of Nicomen Island was under six feet of water, but 20 families yet remained, though their cattle were being transported elsewhere.

In other areas it was the same story: There was water in the basement of the elegant Harrison Hot Springs Hotel, many lumber mills in the New Westminster area were closed down, a fire occurred at Agassiz when water reached lime stored in the warehouse of a building supplies firm. In the northern part of the province the railway line from Smithers to Prince Rupert was out of operation. The general situation was summed up by the daily press:

"Agassiz, Nicomen Island, and Dewdney are flooded. Dykes have broken near Fort Langley. Glendale, near Chilliwack, and the Trans-Canada Highway there are under water. Pitt Meadows is endangered. Water is across the CNR at Port Mann. Barnston Island is fighting to build up its dykes. Lulu Island is threatened. Ladner watches the ocean tides as well as the river, and prepares for a fight."

May 30 saw the crisis intensified as the river tore a gap 200 feet wide through the dyke at Matsqui, and the rapid evacuation of that area began. By this time 4,000 soldiers, 400 sailors and 40,000 civilians were either toiling on the dykes, removing people to safer areas, or milking cows.

One of those packing sandbags at this time was Cornelius Kelleher, who had been in the Matsqui area since 1891, and who had helped to fight the flood of 1894. Another old-timer, Edward Barrow, who at one time had been provincial minister of agriculture, also took his place in the front line. As he later recalled, "It was just after noon Tuesday that I went out to take some levels and noticed a trickle at my feet. In a few minutes it was a stream, and then the flood was on us. I got most of the 50 head of dairy stock out; then we swam the sheep to the barn. There were 22 ewes and 25 lambs. The purebred Guernsey bull is still in the barn. Some men have gone with a boat to bring out the sheep.

"I couldn't estimate the loss. The water will likely rise to the level of the dining-room table. I don't think it will go higher. We moved a lot of furniture upstairs. If these waters rise to the top of the dining-room table, they will be on the same level as the flood of 1894.

"I can stand a lot of water. I've been up to my waist in floods during the past. Even at 81 I have a busy life."

The disaster was soon having repercussions in other parts of the country. Vancouver began running short of milk and butter. In Ottawa the cautious Prime Minister Mackenzie King, then in

his last year of office, asserted, presumably on advice from the
spirit world, that the flood was a provincial rather than a federal
responsibility. Premier Byron Johnson declared a state of
emergency and placed Colonel T. Snow in command of
"Operation Overflow." From his headquarters aboard the frigate
HMCS *Antigonish*, berthed at New Westminster, Snow directed
a combined force of army, navy, air force, provincial and local
police, and Red Cross workers. The RCAF flew thousands of
sandbags from eastern Canada to the stricken area, as well as
large quantities of bread from Calgary. The navy ferried 500
people from the Matsqui area to Abbotsford, while the tug
Heatherton, under Ted Beckstron, also did much useful work in
moving people and livestock to higher ground. Most radio
stations in the area remained on the air 24 hours a day, and
station CHWK in Chilliwack was used as a command post in the
fight against the flood. Meanwhile a "B.C. Flood Committee"
was formed, with the province making the first contribution of
$100,000 toward rehabilitation of victims of the flood. Under
strong pressure from Premier Johnson and British Columbia
members of parliament, the Prime Minister agreed that the
dominion government would, after all, take some responsibility
for aiding in the work of reconstruction.

Many Vancouver citizens were volunteering for duty in the
emergency, and one of them later gave some account of his
experiences:

"Half an hour after I applied to the Beatty Street armories I
was on my way to the flood control headquarters in Pitt
Meadows with 32 others. They came from school, from their
jobs, from every part of Vancouver.

"We reached Pitt Meadows at 9 a.m. and were told to get
some chow—we might not be getting back for a while.

"The dining room was located in the Community Hall. The
service was much faster than any cafe I have been in. We were
served a large wholesome meal cooked by housewives, mothers
and grandmothers of the community. High school girls waited
on us with professional proficiency.

"Just as we were finishing, the P.A. system blared out a call
for 50 men for the dykes. In five minutes we were on our way.

"When we reached the dykes we were told to fill and carry
sandbags to the weak spots. It was hard going. Most of us were
not used to it. There is a knack in toting those bags. If you don't
get them on your shoulder just right, you're liable to sprain an
arm or your back.

"I worked for five hours in the hot sun, and was ready to
drop. Most of the others were in the same condition.

"We used up seven truckloads of sand. Then we ate again."

Despite these valiant efforts by thousands of people, the river continued to rise, the gauge at Mission passing 24 feet. On the first of June a tree in the dyke near Sumas Prairie fell over, weakening the dyke sufficiently for the river to tear an 80-foot-wide breach. A thousand people had to flee as 1,200 acres were flooded. Meanwhile the Great Northern railway line was washed out, cutting railway communication with the United States. Some residents of the state of Washington were by this time making their way north to aid in rescue efforts, even though large parts of the northwest United States were also in serious trouble. The Columbia, for example, was in flood all the way to the coast. In the British Columbia interior such towns as Trail were suffering heavy damage.

The weather intensified the disaster, as rising temperatures throughout the province increased the run-off. For the first time on record, the Fraser forced its way up its tributary, the Harrison, into Harrison Lake, some 10 miles away. The railway embankment at Hatzic crumbled. and more hundreds became refugees. Barnston Island, a mile and a half wide and nearly three miles long, vanished beneath the waters of the Fraser, and there was a big break in the dykes at Hatzic Lake. Another 6,000 acres were flooded, telephone and telegraph lines were washed away, and the little community of Dewdney was isolated, with four feet of water in its main streets. All train service out of the stricken area had now ceased.

By June 5, as 30,000 men and women fought to contain the disaster, the Mission gauge stood at 24.36 feet, 50,000 acres of the best arable land in the province were under water, and the worst was not over. The hottest day of the year coincided with a high tide, which forced water to back up the swollen river and into the flooded area. Colonel Snow called out Vancouver Island reservists, 200 men arriving from Victoria and 100 from Nanaimo, as troops from Lord Strathcona's Horse were airlifted from the prairies to strengthen the dykes of Lulu Island. Meanwhile Mayor Peter Barbeau of Blaine, Washington arrived with 100 men to fight the flood. By this time dead livestock were being washed up on the beaches of Vancouver Island, and the entire Gulf of Georgia was a dark brown. Bathing was prohibited on Vancouver beaches, and many people were inoculated against typhoid. A few people who saw the flood as a golden opportunity to make money, cruised about the devastated area and bought up cattle at 10 dollars a head.

By June 10 the situation was steadily worsening. The main dykes at Sumas Prairie were expected to fall, and those not actually engaged in strengthening them were evacuated. A large number of people were quartered in the old Hotel Vancouver, where the Red Cross and other charitable organizations looked after them. Heavy rains increased the danger that a still greater disaster lay ahead.

Then, when almost all seemed lost, the situation eased. Bright sunshine soaked up some of the water, while the gauge at Mission, which had reached a peak of 24.73 feet on June 10, for the first time recorded a slight drop. The next day it fell a little further, and from reports received from the interior it was plain that the crest of the flood had passed.

Slowly the situation returned to normal, and the province counted the cost. Almost 10 per cent of the area of the Fraser Valley, 55,000 acres, had been flooded. Ten people had died, and 200 families were homeless. Many houses were full of mud when their owners returned, and their furniture was ruined. Three thousand buildings had been destroyed, as well as much valuable farm machinery. The ground was littered with the corpses of dead animals which festered in the sun. Regular railway service was not restored for some weeks. Eighty-two bridges had been washed out, and it would be many years before some agricultural areas were restored to full production. The total cost of the disaster was estimated at $15 million. Had the dyke along the Vedder Canal not held, the cost would have been much greater.

The work of reconstruction began almost at once. After consultations between the federal, provincial and municipal authorities, the dominion government agreed to pay $5 million toward relief and rehabilitation of flood victims, in addition to 75 per cent of the cost of repairing and strengthening the dyking system. This was estimated at over $10 million. A "Fraser Valley Dyking Board," a joint federal-provincial group of 10 members, was established, and charged with the task of making a detailed report on all the factors involved in the flood, together with recommendations for preventing any repetition.

In the meantime the Vancouver *Province* offered the board some suggestions:

"It is not going too far to say that the Fraser was responsible for making British Columbia, and that it has been a major factor in the province's development. But today it is a destroyer instead of a creator.

"One doesn't have to be an engineer to know that the place to control the Fraser is not on its lower reaches, and that the filling and piling of sandbags is a desperate and very temporary necessity.

"The Fraser is a system rather than a river. Some of its tributaries are great rivers in themselves. Its lakes and creeks run into the thousands. The place to control the Fraser is up above,

where the water comes from. The way to control it is to control
its tributaries. For this we need a Fraser River authority—a board
with authority enough and resources enough to take the river in
hand, control its transports, co-ordinate its industries, and make
it work consistently for the benefit of the public as a whole.

"The Fraser is satisfied with an outburst once in 10 years or
so, so there will be probably time to take action before another
great flood. But the authority should be created without delay
and set to work."

The problem was plainly a complex one, as conflicting
interests were involved. For example, municipalities along the
river, in search of tax revenues, continued to urge home-owners
and industries to settle in the areas most susceptible to flooding.
Constructing dams across the tributaries of the Fraser might
prevent salmon from reaching their spawning grounds, and thus
damage a major provincial industry. The rights of the Indians to
their traditional fishing areas would also have to be considered.
There was even a psychological problem involved in maintaining
a high level of vigilance against a threat which would probably
only become real at long, irregular intervals.

While these matters were being considered by the board, the
immediate work of reconstruction went ahead. Almost 170 miles
of dykes were rebuilt, and "borrow pits" behind them, from
which earth had been taken to build the original dykes, were
filled in. The level of the dykes was raised to two feet above the
highest point reached in either 1894 or 1948. Considerable
sums were paid to farmers to buy feed and fertilizer, as well as to
nurserymen and bulb-growers to re-establish their businesses.
Vouchers were given to householders to replace ruined
furniture.

The Dyking Board spent several years examining the whole
question of flood control on the Fraser, and eventually issued a
preliminary report in 1955 and a final report in 1963. It
recommended that nine dams be built on the upper Fraser to
hold back the late spring freshets, and that five of them should be
used to generate electric power. It urged that closer attention be
paid to the depth of the annual winter snow-pack, and that more
weather forecasting stations should be established in the interior.
By the time the board had issued its final report, the dyking
system had been rebuilt, with dykes 12 feet wide at the top and
capable of being used by emergency vehicles. The board urged
governments to proceed on the assumption that some future
flood might reach a level of 26 feet on the Mission gauge, and
noted that the steady increase in the population of the lower
Fraser Valley would make any future collapse of the dykes more
disastrous than ever.

So the great flood of 1948 gradually slipped into the past, and the province entered a period of prosperity which was destined to last for nearly three decades. During this time there were occasional setbacks and calamities, but none of major proportions. As the province moves into the last quarter of the century, no one can tell what the coming years will bring. One thing, though, could be said with some confidence: Any new emergency or disaster would draw from British Columbians the same reserves of fortitude and endurance which they have so often displayed in the past. ●

Bibliography

1862: The Smallpox Epidemic

COOK, S.F., *The Epidemic of 1830-1833 in California and Oregon;* University of California Press, Berkeley, 1955.

DUFF, Wilson, *The Indian History of British Columbia: Volume 1: the Impact of the White Man;* Provincial Memoir No. 5, Victoria, 1964.

PALMER, H.S., *Report of a Journey of Survey From Victoria to Fort Alexander* (sic) *via North Bentinck Arm.* Royal Engineers Press, New Westminster, 1863 (also printed in the *British Columbian,* New Westminster, March 11, 1863 and subsequent issues).

SMITH, Dorothy Blakey (ed.), *The Reminiscences of Dr. John Sebastian Helmcken,* UBC Press, 1975.

YARMIE, A.H., "Smallpox and the British Columbia Indians epidemic of 1862," *B.C. Library Quarterly,* January 1968.

Victoria *Colonist,* beginning with the issue of March 19, 1862.

Letters—Brown to Douglas, dated February 18, 1863 and Elwyn to Colonial Secretary, December 17, 1862.

1864: The Bute Inlet Massacre

BANCROFT, H.H., *History of British Columbia;* San Francisco, 1890.

BROWN, R. Lundin, *Klatsassen and Other Reminiscences of Missionary Life in British Columbia;* London, 1873.

DOWNIE, William, *Explorations in Jervis Inlet and Desolation Sound, British Columbia, Journal of the Royal Geographical Society, London,* 1861.
Hunting for Gold; San Francisco, 1893. Reprinted by American West Publishing Company, Palo Alto, California, 1971.

GRANT, G.M., *Ocean to Ocean.* Toronto and London, 1873.

213

HEWLETT, E.S., "The Chilcotin Uprising: a Study of Indian-European Relations in Nineteenth Century British Columbia," M.A. Thesis, UBC, 1972.

HOMFRAY, Robert, "A Winter Journey in 1861," *Canadian Frontier*, Vol. 1, No. 1, Garnet Publishing Co., Vancouver 1972.

MORICE, A.G., *The History of the Northern Interior of British Columbia*; Toronto, 1905. Reprinted by Ye Galleon Press, Fairfield, Washington, 1971.

ORMSBY, Margaret, "Some Irish Figures in Colonial Days," *B.C. Historical Quarterly*; 1950. Brew's report to Seymour is attached to the governor's despatch of July 7, 1865.
"Frederick Seymour, the Forgotten Governor;" *B.C. Studies*; Summer 1974.

PALMER, H.S., *Report of a Journey of Survey from Victoria to Fort Alexander via North Bentinck Arm*. Royal Engineers Press, New Westminster, 1863.

REID, R.L., "Alfred Waddington;" *Royal Society of Canada Transactions*, Third series, Ottawa, 1932.

SHANKS, Robert N., *Waddington: A Biography*; North Island Gazette, Port Hardy, B.C., 1975

WADDINGTON, Alfred, *The Fraser Mines Vindicated*; Victoria, 1858; reprinted in facsimile by Robert R. Reid, Vancouver, 1949.
The Necessity of Reform; Victoria, 1859.
Overland Communication by Land and Water Through British North America; Victoria, 1867.
Overland Route Through British North America, or, the Shortest and Speediest Road to the East; London 1868.

WYMPER, Frederick, *Travel and Adventure in the Territory of Alaska*; London, 1868.

The Dictionary of Canadian Biography, Volume 10,

Correspondence between Waddinton and the Colonial government, as well as his petition to the Secretary of State for the Colonies, asking for redress.

Extracts from Tiedemann's journal of his exploration in 1862, "A Coast Range Pioneer," *Canadian Alpine Journal*, 1949.

The reports of J.W. McKay and Major Downie are attached to Douglas' despatch of March 25, 1859, to the Colonial Office. *Papers relative to the affairs of British Columbia*, Queen's Printer, London, 1859. Downie's report is also printed as an appendix to R.C. Mayne's *Four years in British Columbia and Vancouver Island* (London, 1862; reprinted in facsimile in 1969 by Johnson Reprint Corporation, New York).

Details of Waddinton's agreement with the colonial government are printed in the *British Columbia and Victoria Directory*, Victoria, 1863, p. 191. The prospectus issued by Waddinton late in 1863 is in the Provincial Archives, Victoria.

Progress reports on the building of the Bute Inlet road appeared from time to time in the *Colonist* (see issues of Aug. 1 and 27, Nov. 7 and 15, 1862). A useful account of the building of the road and of the massacre may be found in F.J. Saunders, "Homatcho, or the story of the Bute Inlet Expedition and the Massacre of the Chilcotin Indians," *The Resources of*

British Columbia, Victoria, March and April 1885.

The massacre and punitive expeditions were covered in detail by the following:

Victoria *Colonist*, especially issues of May 12, June 13 and 28, September 7 and 28, December 14, 1864; July 12 and 13, 1865.

The *British Columbian*; New Westminster, especially issues of May 28, June 1 and 8, August 6 and 24, 1864; March 4 and July 18, 1865.

The Government Gazette; New Westminster, August 13, 20, 27, 1864.

Governor Seymour's despatches and the replies made to them by the Secretary of State for the colonies are on microfilm in the Provincial Archives, Victoria. Seymour's despatches of May 20, August 30 and Sept. 9, 1864 and July 7, 1865 are the most useful. This microfilm also contains some interesting material regarding Governor Kennedy's delay of two days in informing Seymour of the massacre. It would appear that the authorities in London considered reprimanding Kennedy, but decided in the end to refrain. It is evident from Seymour's correspondence with Kennedy that relations between the two governors were somewhat cool.

An address by Governor Seymour to the Legislative Council of B.C. is printed in the *Government Gazette* for December 17, 1864. In it the governor declared "A party of road makers, well provided with food, but unarmed, lay down asleep among a number of armed Indians who were almost in a state of starvation. Let me do justice to the dead; on the scaffold at Quesnelmouth it was stated that they gave no provocation."

Much useful material may be found in E.S. Hewlett, "The Chilcotin Uprising: a Study of Indian-European Relations in Nineteenth Century British Columbia" (M.A. Thesis, UBC, 1972).

Material on Chartres Brew appears in Margaret Ormsby, "Some Irish figures in colonial days," B.C. *Historical Quarterly*, 1950. Brew's report to Seymour is attached to the governor's despatch of July 7, 1865. See also Miss Ormsby's article "Frederick Seymour, the Forgotten Governor," in *B.C. Studies*, Summer 1974.

Other details of the massacre and opinions regarding its causes may be found in the following:

BANCROFT, H.H., *History of British Columbia*, San Francisco, 1890.

BROWN, R. Lundin, *Klatsassen and other reminiscences of missionary life in British Columbia*, London, 1873.

GRANT, G.M., *Ocean to Ocean*. Toronto and London, 1873.

MORICE, A.G., *The history of the Northern Interior of British Columbia*, Toronto, 1905. Reprinted by Ye Galleon Press, Fairfield, Washington, 1971.

WHYMPER, Frederick, *Travel and Adventure in the Territory of Alaska*. London, 1868.

Judge Begbie's Notes taken by the court at the trial of six Indians" are in the Provincial Archives, Victoria. Unfortunately, some of the notes are in the judge's private shorthand.

1868: The Barkerville Fire

BESCOBY, Isabel, "Some Aspects of Society in the Cariboo from its Discovery until 1871; thesis, UBC, 1932. Also, "Some Social Aspects of the American Mining Advance Into Cariboo and Kootenay;" thesis, UBC, 1935.

CORNWALLIS, K., *The New El Dorado;* London, 1858; reprinted by Arno Press, New York, 1973.

DOWNS, Arthur, *Wagon Road North:The Story of the Cariboo Gold Rush in Historical Photos;* Northwest Digest, Quesnel, 1962.

DUTHIE, D.W., *A Bishop in the Rough;* London, 1909.

ELLIOTT, G.R., *Quesnel, Commercial Centre of the Cariboo Gold Rush;* Cariboo Historical Society, Quesnel, 1958.

HOWAY and SHOLEFIELD, *British Columbia from the Earliest Times to the Present;* 4 volumes, Vancouver, 1914. See also Howay's *Early History of the Fraser River Mines;* Provincial Archives Memoir No. 6, Victoria, 1926.

HUTCHISON, Bruce, *The Fraser;* Clarke Irwin, Toronto, 1950.

LUDDITT, Fred, *Barkerville Days;* Mitchell Press, Vancouver, 1969.

RAMSEY, Bruce, *Barkerville: A Guide in Word and Picture to the Fabulous Gold Camp of the Cariboo;* Mitchell Press, Vancouver, 1961.

WADDINGTON, Alfred, *The Fraser Mines Vindicated;* Victoria, 1858.

Papers Relative to the Affairs of British Columbia; Queen's Printer, London, 1859. *Cariboo Sentinel.*

Reminiscences in the Provincial Archives by old-timers include: Harry Jones (1840-1936), John Bowron (1837-1906), Ithiel Nason (1839-1893) and Edward Stout (1825-1924).

There is an interesting article on Billy Barker by Louis Le Bourdais in the *B.C. Historical Quarterly* for 1937. There are brief biographies of Barker and Judge Begbie in my *Men of British Columbia,* Hancock House, Saanichton, 1975.

1875: The Loss Of The S.S. Pacific

Books dealing with the loss of the *Pacific* include:

BAILEY, Hilda Ruth, "British Columbians Enraged at *Pacific-Orpheus* Disaster of 1875." *Harbour and Shipping;* Vancouver, Jan. 1967; "Moodyville Once Rated Among World's Great Timber Ports." *Harbour and Shipping;* March 1967.

HIGGINS, D.W., *The Mystic Spring;* Toronto, 1904.

HOWAY, F.W., "Early Settlement on Burrard Inlet" and "Early Shipping on Burrard Inlet 1863-1870." *B.C. Historical Quarterly;* 1937.

LAMB, W.K., "Early Lumbering on Vancouver Island," *B.C. Historical Quarterly;* 1938.

LEWIS and DRYDEN, *Marine history of the Pacific Northwest;* Superior Publishing Company, Seattle, 1967.

NEWELL, G.R., *S.O.S. North Pacific;* Binford and Mort, Portland, Oregon, 1955.

There is an article on Sewell Moody in the *Dictionary of Canadian Biography,* Volume X, and an obituary of Captain Charles Sawyer in the Victoria *Colonist* of October 9, 1894.

The seven volumes of interviews recorded by J.S. Matthews (copies in the Provincial Archives and Vancouver City Archives) contain scattered recollections of Moody by some of those who remembered him.

A copy of Governor Kennedy's despatch of August 17, 1865, regrading the *Brother Jonathan,* is in the Provincial Archives.

The loss of the *Pacific* and the subsequent investigations are dealt with in detail in the Victoria *Colonist* for November 9, 1875 onward.

1886: The Vancouver Fire

The seven volumes of interviews recorded by Major Matthews contain numerous first-hand accounts by survivors of the fire. Selections from them may be found in my *Vancouver Recalled*; Hancock House, Saanichton, 1974.

There are articles about the fire in the *Mainland Guardian;* New Westminster, for June 16, 1886; the Vancouver *World* of June 20, 1896; the Vancouver *Province* of May 30, 1936, and March 18, 1942; and the Vancouver *Sun*, March 18, 1942.

Vancouver *Historical Journal*, Vol. 3, January 1960.

1887: The Nanaimo Coal Mine Disaster

Books about the Dunsmuirs and the early days of the Vancouver Island coal mining industry include:

AUDAIN, James, *From Coal Mine to Castle;* New York, 1955.

Alex Dunsmuir's Dilemma; Victoria, 1964

BATE, Mark, "Brief Descriptive Notes of Nanaimo in 1874," *Nanaimo Free Press;* April 15, 1924.

GOULT, Barrie, "First and Last Days of the *Princess Royal*," *B.C Historical Quarterly*, 1939.

JACKMAN, S.W., *Portraits of the Premiers*; Evergreen Press, Vancouver, 1969.

JOHNSON, Patricia M., *A Short History of Nanaimo*; Nanaimo, 1958.

"Fort Rupert," *Beaver*; Spring 1972.

KEMBLE, J.H., "Coal from the Northwest Coast 1848-1850," *B.C. Historical Quarterly;* 1938.

McKELVIE, B.A., "The Founding of Nanaimo," *B.C. Historical Quarterly;* July 1944; "Coal for the Warships," *Beaver;* Winnipeg, June 1951.

RICKARD, T.A., "A History of Coal Mining in British Columbia," *The Miner;* Vancouver, June 1942.

YOUNG, Patricia, "The Fabulous Dunsmuirs," *Chatelaine*; Sept-Nov. 1961.

See also the article on the Dunsmuirs in Scholefield and Gosnell, *History of British Columbia*, 1913.

Unpublished material includes:

BRYANT, Cornelius, Diary, 1857-1860. Provincial Archives.

BUCKHAM, A.F., "The History of Coal Mining Companies, Vancouver Island." Unpublished pamphlet dated March 1966, on file in the Ministry of Mines and Petroleum Resources, Douglas Building, Victoria.

JAMES, A.R., "The Coalfields of Vancouver Island." Unpublished pamphlet dated Oct. 1969, on file in the Ministry of Mines and Petroleum Resources, Douglas Building, Victoria.

MATHESON, Marion, "Some Effects of Coal Mining on the Development of the Nanaimo Area." M.A. thesis, UBC, 1950.

MUIR, Andrew, Diary, 1848-1850. Provincial Archives.

SMITH, Brian R., "A Social History of Early Nanaimo." B.A. thesis, UBC, 1956.

Copies of Governor Douglas' despatches to Archibald Barclay, secretary of the HBC in London, concerning the Vancouver Island coal discoveries, are in the Provincial Archives. So are Douglas' despatches to the British government. Correspondence between Douglas and Joseph McKay may be found in the "Nanaimo correspondence," Provincial Archives. There is some material on McKay in "Notes and comments," B.C. *Historical Quarterly*, for 1945.

The Vancouver Island census of 1854 is summarized in the *B.C. Historical Quarterly* for 1940.

The report of Archibald Dick, provincial inspector of mines, for the year 1887 is in the B.C. *Sessional Papers* for that year. This report deals not only with the disaster of May 3, but lists all other coal mining accidents in 1887.

1894: The Fraser Valley Flood

More detailed accounts of the development of the Fraser valley from earliest times may be found in:

DEWDNEY, Edgar, report to the B.C. government, *Sessional Papers*; 1877.

GIBBARD, J.E., "Early History of the Fraser Valley 1808-1885." M.A. Thesis, UBC, 1937.

HUTCHISON, Bruce, *The Fraser*; Clarke Irwin, Toronto, 1950.

KITTO, R.H., "The Settlement of the Lower Fraser River Valley, British Columbia." M.A. thesis, University of Southern California, 1932.

SEWELL, W.R., "Economic and Institutional Aspects of Adjustments to Floods in the Lower Fraser Valley." PhD thesis, University of Washington, 1965.

SINCLAIR, F.N., "A History of the Sumas Drainage, Dyking and Development District." Unpublished MS in Provincial Archives, Victoria.

WELLS, Oliver, "Early Times in the Fraser Valley," *Butter-Fat*; Burnaby, Dec. 1963.

WHITE, G.B., "A History of the Eastern Fraser Valley Since 1885." M.A. Thesis, UBC, 1937.

Victoria *Colonist*, beginning May 29, 1894.

Correspondence between the provincial and federal governments concerning the flood is in the *Sessional Papers* for 1894 and 1895.

1896: The Point Ellice Bridge Disaster

BINNS, Richard M., "The Point Ellice Bridge Disaster," *Canadian Rail*; Montreal, April 1969.

An exhaustive investigation into the disaster may be found in Government of B.C., Attorney-General's department, "The Point Ellice Bridge Disaster Inquest." Two Volumes.

Detailed accounts may be found in the Victoria *Colonist*.

1898: The New Westminster Fire

The following are useful:

COPE, Mary, "Colonel Moody and the Royal Engineers in British Columbia." M.A. Thesis, UBC, 1940.

HOWAY, F.W., *The work of the Royal Engineers in British Columbia 1858-1863*; King's Printer, Victoria, 1910.

MATHER, Barry, and McDonald, Margaret, *New Westminster, the Royal City*; J.M. Dent, Vancouver, 1958.

McDONALD, Margaret Lillooet, "New Westminster 1859-1871." M.A. Thesis, UBC, 1947.

SAGE, Walter N., "The Birth of British Columbia." *Beaver*; Winnipeg,

Spring 1958.

WOLFENDEN, Madge, "Sappers and Miners." *Beaver*; Spring 1958.

WOODLAND, Alan, *New Westminster, the Early Years 1858-1898*; Nunaga Publishing Company, New Westminster, 1973.

Moody's impressions of life along the Fraser in gold rush days may conveniently be found in my *James Douglas: Servant of Two Empires.* (Mitchell Press, Vancouver, 1969).

The *Daily Columbian's* plant was destroyed by the fire, but a retrospective account of the disaster may be found in its later files.

1910: The Victoria Fire

The fire was covered in detail in the Victoria newspapers of the day.

1913 & 1914: The Hell's Gate Slides

HUTCHISON, Bruce, *The Fraser*; (Clarke Irwin, Toronto, 1950)

Detailed reports to the provincial government concerning the slides by J.P. Babcock, G.P. Napier (uncle of the present writer) and others may be found in the B.C. *Sessional Papers* for 1914 and 1915.

Publications by Babcock include *The Game Fishes of British Columbia* (Victoria, King's Printer, 1910) and *The Pacific Salmon* (Victoria, King's Printer, 1931). Babcock's obituary may be found in the Victoria *Times* and Vancouver *Province* for Oct. 13, 1936.

1918: The Loss of the Princess Sophia

HACKING, Norman and Lamb, W.K., *The Princess Story: a Century and a Half of West Coast Shipping*; Mitchell Press, Vancouver, 1974.

LUTHER, Capt. Phil, "Princess Sophia on Vanderbilt Reef," *The Sea Chest*; Seattle, June 1977.

MCFADDEN, Louise, "B.C.'s Worst Marine Disaster," *B.C. Outdoors*; Cloverdale, Sept. 1973.

PATERSON, T.W., *British Columbia Shipwreck*; Stagecoach Publishing, Langley, October, 1976.

The *H.W. McCurdy Marine History of the Pacific Northwest.* Superior Publishing Company, Seattle, 1966.

ROGERS, A.C., *Shipwrecks of British Columbia*; J.J. Douglas, Vancouver, 1973.

Seattle *Times*, Nov. 10, 1918.

Vancouver *Province*, Oct. 26 and Nov. 4, 1918.

Victoria *Colonist*, Oct. 27 and Nov. 8, 1918.

Victoria *Times*, Oct. 26 and Nov. 6, 1918.

1918-1919: The Influenza Epidemic

ANDREWS, Margaret W., "Epidemic and Public Health: Influenza in Vancouver 1918-1919," *B.C. Studies*; UBC Press, Summer 1977.

CROSBY, Alfred W., *Epidemic and Peace, 1918*; Greenwood Press, Wesport, Conn., 1976.

McKECHNIE, Robert E., *Strong Medicine*: J.J. Douglas, Vancouver, 1972. *Canadian Medical Association Journal,* November 1919.

Official reports include City of Vancouver, financial and departmental reports for the year ending Dec. 31, 1918 and Twenty-third report of the

Provincial Board of Health, *Sessional Papers*, King's Printer, Victoria, 1920.

Material in manuscript form is contained in "Memories of Sixty Years" by Dr. H.N. Lidster (MS in Provincial Archives); "Early Vancouver," Volume One, by J.S. Matthews (typescript copies in Provincial and Vancouver City Archives); Margaret Butcher, "Journal of Life as Nurse Among the Indians of Kitimat," 1916-1919 (MS in Provincial Archives).

Cranbrook *Courier*, Jan. 12, 1972.

Kelowna *Daily Courier*, Nov. 23, 1968

Prince Rupert *Daily News*, Oct. 24, 1968

Vancouver *Sun*, March 31, 1976

Vancouver and Victoria newspapers of the period carried detailed accounts of the epidemic.

Fictional works containing references to the epidemic include Katharine Anne Porter, *Pale Horse, Pale Rider* (New York, 1939) and Thomas Wolfe, *Look Homeward, Angel* (Scribners, New York, 1939).

1929-1939: The Great Depression

ALLEN, F.L. *Since Yesterday*; Harpers, New York, 1940.

FOSTER, V.W., *Vancouver Through the Eyes of a Hobo*; Vancouver, 1934.

LAWRENCE, J.C., "Markets and Capital: a History of the Lumber Industry of British Columbia." M.A. thesis, U.B.C., 1957.

LIVERSEDGE, Ronald, *Recollections of the On-to-Ottawa Trek*, 1935; Vancouver, 1961.

MATTHEWS, J.S., "Early Vancouver," (Typescript in Provincial and Vancouver City Archives).

MORLEY, Alan, *Vancouver From Milltown To Metropolis*; Mitchell Press, Vancouver, 1961.

ORMSBY, Margaret, *British Columbia: a History*; Macmillan, 1958.

WRIGHT, Arthur James, "The Winter Years in Cowichan; a Study of the Depression in a Vancouver Island Community." M.A. thesis, U.B.C. 1966.

1948: The Fraser River Flood

HUTCHISON, Bruce, *The Fraser*; Clarke Irwin, Toronto, 1950.

PATERSON, T.W., "The Fraser Flood of 1948," *B.C. Outdoors*; June 1969.

SANDERSON, Eric, *Nature's Fury*; Vancouver, 1948.

SCOTT, Jack, "Flood Town," *Vancouver Sun*; supplement to issue of August 28, 1948.

Official reports include Fraser River Board, "Interim Report on Flood Control in the Fraser River Basin," Queen's Printer, Victoria, 1955; and "Fraser River Board, Final Report," Queen's Printer, Victoria, 1963.

British Columbia *Sessional Papers* for 1949.

Much valuable material may be found in W.R. Sewell, Economic and industrial aspects of adjustment to floods in the lower Fraser Valley. (PhD thesis, U. of Washington, 1964).

GOLD PANNING IS EASY
Young or old, an enjoyable and profitable hobby.
ROY LAGAL

In this book Roy Lagal, inventor of the "Gravity Trap" gold pan, proves that gold panning is easy! He does not introduce a new method; he just removes confusion surrounding old established methods. The author, an expert at his craft, spends countless hours in the field, testing and updating prospecting equipment and sharpening up field search techniques. This book is sure to be as successful and popular as *Gold Panner's Manual.*

$3.95 NON-FICTION   0-919531-00-8   80 pages

GOLD FIELDS OF THE KLONDIKE
ERNEST INGERSOLL

Originally published in 1897 at the beginning of the world's greatest gold rush, this book is a masterly and fascinating description of the then newly discovered gold mines. It details how they were found, how worked, and what fortunes were made. It also describes the richness of the gold fields and outlines the various routes used by miners to get there. Completely re-designed and re-typeset in a crisp modern style for easy reading. A factual historic event reported when it happened.

$3.95 NON-FICTION   0-88983-040-1   128 pages

OUTLAWS OF WESTERN CANADA
A Collection of Western Canada's Most Villainous Outlaws
T.W. PATERSON

Through television, books and movies, Canadians have long been saturated with the heroes and villians of the American West, while remaining totally ignorant of our own desperadoes. This book shatters the myth that the Canadian West was placid or dull, with a collection of 20 chapters on Western Canada's most villainous outlaws—Cannibals, thieves, murderers, etc. An enlightening look at what the Canadian West was really like.

$4.95 NON-FICTION   0-919531-01-6   160 pages

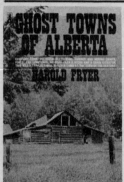

GHOST TOWNS OF ALBERTA

Company town, religious settlement, lumber and mining camps, forts, and sometimes, no more than a store or grain elevator, this was a typical small Alberta town at the turn of the century.

HAROLD FRYER

A warm-hearted look at the small communities which blossomed in Alberta, then fell into ruin when residents moved away. Relocated railway tracks, that lifeline of all Prairie communities, spelled the end for many. For others, it was the very reason for existence and prosperity.

$5.95 NON-FICTION   0-88983-039-8   192 pages

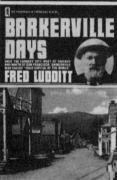

BARKERVILLE DAYS

Once the largest city west of Chicago and north of San Francisco, Barkerville was called "Gold Capital of the World."

FRED LUDDITT

This book, rich in fact and anecdotal history, is the work of a do-it-yourself style miner-historian, a mining man who talked the language of the last of the originals and their first descendants. A dedicated gatherer of the authoritative story of the Cariboo, centering on Barkerville, Fred Ludditt has done an admirable job of preserving the rich heritage of the region. Here is the priceless product of interviews which can never be done again.

$3.95 NON-FICTION   0-88983-032-0   158 pages

THE BEST OF CANADA WEST

Canadian History Dull?

Since 1969, when *Canada West* was first established, the magazine has published numerous fascinating and interesting stories on ghost towns, pioneers, mines & mining camps, great achievements, lost treasure, railroad, Indians, shipwrecks, and a host of others. In the tremendously successful *The Best Of Canada West* (Volume 1), we presented 34 of the articles written by Mr. N.L. Barlee from 1969 to 1977. In Volume 2, we have complied another fascinating collection of 25 stories spanning the years 1970 to 1979. These were written by a variety of authors. After reading this book you will convinced that Canadian history was anything but dull.

$3.95 NON-FICTION   0-88983-033-9   184 pages

$3.95 NON-FICTION

GOLD PANNER'S MANUAL
Now in its 7th Printing With Nearly 75,000 Copies in Print!
GARNET BASQUE
The complete guide for the gold panner. With gold becoming increasingly more valuable, more and more people are panning the gold-bearing creeks of B.C. and the Yukon, both for fun and profit. This book includes chapters on: *Gold Throughout The Ages; Some Facts About Gold; How To Locate Placer Gold; The ABC's of Gold Panning; How To Recover Fine Gold; Methods Of Placer Mining; Equipment;* etc.
0-88983-003-7   112 pages

$3.95 NON-FICTION

EAST KOOTENAY CHRONICLE
A story of settlement, lawlessness, mining disasters and fires stretching across southern British Columbia from the Alberta border to Creston on Kootenay Lake.
DAVID SCOTT & EDNA HANIC
Two years of extensive research have resulted in an engrossing story of the Kootenay Indians; the first explorers and missionaries, the gold rush at Wild Horse Creek; the construction of the Dewdney Trail; and the beginnings of settlements like Fisherville, Fort Steele, Fernie and more. It is also the story of such men as David Thompson, Colonel Baker, Father de Smet, William Baillie-Grohman, Edgar Dewdney, Colonel Steele, Father Coccola and others.
0-88983-028-2   170 pages

THE CHILCOTIN WAR
The True Story of a Defiant Chief's Fight To Save His Land From White Civilization
MEL ROTHENBURGER
Just before daybreak on April 30, 1864, a work party engaged in constructing a new road to the Cariboo goldfields was attacked without warning by a band of Chilcotin warriors. Wielding knives and axes, and firing muskets, they butchered the men while they slept. Only three escaped. Fully documented for the first time, this book relates the terrifying events of one of the bloodiest chapters in British Columbia history.
0-88983-011-8   208 pages

$2.95 NON-FICTION

ORDER FORM

If the store where you obtained this book does not have the other books you require, simply fill in this Order Form, or send a list of titles wanted, to:

SUNFIRE
PUBLICATIONS LIMITED
P.O. Box 3399, Langley, B.C. V3A 4R7

ALL PRICES SUBJECT TO CHANGE WITHOUT NOTICE

NAME & ADDRESS (Please Print)

_____

_____

_____

DO YOU WISH TO BE PLACED ON OUR MAILING LIST TO RECEIVE FUTURE CATALOGUES?
☐ YES   ☐ NO

MR. PAPERBACK series

QU.	TITLE	PRICE	AMOUNT
_____	Barkerville Days	$ 3.95	_____
_____	British Columbia Disasters	6.95	_____
_____	Best of Canada West (Vol 2)	3.95	_____
_____	Chilcotin War	2.95	_____
_____	East Kootenay Chronicles	3.95	_____
_____	Ghost Towns of Alberta	5.95	_____
_____	Gold Fields of The Klondike	3.95	_____
_____	Gold Panner's Manual	3.95	_____
_____	Gold Panning Is Easy	3.95	_____
_____	Outlaws Of Western Canada	4.95	_____

OTHER TITLES

QU.	TITLE	PRICE	AMOUNT
_____	Best of Canada West (Vol 1)	$ 7.95	_____
_____	British Columbia Ghost Town Atlas	6.95	_____
_____	British Columbia—The Pioneer Years	7.95	_____
_____	British Columbia Shipwrecks	7.95	_____
_____	Canadian Battles & Massacres (CL.)	15.95	_____
_____	Canadian Battles & Massacres (PA.)	8.95	_____
_____	Ency. of Ghost Towns & Mining Camps of B.C. (Vol 1)	9.95	_____
_____	Ency. of Ghost Towns & Mining Camps of B.C. (Vol 2)	9.95	_____
_____	History Of The Canadian West	4.95	_____
_____	Yukon Ghost Town Atlas	4.95	_____

TOTAL _____

ADD $1.00 FOR POSTAGE & HANDLING _____ **+ $1.00**

AMOUNT ENCLOSED _____